PARIS
BY BISTRO

PARIS
BY BISTRO

A Guide to Eating Well

by Christine and Dennis Graf

ARRIS BOOKS
An imprint of Arris Publishing Ltd
Gloucestershire

First published in Great Britain in 2004 by

Arris Books
An imprint of Arris Publishing Ltd
Unit 1A Fosseway Business Centre
Stratford Road
Moreton-in-Marsh
Gloucestershire GL56 9NQ
www.arrisbooks.com

ISBN 1 84437 009 7

Printed and bound in Korea

To request our complete catalogue, please call us at **01608 652655**, visit our web site at: **www.arrisbooks.com**, or e-mail us at: **info@arrisbooks.com**

CONTENTS

acknowledgments vi
introduction: about bistros vii

1. UPTOWN: THE 1ST & 2ND ARRONDISSEMENTS—1

2. THE MAGICAL MARAIS: THE 3RD & 4TH ARRONDISSEMENTS—20

3. WRITERS' WATERING HOLES: THE 5TH & 6TH ARRONDISSEMENTS—52

4. AFRICAN-AMERICANS IN PARIS: THE 6TH ARRONDISSEMENT & BEYOND—81

5. MOVERS AND SHAKERS: THE 7TH & 8TH ARRONDISSEMENTS—97

6. PARIS WITH A PAST: THE 9TH & 10TH ARRONDISSEMENTS—121

7. MOVING UP IN THE WORLD: THE 11TH & 12TH ARRONDISSEMENTS—139

8. LEFT BANK SOUTH: THE 13TH & 14TH ARRONDISSEMENTS—164

9. PRIVILEGE & PROSPERITY: THE 15TH & 16TH ARRONDISSEMENTS—177

10. ESCAPE FROM CONVENTION: THE 17TH & 18TH ARRONDISSEMENTS—191

11. OUT OF THE LOOP: THE 19TH & 20TH ARRONDISSEMENTS—207

12. MAIGRET'S BISTROS—216

13. ROMANTIC BISTROS—233

bibliography 247
glossary 249
index 258

ACKNOWLEDGMENTS

To all of the people who have so generously shared their enthusiasm for Paris and insights into good food with us, including Lucy Brennan, Lisa Bernard, Susan Cole, Sheila Coxe, Christine Estruga, Dominique Grangeon, Fabio Lopes, Jacqueline Nonglaton, Charles and Katherine McCracken, Stewart Rayment, François Rhein, and other Parisians and longtime residents of the City of Light whose names escape us.

To David Shumway, who eschews artichokes and foreign travel, but is an inspiration to his friends just the same.

A special thank-you is due to Anita and Albert Cesbron, and Marie Louise and Bob Sigel for opening their homes to us and making their Paris ours, and to Elizabeth Porto and Juliana Spear at Interlink.

Finally, we thank the bistro, brasserie, and restaurant chefs and other workers who have made this study so enjoyable. We've tried to emphasize bistros in areas popular with tourists, but a few special favorites happen to be in less visited areas, in hard-to-find places. They are well worth the trouble of seeking out.

You will not find the most famous and expensive bistros, like Chez Georges, L'Ami Louis, or Benoît in these pages—they are well beyond our cut-off point for expense.

We have not solicited or accepted free meals from bistro chefs or proprietors, and we have not identified ourselves, so the food and service we describe should be the same that you, the reader, will receive. We think that our findings will delight you.

INTRODUCTION:
ABOUT BISTROS

Are you intimidated by artichokes? Do you flinch beneath the stares of waiters? Are you stopped short by the major questions of life, like which fork to reach for next? If so, what you need is not another classic French restaurant, but a bistro.

Restaurants are serious business—most bistros are not. Restaurant chefs become household names. But nobody makes a fuss about the Paul Bocuse of the bistro. Nobody did, that is, until the "new" bistros appeared.

Three hundred or so years ago, Vatel threw himself on his sword when an expected shipment of fish for the king's dinner failed to arrive. (The fish eventually arrived late, but by then it was too late for Vatel). As Waverley Root informed us, Vatel was not a cook, as most people thought, but a sort of manager; in any case, he blamed himself for the scarcity of food for the king's table. Thirty or so years ago, a chef in a well-known Paris restaurant committed the same act, doing himself in over a little matter involving the *Guide Michelin*, which had taken away one of the establishment's stars. A bistro chef's response to such a loss would be a shrug. He'd probably put it down to the bad taste of the Michelin man on that particular day, make a joke about the situation, and go on.

If you're like us, you don't want any chef to get that serious. Food is meant to be a celebration of life. It should be associated with good times. We don't want people to harm themselves on our account.

Still, bistro food can be great food. One of the most memorable meals we've ever had in Paris was years ago at the bistro Allard, in the 6th arrondissement. We recommended it to friends from the midwest who were about to make their grand tour of Europe. In addition to Allard, they went to the famous Tour d'Argent, what the French would call a *temple de gastronomie,* and compared the cuisine of the two restaurants favorably.

One warm summer evening years ago, my husband and I were passing the bistro and I saw an attractive brunette who turned out to be Fernande Allard herself standing outside. I stopped, greeted her, and briefly repeated the story I'd heard comparing her place with the Tour—and was rewarded when she asked me to come inside. "Tell the cooks what you just told me," she insisted, and I got the chance to repeat the story to two scrawny, perspiring young men in the kitchen. Smiles lit up their faces.

What is a Bistro?

> *Until you have wasted time in a city, you cannot pretend to know it well. The soul of a big city is not to be grasped so easily; in order to make contact with it, you have to have been bored, you have to have suffered a bit in those places that contain it. Anyone can get hold of a guide and tick off all the monuments, but within the very confines of Paris there is another city as difficult of access as Timbuktu once was.*
>
> Julien Green, *Paris*

What is a bistro anyway? Some have said that the word came to us from the Russians, who called out "bystra, bystra" to mean "quickly, quickly" when they wanted fast service. We would not always recommend this technique. Quite often it has the opposite result.

An American friend remembers an incident which occurred one evening in a Left Bank bistro. He and his wife were sitting at a side table, receiving impeccable service. During their meal they were embarrassed to observe a large group of their countrymen behaving in full "ugly American" mode—waving their hands, snapping their fingers, and shouting "Garçon, garçon," at a dignified-looking man who was none other than the proprietor. The louder their shouts and more frantic their gestures, the less notice the proprietor paid to them. Instead, with a little smile on his face and effortlessly balancing a tray, he sauntered right past their table. He did this several times, completely ignoring the shouts and the glares. But he did make his way quite often to our friend's table, using a little French, a little English, and a lot of sign language to help them order something they would really enjoy, and, later, to make sure that everything was right.

In reading about the history of bistros, the word "café" keeps cropping up. In an introductory French textbook, *Cours de Langue et de Civilisation Française*, G. Mauger described a bistro as "un petit café du quartier," a little neighborhood café. Books about bistros include establishments with the word "Café" blazoned on their exterior. Café or bistro? They are ultimately the same. Sometimes we think of a bistro as a café with a greater emphasis on food. But there are places called cafés with good food, and others called bistros with mediocre offerings.

In W. Scott Haine's scholarly research on cafés, he has noticed a looseness in the way the terms "bistro," "bar," "café," and "restaurant" have been used in the past. This extends to our own time. The Larousse *Histoire des Cafés et des Cafetiers* gives Humphrey Bogart's Casablanca nightclub and the Berlin cabaret where Liza Minelli performed as examples of cafés in the movies.

More recently, a bistro is thought of as a small, individually owned restaurant, often run by a family and patronized by regulars. There will almost always be a small bar and a number of small tables. The food will be simple country classics, *la cuisine grand-mère*, the sort of things grandmother used to serve. Prices are usually reasonable, although some famous bistros can be quite expensive. Most bistros have their own specialties, often regional dishes, which people ask for again and again.

Brasseries are larger, noisier, and less formal places, often with many square meters of brass and chrome, and a long bar dispensing a number of beers on tap. A brasserie was originally the retail outlet of a brewery; many in Paris were founded by Alsatians who came to Paris in the 1870s, after the Franco-Prussian War.

Many brasseries still serve Germanic-influenced food and wine—sauerkraut, sausages, and the white wines of the southeast. You will also find typical French country bistro food in addition to the classic brasserie fare of seafood. Brasseries are usually open late at night. In Paris, many of the classic brasseries have been taken over by the Groupe Flo, sometimes to the consternation of the long-time regulars—see our discussion of the Balzar, in the 5th arrondissement.

The New Bistro

In recent years, there has been a trend toward something that is neither a café nor a traditional bistro, nor yet a classic restaurant. This new sort of eating place is not open for business all day like a café; you can't get a drink there at all hours, and the food is most definitely something grandmother would not even think of attempting—unless she were energetic and inspired, a Julia Child, perhaps, or a Simone Beck. What has been happening is that young chefs, formerly *sous-chefs* in the most famous Parisian restaurants, have been leaving and starting up little restaurants of their own, places that they call "bistros." The absence of grand restaurant frills and fussiness, the minimalist decor, the limited wait staff—no maître d', just one or two friendly and helpful servers—make the place appealing, while keeping prices down to a level where these restaurants can compete with other bistros. Thus, you can dine for a reasonable price at a modest-looking restaurant where the chef has worked in the kitchens of Le Crillon, the Tour d'Argent, or even the Elysée Palace. And the cuisine reflects it: you taste outstanding food, you get a chance to sample the fare of someone who's on the cutting edge of the most recent developments in cuisine, and who has a chef's classical training lending substantial background to his or her ideas.

Why is this revolution in bistros happening now? Maybe it's a result of the natural urge that most of us feel to be independent and in charge, to use our skills for our own benefit and not just for the company. Maybe it is what one could call the Paul Bocuse phenomenon: the dream that a young chef could become a "name" and not have to keep on toiling anonymously for the glory of the establishment.

Another motive that nobody seems to mention is the atmosphere in the back room where the work gets done. If you've ever read George Orwell's *Down and Out in Paris and London*, you'll remember his horrifying description of working in the kitchen at the Hotel Lotti, where he toiled as a *plongeur* (dishwasher) in the 1930s.

By the time British designer and restaurateur Terence Conran made his own journey to the kitchen of a Paris restaurant to learn about food two decades later, conditions were not much better. He wrote: "La Méditerranée in Paris has changed little in its appearance since I worked there as a 'plongeur' in the early 1950s. But in those days, whilst the restaurant the customers saw was really quite grand, the kitchen was an eye-opening thieves' den of squalor and cruelty."

We would hope that restaurant conditions have substantially improved, that the helpers, whether they are *sous-chefs* or merely *plongeurs*, get decent treatment, but cooking is a high-pressure job anywhere. It must be particularly so in a culture as food-centered as the French, and one can imagine that in famous kitchens all over the city there must be *sous-chefs* who dream of the day when they may escape from the local tyrant and be the one in charge at their own small place.

Bistro Etiquette

Recently we picked up a French guide to travel, *Voyager aux Etats-Unis* (*Travel to the United States*) giving helpful—and unintentionally hilarious—hints to the French person planning a trip. The potential tourist is told how to manage in the country of "les Anglo-Saxons." Our puritanical streak, our strange foods, our disconcerting habit of addressing people by their first names, it's all in there. Warnings about the food *chez nous* focus on overcooked meat and undercooked vegetables, and the reader is cautioned against patronizing French restaurants abroad because they tend to be pretentious and overpriced.

With these cultural differences in mind, a few reminders on how to manage in the French capital. A nice surprise about bistros is that you often find great courtesy there. Even in a city the size of Paris, it's customary for people to greet and be greeted when they enter and leave a bistro; you'll hear "Bonjour, Monsieur, Madame, au revoir M'sieu, Madame" all the time. In return, you'll want to manage a polite "Bonjour"[bawnsjure] and "Au revoir" [oh-vwahr].

In many of the bistros we recommend, people dress informally: good jeans or slacks with an appropriate shirt or top would not be out of place. Women can wear slacks but usually wear skirts or dresses. Still, we were surprised to see a middle-aged man, a tourist, leave an attractive restaurant in the 6th district wearing, among other things, a baseball cap and short shorts. At the time, we were sitting near some very well-dressed Parisians.

The French respect each other's privacy; conversation in a bistro will generally be in hushed tones. You normally do not hear loud talk or raucous laughter. On a few occasions during our research, we found that a restaurant could be completely dominated by one or two loud English-speaking tourists relating their stories. This is not typical, but it does change the ambiance in an unfavorable way. (There were many more savvy Anglophones who'd learned to adjust the volume of their conversation to Parisian levels).

Eating in Paris

Yes, it is possible to get a bad meal in Paris, and, unfortunately, it's getting easier and easier. Sad to say, many visitors to the French capital find themselves in fast-food restaurants, self-service cafeterias, and conveniently located chain restaurants, eating thin flavorless steaks and soggy fries while not knowing that a few blocks away there is a legendary bistro packed with local gourmands joyously wolfing down extraordinary food. Price is not always a good guide, although food of high quality can never be cheap.

Some observations:

⁂ The best-value restaurants are often on obscure side streets. For this reason we urge you to equip yourself with a detailed street-by-street map, available at any Paris newsstand.

⁂ Very simple-looking places can serve quite sophisticated food.

☙ What we call a menu, the French call the *carte*. Most French restaurants have a fixed-price (*prix fixe*) meal with two or three courses called the *menu*, offering a limited choice of what is listed on their *carte*. This is usually a good value, and many patrons will order from it.

☙ By law every French restaurant must have the menu, or *carte*, posted outside along with the prices so you know what's available before you enter. Most waiters can speak at least a few words of English, although they may not know enough to discuss the fine details of ingredients or preparation of a specific dish with you.

☙ French law requires each restaurant to provide ordinary tap water. If you don't see it on the table, ask for "Un carafe d'eau, s'il vous plaît," (ahn kah-raff dough, seel voo play). Most French people prefer to drink bottled water, and if you've never been to Paris before and are worried about the possibility of digestive disorders, you might want to stick to bottled water for the first few days. The tap water is perfectly safe and is purified by ozone, not chlorine, so has none of that unpleasant chlorinated taste.

☙ Tipping is usually included in the price of the meal, indicated by the term *service compris* (service included) on the menu. You need not leave anything else, although if there are a few coins left over after you've paid your bill, you may want to show an unexpected generosity.

Words, Words Words—
Avoiding Misunderstandings

French and English share a great vocabulary when it comes to food. Where did we get the words "hors d'oeuvres," "soup," "quiche," "beef," "carrots," "cream," "dessert," and a host of other terms for edibles if not from the French? But similarities can create confusion. It's important to remember:

☙ *entrée* means hors d'oeuvre, not main dish, in France.

☙ *plat* (think of "plate") is the word for the main course.

☙ after that, it's easy: dessert is the same word in both languages.

Ordering Wine

Even people who are familiar with California wines sometimes freeze when confronted with a wine list in France. Virtually all of the wines will be carrying names unknown to them. Few

bistros have a wine specialist, and many waiters' level of English is minimal.

You don't actually have to order wine, of course. If you don't, you may wish to get bottled water with your meal. Coffee is always drunk only after the meal, and, of course, unless you're ten years old, don't ask for Coca-Cola.

Most wine in bistros is not as expensive as it would be in British or American restaurants. Wine lists are usually short, and there's often a "house wine," a decent and low-priced alternative to the bottled wine. This may arrive in a "carafe," "demi" (half liter), or a "quart." Sometimes it's included in the price of the *formule*, or fixed-price menu, but usually not. A few restaurants will have choices of half-bottles, but in general you'll have to order a full bottle or a glass.

Some observations:

✤ In the United States and, to a lesser extent, Britain, the name of the grape used to make the wine is all-important. People will ask for a Chardonnay, or Merlot or whatever, but in France, the place where a wine is made is most significant. The French seem to have an almost mystical attachment to the soil, the *terroir*, and they think this is what's important to know. A wine specialist would know, of course, which wines were made with Chardonnay grapes and which were made primarily with Merlot, but the average waiter would consider that information trivia.

❧ The old advice about red wine with meat and white wine with fish is generally useful, though any "foodie" can think of exceptions. Most French chefs make great use of sauces, and these can affect your choice of wine. It's very common for a couple to go into a bistro and find that one wants fish, the other, meat. When this happens it might be possible to order a *demi* of red and another of white, or to order the wines by the glass.

❧ In most bistros there will be a minimum of wine-serving ceremony, but the waiter should show you the bottle before opening it and, after opening it, may give you the cork for your inspection. This is a bit of tradition—you don't have to sniff the cork or anything like that. Just look at it and put it down. He'll then pour a small amount in your glass and you'll taste it. Unless there's something terribly wrong—and that's unlikely—you'll nod and keep the wine. The only wines which are likely to have "turned" might be the oldest, most expensive vintages, and if you're in a position to order these, you'll know when they're not satisfactory.

❧ If the wine list looks really unfamiliar and the waiter seems to have no English, don't panic. If you're ordering meat, find the *rouge* or red wines on the list. An inexpensive Côtes du Rhône should not be much over fifteen euros or about fourteen dollars, and you'll probably like it. Another possibility is Beaujolais, which most people have heard of, and while the type served in most bistros is not terribly high in quality, it's not especially expensive either. In most bistros, there's a strong correlation between the price of wines and the quality, but for most of us their less expensive offerings are perfectly adequate. If you order the dish that's one of the specialties of the restaurant, the waiter will usually be able to suggest the best wine to go with it. Unless the recommended wine is far beyond your budget, you should try it.

An Embarrassment of Riches

There are many good bistros in Paris and a few great ones. The French traditions of producing first-rate ingredients for the cook, from raising free-range animals to bringing fresh produce to market only when it is ready to be eaten; undergoing a long and demanding apprenticeship that will sometimes result in a top chef whose talent is worthy of his toque; making use of specialized sources for obtaining the finest of what is needed; more recently being willing to experiment and open to foreign cuisines, a combination yielding such inspired results—this is what you will experience as you try the bistros in this book.

The remembered pleasure of eating thoughtfully prepared meals in our own country or in France should influence us to try to keep our best traditions intact, even to have an influence upon the future. Above all, what we should try to deter is the sort of brave new world of profit-driven food engineering so well described by Eric Schlosser in his impressive book, *Fast Food Nation.* Just one experience in a food laboratory changed his view of processed foods:

> Grainger had brought a dozen small glass bottles from the lab. After he opened each bottle, I dipped a fragrance-testing filter into it... Before placing each strip of paper in front of my nose, I closed my eyes. Then I inhaled deeply, and one food after another was conjured from the glass bottles. I smelled fresh cherries, black olives, sautéed onions, and shrimp. Grainger's most remarkable creation took me by surprise. After closing my eyes, I suddenly smelled a grilled hamburger. The aroma was uncanny, almost miraculous—as if someone in the room were flipping burgers on a hot grill. But when I opened my eyes, I saw just a narrow strip of white paper and a flavorist with a grin.

This is the science behind the *cuisine industrielle* that seems to be taking over the food preparation industry, in France as well as at home. When large conglomerates buy up restaurants and establish chains, what they market is an innocuous, standardized product that might not be far removed from airline food. You can be sure that there's no individual chef in these kitchens exercising his or her creativity.

We have reviewed a few eating places that happen to be owned by large companies: it's impossible to describe the brasseries, for example, without doing so. Some of these places are worth visiting, for the decor if not the food. But in none of them will you get food at the level attained by a good chef working with fresh ingredients. We urge you whenever possible to try some of the choice small bistros where the menu changes daily, to get an idea of what fresh food can taste like when prepared by a master chef.

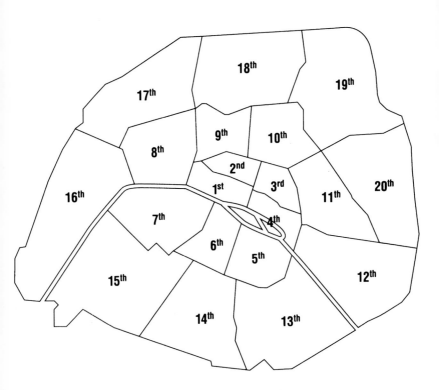

PARIS ARRONDISSEMENTS

UPTOWN: THE 1ST & 2ND ARRONDISSEMENTS

> Outside, the fire-red, gas-blue, ghost-green signs shone smokily through the tranquil rain. It was late afternoon and the streets were in movement, the bistros gleamed. At the corner of the Boulevard des Capucines, he took a taxi. The Place de la Concorde moved by in pink majesty, they crossed the logical Seine....
>
> —*F. Scott Fitzgerald*

Apart from the Eiffel Tower and the Arc de Triomphe, what comes to mind when people think of Paris is usually something in the 1st arrondissement. Possibly you picture Paris with the Ritz Hotel and the great column of the Place Vendôme. You may remember the Louvre, once a royal palace itself, now an impossibly vast treasure house of art.

Marcel Proust dined often at the Ritz Hotel and liked to gossip with the waiters, who often provided him with ideas for his work. A dinner in July 1917 was interrupted by a German air raid. Proust watched it from a balcony and used the experience later in *Le Temps Retrouvé*.

We associate Paris with luxury, although Janet Flanner, the *New Yorker's* famous Paris correspondent, once wrote to a friend: "I moved over here this afternoon into the room you occupied with me. The shabbiness of the Ritz is a great comfort after the garish modernism of the Inter-Continental."

The premier shopping district in the world starts in the 1st arrondissement on the rue St.-Honoré, the longest street of first-rate shops in Paris. In the Place Vendôme, Cartier and Van Cleef and Arpels have watches and jewelry fit for the nobility. The rest of us enjoy them vicariously, in the way that Audrey Hepburn enjoyed breakfast at Tiffany's, peering into the window of the exclusive jewelry store as she sipped coffee and munched a pastry.

The 2nd arrondissement adjoins and continues the first. There is a strong financial flavor about this district—here are the Bank of France and the Bourse, the French version of Wall Street. Moneychangers line the streets, and little wine bars fill up at noon with men and women who whisper important information. It is no accident that Legrand, the best winesellers in the city, have their shop here. So does the avant-garde designer Jean-Paul Gaultier. Agence France-Presse, the center of French journalism, is across the street from the Bourse. That, too, was probably not without design.

In his writing F. Scott Fitzgerald sketched a romantic Paris, the Paris of the Right Bank. But for Parisians, the 1st and 2nd arrondissements are not primarily places of romance, or of apartments and families. It's business, money, and work. It's strong coffee and high tension.

Some good addresses in central Paris:

L'Ardoise
28 rue du Mt. Thabor 75001 Paris (01.42.96.28.18)
Métro: Tuileries
Tue–Fri noon–2:15 P.M., Tue–Sat 7:00 P.M.–11:00 P.M.,
closed August

L'Ardoise is small. On the main level, there are only ten tables. Recently they were crowded with Americans and Japanese—and a few French people who had somehow managed to escape the obligatory Sunday lunch with the family.

There is nothing special about the decor: white tablecloths, cream walls with enlargements of old French postcards, and tiled floor. Your interest starts to peak when the waitress comes to your table bearing the 28-euro menu, scribbled in chalk on a section of old blackboard—they call it an *ardoise*—and you see a stunning variety of outstanding choices. Before the time came to order, we noticed pigeon, quail, and several other intriguing possibilities.

As appetizers, we chose shrimp set off with grapefruit, and *langoustines*. The shrimp arrived in a flower-like arrangement, the shrimp set off with scallions in a light vinaigrette in the center, sections of dark red grapefruit arranged like petals around it. The *langoustines* were large and aggressive-looking, in a light mustard-flavored mayonnaise, accompanied by a finger bowl with lukewarm water and lemon slice.

In between the hors d'oeuvres and main course, we could relish the ambiance at L'Ardoise—relaxed and friendly with everyone talking at once.

Our *plats* were not only good, they were memorable: a *porc rôti* (roast pork) done just right, with spinach in a sauce lightly flavored with citrus, and *barbue* or brill, a fish resembling turbot, in a rich sauce involving balsamic vinegar, with snow peas and *haricots verts* (green beans), and topped with tiny morsels of crisp fried onion.

To go with the meal we chose a rich Les Bastides, Côteaux d'Aix 1995 at 20 euros. Other wines were available by the bottle from about 14 euros.

Service was friendly: the two young women who waited on the tables were smiling and courteous. One even risked a trip to the kitchen to ask the chef about the ingredients of a sauce. A little later I heard the other cheerfully translating the dessert menu for a group of American diners.

We had ordered similar desserts: crisp little caramelized squares, one filled with a rich, dark chocolate mousse, the other with raspberries and a heavy crème, garnished with an impressionistic splatter of sauce.

The chef, Pierre Jay, originally from Savoie, finally appeared, slightly flushed from his exertions. He looked a little as you might expect Austin Powers's younger brother to look. A consummate professional, he used to work at La Tour d'Argent.

❖ *L'Ardoise: outstanding food you remember and tell friends about, but hope there'll be a table available when you need it.*

Aux Bons Crus
7 rue des Petits Champs, 75001 Paris (01.42.60.06.45)
Métro: Palais-Royal
Open daily 9:00 A.M.–2:00 A.M.

Aux Bons Crus is a *bistro à vins* nearly a century old which might not attract one at first glance. There's nothing especially fetching about the long, narrow room, the new-style bar with wildly colored marble, and the deco-shaped cutouts on the ceiling for lighting.

But Aux Bons Crus deserves a second look. Besides some stunning historic gear—a formidable machine for bringing bottles up from the cave—and a good selection of wines, this wine bar offers attractive meals at reasonable prices in this high-priced arrondissement.

Here near the stock exchange since 1905, Aux Bons Crus has changed little over the years. Prewar wine barrels are stacked to the ceiling, although the original zinc bar may have been lost to the forces of the Occupation in the same war. Here the nonsmoking section is clearly preferable—it's in front by the window and the breezes. The smoking section, a dark and larger room at the back, must have one of the lowest ceilings in Paris. If you are anything approaching six feet in height, you will have to stoop.

Most of the wines are lower-cost regional varieties and recent vintages in the 16- to 31-euro range, but we chose the wine of the month, a *pichet* (pitcher) of young, chilled red Bergerac. It went beautifully with a *tartine saucisson de montagne*, an open-faced sandwich with spicy salami on a slab of *poilâne* bread, with a large dab of chutney. In the course of a conversation we asked the man next to us, a magazine publisher, about the popularity of foreign foods in Paris. He didn't have to reply, as just then the waitress brought him the day's special, *poulet au curry*, not something a wine bar would have served years ago.

Salads run from 7 to 9 euros, but you may wish to try *tartines*—open-faced sandwiches—on the tasty and filling *pain poilâne*. They include *rillettes à l'oie* (minced spread of goose), *jambon cru* (smoked cured ham), *saucisson de montagne*, and Cantal or Camembert, served with vegetables and *confit d'oignons*—a sort of onion chutney.

If you like salami and sausages, you'll be delighted with Aux Bons Crus. There is a varied assortment of *charcuterie*, a high-quality type of dry salami, *tarte chaude du jour* (hot quiche of the day), and salad, as well as the classic desserts *mousse au chocolat* and *crème caramel.*

Wines come by the glass, from 3 euros on up, or by the bottle starting at 10 euros. There's also a *vin du mois,* a young red Bergerac when we were there, available in a 46-cl carafe.

An open-faced sandwich doesn't sound like anything special, but at Aux Bons Crus they know how to make it: our *saucisson* with *pain poilâne* was appealing, with pickles, onion chutney, and the pleasing contrast of vegetables to add color and crunch.

Aux Bons Crus enjoys a clientele of unusual sophistication, attracting journalists from Agence France-Presse and *Le Figaro*, as well as shoppers from the chic Place des Victoires. Our neighbor, the magazine publisher, had to leave before we did, and as he got up we noticed his magnificent briefcase. Priding myself on my knowledge of the latest high-priced French status symbols, I looked at it and said to him, "Louis Vuitton?" He smiled, and opening it discreely, showed us the gold lettering: "Harry Winston, New York."

❖ *Aux Bons Crus: if you lunch there, you'll be in very good company.*

Café Noir
65 rue Montmartre, 75002 Paris (01.40.39.07.36)
Métro: Sentier
Mon–Fri 10:00 A.M.–2:00 A.M., Sat 4:00 P.M.–2:00 A.M.

Not a bistro, not even a conventional café, the Café Noir is a bar on the rue Montmartre in the banking district. With a highly individual decor—old chipped tiles in pastel colors cover a black-lacquered wooden bar and a circle of orange and white neon edges the picturesque old mural high up on the walls—Café Noir draws a young and artistic crowd. Soft rock music thumps away and locals gather for

after-work pick-me-ups and liquid sustenance at any time of the day or night. This café is a fun and friendly place: an old bicycle is displayed above the entrance, an illuminated heart shines forth in red plastic, mirrors are plastered with stickers for unconventional causes. The young barman, head shaved in obedience to the current fashion, barely glances up from his crossword puzzle when a new arrival comes by—but soon he glides over to offer good-natured service. Drinks are fairly priced, the coffee that's a euro at the bar will be 1.50 at a table and 2 on the terrace outside. A large beer starts at 3 euros, with *plats* at lunch around 10 euros.

❖ *Café Noir: fun and funky, a rest from the serious-suited financial district.*

Les Cartes Postales
7 rue Gomboust, 75001 Paris (01.42.61.23.40)
Métro: Opéra
Mon–Fri lunch, Tue–Sat dinner, closed Mon eve, Sat
lunch, and 2 weeks end of July-early August

Bright walls and the white linen of the tablecloths lend a cheerfulness to this little hideaway tucked into an Asian-influenced street in the 1st arrondissement. Across the street are a Korean restaurant and an Asian caterer. Within, a welcome feeling of calmness and serenity—it is possible to have a quiet conversation here. Spot lighting focuses on the tables but is not harsh. The service is efficient and quietly polite. Except for one table of French people and ourselves, most of the customers were Asian.

The only thing not minimalist at Cartes Postales is the food, prepared by a Japanese chef trained in France. From the 23-euro menu (other menus are available at 38 and 53 euros), two of us ordered crab cakes to start, the third a salmon hors d'oeuvre. The salmon was the largest plate of artfully arranged smoked salmon we have seen; it was marinated with dill and accompanied by tomatoes, chives, and greens. The crab cakes were warm rice- and crab-filled spring rolls, lightly cooked and served with a rice vinegar and oil dressing, given piquancy by a sprinkling of grapefruit juice.

The 23-euro menu is simple: after the hors d'oeuvre, fish—depending on the catch of the day—or an *entrecôte*, for non-fish eaters who happen to be taken here, we suspect. Anyway, it would be a shame to order anything but fish at Cartes Postales, although two Japanese businessmen were tucking into the steaks with enthusiasm. A large plate of various kinds of fish was served: *saumon, thon, dorade, barbue* (salmon, tuna, John Dory, brill) on a bed of tiny *haricots verts* (green beans) with little slices of leeks, and carrots, all in a subtly sweet sauce enriched with cream and chives. Never had we had such a variety of fish at one time, and never have we felt that it was so perfectly cooked.

A cheese plate consisted of ripe Camembert and *chèvre* artistically arranged on leaves of lettuce and watercress. A short dessert list: one *crème brûlée* was still available, but we settled for sorbet and *salade de fruits*, the fruit poached in a light syrup but still crunchy.

❖ *Les Cartes Postales: Japanese precision and French attention to detail make it a special place.*

Le Dauphin
167 rue St.-Honoré, 75001 Paris (01.42.60.40.11)
Métro: Palais-Royal
Open daily

Le Dauphin is modern—even with the old zinc bar to your right as you enter—and has a great location looking out on the Place André Malraux. The decor at the Dauphin is simple too, with reddish-brown banquettes, ochre walls, and small oak tables. On the walls are cartoon-like renderings of curvacious, underdressed ladies in different roles, one in net stockings and bunny ears, another with a feather fan and a chef's toque, and another with cigar, cane, and the jacket part of a tuxedo.

It's a place for a substantial, old-fashioned meal, with rich broths bubbling away in cast-iron pots, and intriguing blends of vegetables and meats.

Even on a Sunday night in August, some *formules* (fixed price menus) are available: an hors d'oeuvre and *plat* for 23 euros, and a dessert and *plat* for 21 euros. Off the fixed-price menu, the specialty of the house is *parrilladas*, grilled meat or seafood, like an assortment of grilled fish or well-aged prime rib for two, at 20 euros per person. Three of us chose the first alternative, and some unusual possibilities were there before us.

Huge plates of hors d'oeuvres appeared: the *paella* was not the classic Spanish dish, but a base of fish *fumet* in aspic, with saffron rice and seafood, and bright touches of red pepper and zucchini. *Escargots* were served on a little plate, without shells, in the traditional garlic-and-butter sauce with artichoke hearts and olives. A *salade royale* was beautifully arranged with slices of melon and grapefruit on a plate of zucchini, roasted red pepper, tomatoes, and snow peas, with a pesto sauce and *frisée* lettuce.

The *cabillaud* (fresh cod) and *joues de porc* (pork cheeks) were served in little, black cast-iron casseroles. The cod came in a rich delicate sauce of butter and chives in a base of fish *fumet*. Described as "Louisiane," it was more complex than any Creole sauce we've tasted. The *joues de porc* were small pieces of tender pork flanked by carrots and little onions, in a rich garlicky broth that seemed to have been simmered for hours before being flambéed with armagnac.

The *entrecôte* was an enormous steak with tomatoes, zucchini, and fennel, sprinkled with parsley and accompanied by two sauces. Unfortunately, although promising in appearance, the steak turned out to be tough and stringy. The friend who'd ordered it was finally persuaded to send it back and get something edible, the *cocotte d'agneau* (lamb stew), very tender in a broth with fennel, zucchini, black olives, carrots, and tomatoes.

Service at Le Dauphin was adequate, if not outstanding. The waiter extolled the virtues of French beef when we made our complaint about the toughness of the *entrecôte*, but finally did return it to the kitchen.

A good vin du Pays d'Oc was a satisfactory accompaniment to the hearty meals.

❖ *Le Dauphin: substantial and well-cooked fare. Worth a visit.*

La Fresque
100 rue Rambuteau, 75001 Paris (02.42.33.17.56)
Métro: Rambuteau
Mon–Fri, Sat eves, Sun, closed 1 week in August.

Old white tiles accented with a broad stripe of blue above the maroon banquettes; naive paintings in the style of Henri Rousseau—jungles, cats, women and a cherub—are here, there, and down the narrow stairway. This is a narrow space with ochre in a glossy finish on the ceiling.

The 12-euro lunch menu started with large plates of cold gazpacho, its intense tomato flavors reviving us as we sat in this narrow little hallway of a main room, diverted by business people talking and gesturing energetically on the banquettes against the wall.

When we arrived we saw mostly young women, business people enjoying the incredible value of this little bistro. We chose a refreshing rosé which arrived chilled in a *pichet*, just right to accompany the *filet de rascasse* (gunard or scorpion fish) in a white-wine sauce and the *sauté de veau provençale* (sautéed veal with Provençal sauce). Both *plats* were generous, the fish garnished with vegetables, purée of carrots, cooked endive, and overcooked peas—a detail, considering the value received here. The *sauté de veau*, in a hearty sauce of tomato, zucchini, and black olives, was well-flavored and filling.

We were entertained by the service; no stiff-looking waiters' uniforms here, the servers romp past in slacks and T-shirts, suitable for the heat of the day. Their manner is friendly and informal: "Vous-avez choisi, les gars?" (Made your choices, fellas?) one of them queried a table of businessmen.

❖ *La Fresque: All of us who appreciate the Pompidou Museum will be pleased to find this good little restaurant a few blocks away.*

Lescure
7 rue Mondavi, 75001 Paris (01.42.60.18.91)
Métro: Concorde
Mon–Fri lunch and dinner, closed in August

Lescure has an enviable location, just off the Place de la Concorde. And it must be doing something else right, because on a Wednesday night it was packed.

Lescure transports the diner to provincial France: you might forget you're in central Paris in this main room with its pastoral look of warmth and intimacy. The stone wall near us was covered with a large oil painting of a country scene; at the top of the painting were hung, improbably, straw hats. Wreaths of garlic drape from the beamed ceiling and in the corners of the room. The tiled floor hints at Provence. On the old zinc bar, a large bouquet of lilies and a lamp covered in burlap give light and warmth.

A bargain 19-euro menu promised a choice of *terrine de foie de volaille* (chicken liver terrine) or *saucisson de campagne ou saucisson sec* (dry salami) to be followed by haddock, *poulet au riz basquaise* (chicken Basque-style), or *boeuf bourguignon* (beef stew in wine), and a choice of cheese or dessert. Also included, a half bottle of wine. Both red and white were very drinkable, probably from one of the small vineyards in the South.

The terrine was a large tasty slice served on a bed of red lettuce with pickles and generous enough for two. The *saucisson sec* came in a good portion on a large plate, to eat with butter and the *pain paysan* (dark country bread).

Tasty chicken croquettes followed, on a bed of saffron rice with a tomato sauce accentuated with basil. The well-flavored *boeuf bourguignon* came with carrots and boiled potatoes. Nothing subtle here, but hearty and good, like our idea of typical country fare. And at Lescure in the 1st arrondissement, you're paying country prices. Amazing.

We love French sorbets, so decided to try the cassis and mandarin orange. Both were refreshing, the cassis with intense black-currant flavor, the mandarin including orange pulp and deep citrus flavors.

Here you keep your cutlery between courses—but who cares? The service is a touch casual in other ways too: we were almost served the *boeuf bourguignon* and then the waiter remembered it was for the table behind us. At first we suspected that the service might be too efficient; as we were being briskly provided with hors d'oeuves, we had the feeling that Lescure tries to accomodate several settings per evening. Still, we were allowed to linger over dessert without being pressured to leave.

❖ *Lescure: country charm and low prices in the center of town.*

Louvre

When you're in the Musée du Louvre (open Mon, Thurs–Sun 10:00 A.M.–5:00 P.M., Wed until 9:00 P.M.) there are places to stop and rest your feet while enjoying a palatial setting. One is the **Café Molière**, a summer terrace open from 10:00 A.M. to 5:00 P.M. on the first floor of the Richelieu wing. It's a better place for a quick cup of sustaining coffee than for a snack, which might include plastic-wrapped sandwiches, the type found in supermarkets, for 6 euros, or a "chef" salad in a small plastic bowl for 8 euros. Reasonably-priced drinks include coffee at 3 and tea for 4 euros.

A prettier café but without the Molière's spectacular view of the courtyard is the **Café Denon**, a restaurant and tearoom open when the Louvre is open. A vaulted ceiling and stone walls set off the tables in this elegant hideaway on the lower ground floor of the Denon wing.

Pharamond
24 rue de la Grande-Truanderie, 75001 Paris
(01.40.28.03.00)
Métro: Les Halles
Open daily except Sun eves

In a city which still has many of its lovely and old-fashioned restaurants, Pharamond, in the old Halles section of Paris, deserves special notice. What astonishes the visitor is the decor—Belle Epoque at its most extravagant. Here are extraordinary century-old tiles in intricate patterns, some picturing yellow apple trees growing out of Delft-like vases, and some forming abstract patterns around the large mirrors. Immense old mirrors make this narrow restaurant with its high ceilings appear much larger and more lively than it is. Most of the decor appears original, with only the light fixtures obvious reproductions.

The old oak bar has five old-fashioned beer pulls, and in large letters the words "Heute-Pharamond" in frosted glass on the mirror dominate the very back of the room. A winding staircase leads up to the first-floor dining room.

The specialty here is *cuisine Normande.* Dishes might contain a reduction of *pommereau,* or you could order a Calvados-spiked dessert. A good variety of main dishes are available from 13 to 15 euros. The vegetable plate of the day is 9, and an assortment of cheeses, 8 euros. *Tripes à la mode de Caen* (beef tripe cooked with vegetables and Calvados) is a house specialty.

Office workers in the area come for the 13-euro lunch special, hors d'oeuvre and *plat* or *plat* and dessert, with the house wine a reasonable 10 euros for a half liter. One day the set lunch was *oeufs mimosa,* a Gallic variation on deviled eggs, served with salad greens, followed by *brandade de morue,* a tasty combination of salt cod and mashed potatoes, whipped together with olive oil, chopped parsley, and a touch of horseradish. A very generous serving came hot in a Le Creuset casserole dish, with a good-sized green salad on the side.

The set lunch included *fondant au chocolat*, a chocolate dessert very much resembling a rich chocolate truffle, the bittersweet flavor well complemented by *crème anglaise*. We couldn't resist the description on the à la carte menu, so also ordered a *moelleux au chocolat*, partially-cooked chocolate cake served hot, the creamy filling intensely flavorful. This too was served with *crème anglaise* and colorful garnishes of fresh raspberries, orange slices, candied orange peel, and mint.

❖ *Pharamond: good value in a setting of Belle Epoque charm.*

Le Rubis
10 rue du Marché St. Honoré, 75001 Paris
(01.42.61.03.34)
Métro: Tuileries
Mon-Fri 8:00 A.M.–10:00 P.M., Sat 9:00 A.M.–4:00 P.M.,
closed August

Before the glamor, before the high-priced houses of fashion had claimed this part of the city, there were little retreats like the Rubis. A simple, old-fashioned wine bar in a chic neighborhood not far from the Ritz Hotel, Le Rubis gives the impression of being out of its time and place, belonging to the past. There's something irrepressibly cozy about this little hangout, with its 1920s-era molding curving above a classic zinc-topped oak bar. Stripes of neon in pink and white zigzag above emphasize the Deco effect. The interior is done in calming ivory tones, with little framed prints here and there.

Permanently posted is a long and impressive list of wines available by the glass, at petite prices at the bar, a little more if you sit on the comfortable red banquettes behind the simple formica tables. This is a friendly place—a motorcyclist stops by for directions and everybody chimes in with advice, the couple behind the bar and an elegant, red-gowned lady with a dozing spaniel on the leash.

Hot food is available at lunch: simple food—*saucisson chaud* (hot salami)on Mondays, *tête de veau* (calf's head) on Tuesdays, *petit salé aux lentilles* (pork rib with lentils) on

Wednesdays—or you can make do very well with a plate of *charcuterie* or one of their good sandwiches, perhaps a *saucisson sec* on *pain poilâne*. In the afternoons peace reigns at Le Rubis, and it's a perfect stop for a snack, a glass of wine, or a coffee, in a part of the city where most bars like this have long since ceased to exist.

❖ *Le Rubis: good* cuisine familiale *in an unspoiled wine bar from the past.*

Le Tambour
41 rue Montmartre, 75002 Paris (01.42.33.06.90)
Métro: Les Halles or Sentier
Open daily, 24 hours a day

If it's late or early and everything else is closed, try Le Tambour, its emblem a sturdy little drummer in Napoleon's army. Here's the possibility of an unbelievably low-priced lunch in the center of the financial district, near the Bourse, or stock exchange. It's only 10 euros for the *formule* of hors d'oeuvre and *plat*, or *plat* and dessert, and à la carte lunch prices are very fair.

Here are low ceilings in the usual faded café ochre, walls decorated with real Paris street and métro bric-a-brac: a genuine old métro map from the Stalingrad stop, plaques of instructions and warnings, and bar stools made from large red-and-yellow bus route signs with "Faire signe au machiniste," along with the name of the specific stop—Emile Zola and Ecoles are two we noticed.

The menu makes it formal: "André Camboulas et son équipe ont le plaisir de vous accueillir 7 jours sur 7, 24 heures sur 24." (André and his team welcome you . . .) In short, Le Tambour is always open. André, his uncombed hair and wild mustache giving him the look of a hippie or *ancien soixante-huitard* (one of those who rioted in '68), tends bar, occasionally calling out greetings and farewells in a resounding, gravelly voice.

The 10-euro lunch offered good variety: among other hors d'oeuvres, we noticed *crudités, oeuf mayonnaise,* terrine of sole, and others. *Plats* included a *pot au feu* (beef stew), *salade nordique* (smoked salmon and shrimp salad), *steak-frites* (steak with fries), and *viande froide* (cold meat plate).

For hors d'oeuvres, we chose artichokes, accompanied by a little pot of vinaigrette. Very good—a better hors d'oeuvre than expected at the price. The *tourte* resembled a hot quiche, with egg, spinach, bits of pork, and a savory cheese topping. An *assiette anglaise*, or cold meat plate, consisted of sliced roast beef, a roasted chicken thigh, hot French fries, and lettuce and tomato—rather like a good picnic lunch with fries. To accompany all of this, the 7-euro carafe of the *vin du mois*, a Touraine, was very drinkable.

Desserts were *tartes*—open-faced pies—and we chose the *poire-chocolat*, a tasty if unlikely-sounding combination.

In the evenings, it's all à la carte. A children's menu is then available, made up of just what appeals to a child: *steak haché, frites, glace* (hamburger, fries, ice cream) for 8 euros.

The mood at Le Tambour, when it's not lunchtime frantic, is pleasantly informal; our waiter sat down with some regulars to figure out their bill, there was jovial bantering at the bar, and occasionally the voice of André would thunder forth. Habitués are more likely to be readers of *Libération* than of the *Figaro*, which has offices just down the street, but a few thrifty stockbroker types stride in from the Bourse.

❖ *Le Tambour: loud and lively; bistro classics and excellent value.*

Le Tir-Bouchon
22 rue Tiquetonne, 75002 Paris (01.42.21.95.51)
Métro: Etienne-Marcel
Mon-Sat noon-3:00 P.M., 8:00 P.M.-11:00 P.M., Sun. eves

L e Tir-Bouchon (corkscrew) would be a great name for a wine bar, but in this case it's an exceedingly pleasant bistro in the garment district of Paris. You enter a large pleasant room with dark beams showing up against an ochre ceiling, exposed old stone on one wall, and elaborate, Second-Empire wainscotting on another. A feeling of warmth is here, coming from old and gleaming copper pots, vintage harness, and framed photos of the area on a wall of sponged apricot. At the back, an unusual bar in gleaming copper has banks of wine bottles stacked nearby.

The 13-euro lunch menu offered a substantial meal with wine. It included starters like a *salade de crudités* (raw vegetable salad) or the *assiette de bulots* (whelks, a marine snail), followed by *coquelet rôti à la sauge* (chicken roasted with sage), *panaché de poisson* (a mixture of fish), and for dessert, *charlotte au chocolat* (molded cream dessert) or fruit, as well as a choice of a quarter bottle of wine, white, red, or rosé according to the diner's preference.

A 19-euro menu offering an *entrée, plat,* and dessert but no wine includes more extravagant classics like foie gras and *steak de gigot* (lamb steak). A varied and interesting wine list is chalked up on a slate board, but you could always try a *pot* of the very drinkable house wine at 9 or 11 euros.

The friendly waiter likes to try out his English. Since we were using our French, what emerged from him was Franglais— "The feesh, pour vous?"—but we liked his attitude.

Crudités were a large, attractive arrangement of tomato, chopped celeriac, cucumber, red and yellow bell pepper, and onion, in a light vinaigrette. The *plats* were served on very hot plates: artfully arranged and very fresh-tasting fish was accompanied by small potatoes and cucumber in a drawn butter sauce, the chicken with carrots and small oven-baked potatoes, in a sauce fragrant with sage.

For dessert, the *charlotte au chocolat,* a light, spongy-textured chocolate mousse with a biscuit base in delicious *crème anglaise,* had a delicate undertaste of *crème fraîche.*

❖ *Le Tir-Bouchon: good food in a charming little bistro.*

A la Tour de Montlhéry (Chez Denise)
5 rue des Prouvaires 75001 Paris (01.42.36.21.82)
Métro: Châtelet
Mon 7:00 A.M.–Sat 7:00 A.M. closed mid-July–mid August

When Les Halles was the great food market of Paris, there were dozens of all-night bistros like this one serving the locals. Most are gone now. The porters and meatcutters have gone to Rungis, and the workers crowding Chez Denise are now artists and young professionals.

You enter a typical bistro with a long bar and are ushered into a second room, a dining room with long tables on both sides. People squeeze in close to each other on the long banquettes. Your first impression is that this place is wild, raucous, exuberant beyond belief, that it recalls Paris student life as it has existed from the time of François Villon to our own.

Wedged in beside a Frenchman devouring a *steak tartare*, we have a few minutes to observe the old stone walls, huge beams above, dark sienna ceiling, framed art work, photographs, and unframed oils—none of which seems to have any relationship to the others. There is joyous flirting and hand-holding on the dark red banquettes across the narrow tables.

The waiter imperiously bangs down a metal basket with dark breads and a large plate of butter. There are *jambons d'Auvergne* and *saucissons* hanging down from the ceiling. An *ardoise* is chalked with the selections of the day—you struggle to interpret the handwriting and the thing is whisked away. But you remember one or two safe items (the menu is heavy on the bistro classics most foreigners are afraid of—tripe, kidneys, brains, and the like), and you succeed in bellowing out an order.

One of us goes for the haddock, which comes in large, orange-gold segments in a delicious sea of *beurre blanc*, with boiled potatoes lightly dusted with parsley on the side. The fish has a slightly smoky, vaguely salty flavor and is wonderful with *beurre blanc*. The other orders beef, *onglet*. The large flank steak is seared and grilled, and served in its own juices with *frisée* lettuce and a large side dish of fries. Easily enough for two diners with modest appetites.

For wine there is the house Brouilly, and you pay only for what you drink. Not especially thirsty, we're charged only 7 euros for the third of a bottle we consume between us.

The waiters could be characters out of a film; asking ours for the usual "carafe d'eau," I was told "Ce n'est pas possible"

(it's not possible), but he relents and comes back later with fresh glasses and water.

Students who come here have to be fairly well-heeled; *plats* are 16 or 19 euros, but servings are large. Afterward we see some brave people nearby digging into great rectangles of *baba au rhum* with large rosettes of whipped cream.

A smiling Chinese gentleman, a longtime regular at Chez Denise, starts speaking to us just as we are paying our bill, and we exchange a few words. "This is where people who don't know each other talk," he says, adding, "Lots of artists, artistic people here. Singers from Opera."

Chez Denise is not a place for those who require a restaurant of refinement and elegance, of opulence and hushed sounds, white linen and obsequious waiters. So what! Chez Denise has old-fashioned charm, good-natured noise, well-cooked bistro food, and a chic and up-to-date clientele. Great fun.

❖ *Chez Denise: a Paris experience that should not be missed.*

THE MAGICAL MARAIS: THE 3RD & 4TH ARRONDISSEMENTS

...sometimes it seemed right to me that the capital should recall its history through the medium of the Marais, perform its intellectual tasks with the aid of the fifth district, and do its sums in the Stock Exchange quarter...

—Julien Green, *Paris*

If you miss the Marais, you miss the best part of Paris. The small streets near the Place des Vosges are vestiges of a human and personal city from before the time of the great boulevards. One of the oldest parts of the city, the Marais is now in some ways new and fashionable again. From the great squares close by comes the boom of rock music when there's a festival or a demonstration; in the Marais, canny street musicians practice their Bach.

The 3rd arrondissement is across the street from us when we live in Paris. Cross the boulevard and you move from the working-class 11th, which for years now has been the area to watch, to the more stable and prosperous 3rd district. In the 3rd can be found buildings that are not high, still on a human scale, and, on some walls, intriguing old signs fading in blues and greens with the lettering partially worn away.

Here is a traditional trade, leatherworking. Skilled craftsmen still create fine garments for the couturiers; they still do impressive work in tiny ateliers, and in hot weather the doors propped open to give them a breath of air supply you with a glimpse of fingers flying over fabric and leather, crowded studios, and feverish activity.

As you go toward the Bastille, you enter the 4th arrondissement. Today this is desirable property indeed. It might

be thought of as the Parisian version of New York's Greenwich Village or London's Chelsea. Many gay people live in the area. So does the bishop of the Episcopal Church. In recent years the 4th has become what the 6th, especially St. Germain-des-Prés, used to be: a place of such charm that it draws like a magnet the highly-placed and the intelligentsia who can afford to live here—Jack Lang, former minister of culture, has an apartment on the Place des Vosges. The district attracts tourists, chic Parisians, a large part of the gay community, and anyone else susceptible to the narrow streets winding between buildings that belong to Victor Hugo's Paris, pre-Haussmann and with a scattering of select small shops, art galleries, and bistros.

In the center is the Place des Vosges, a perfect square, originally called the Place Royal when it was finished in 1612. Walk around this seventeenth-century wonder with the covered passage, admire the dark red brick façades and the vaulted ceilings above. Through an occasional half-open shutter you glimpse noble salons with high ceilings and dark beams.

Here in one corner at number six lived the author of *Les Misérables.* He was visited there once by Charles Dickens, who described Victor Hugo as a genius encumbered with a sinister-looking wife and daughter. He wrote: "Sitting among old armour, and old tapestry, and old coffers, and grim old chairs and tables, and old Canopies of state from old palaces, and old golden lions going to play at skittles with ponderous old golden balls, they made a most romantic show, and looked like a chapter out of one of his own books."

Farther west from the Place des Vosges, the rue Pavée is in the historic and picturesque Jewish quarter, crossing the rue des Rosiers. This street has been the center of a small Jewish community since the 1770s, but became more populated in the late nineteenth century with immigrants arriving from Eastern Europe.

Nowadays the bistros, galleries, and artists' workshops in the Marais still draw visitors. Creative people live here—artists, and workers from the television and film-making world, young people of all colors and countries. Much of the nightlife of Paris spills out onto the streets, especially during the warm months.

Not many streets away, you ask yourself: "Is it a plumber's nightmare? A giant Erector-set construction in primary colors, a broken toy created and discarded by a deranged

child?" Whatever it is, the Centre Georges Pompidou draws more visitors than any other attraction in Paris except, possibly, the Eiffel Tower. Here is street theater: jugglers, acrobats, fire-eaters, all manner of extemporaneous entertainment. And the crowds flock there to admire or scoff at their efforts.

Toward the west, going up the rue de Rivoli, you find yourself nearing two national institutions: on your right is the BHV (Bazar de l'Hôtel de Ville, or "bay-ash-vay" to Parisians), the department store for do-it-yourselfers, including an amazing basement with incredible variety, a sort of super hardware store, fascinating even if you don't happen to need anything they're selling or can't imagine how you'd ever get it home.

Continuing up the rue de Rivoli toward the Seine, on your left you see the soaring façade of the Hôtel de Ville, or Town Hall, a lofty and majestic nineteenth-century structure. Inside, in the reception rooms, are gilt, mirrors, and chandeliers in typical late-nineteenth-century extravagance. Our favorite story about the Hôtel de Ville was told by the late president François Mitterrand in his memoirs. He related an experience that happened right after World War II, when General de Gaulle was attempting to give a speech from the Hôtel de Ville. Since the building has no balconies, he had to lean far out of the window to deliver his speech. Mitterand and his friend were called on for support. Standing behind him, they had to clutch the General's legs as he leaned forward to keep him from toppling out onto his audience. After the experience was over, De Gaulle might have wondered if the effort had been worth it; the crowd, confused about who had been speaking, kept interrupting him with shouts of "Vive LeClerc!"

A profound loss to the city was Les Halles, the wholesale food market, which had existed for over 800 years. In 1969 it was relocated out to the suburb of Rungis. Many observers compared this to ripping out the city's center. In its place, a bland, American-style, covered shopping mall—le Forum des Halles—opened in 1978. It takes up some of the leftover space but will never have the liveliness of the old Halles.

Some bistros in the area:

Au Bascou
38 rue Réaumur, 75003 Paris (01.42.72.69.25)
Métro: République
Tues–Fri lunch and dinner, Mon and Sat dinner only

This is one of those little, out-of-the-way restaurants people collect cards from to give to their friends. The owner is a jovial, mustachioed man looking as if he had just stepped off the train from his town in Southwest France. He rightly prides himself on the richness of the country food and regional wines here.

The interior is warmed with colors of the Southwest: terra cotta, cinnamon, and sun-ripened pumpkin. The walls have the look of a picturesque ruin, with cracks and fissures painted over. Dried red peppers hang in bunches from the beams. In a second dining room is a wall of exposed stone and another terra cotta-colored wall. The look is so inviting that one can almost forgive the naive paintings of a Basque farmer with his cows and another of a pair of starry-eyed young lovers.

Au Bascou gives you a chance to sample outstanding Basque cuisine at reasonable prices which do not vary between lunch and dinner. (Hors d'oeuvres are 9, main dishes 14, and desserts 6 euros).

The *piperade* we sampled was a beautifully presented hors d'oeuvre, rounds of egg in layers with tomato and flat-leafed parsley, as attractive as in a multi-starred restaurant.

Plats were large and impressive: *tloro de Labourd*, a Basque fish soup resembling *bouillabaisse*, was a saffron-colored taste treat, with various kinds of fish, mussels, red bell peppers, tomatoes, onion, garlic, parsley, and potatoes. It was topped with two alarming-looking *langoustines*, which turned out to be delicious. The *magret de canard "Amatxi"*—the friendly waitress explained this as meaning "façon grand-mère" or in the old-fashioned style—was a generous serving of duck breast with crisp, if slightly blackened potatoes in an intensely flavored sauce. A basket of dark, well-textured *pain de campagne* was just right to go with Basque food, and perfect for getting every last bit of the delicious soup and sauce.

Desserts at Au Bascou do not disappoint: we shared a delicious *baba au Patxaran*, which a considerate cook had split elegantly in the kitchen; half a baba each on a base of *crème anglaise* over a *coulis* or sauce of red fruits, with a small *quenelle* of coffee ice cream and a sprig of fresh mint. *Patxaran,* our waitress informed us, is a Basque liqueur made from *prunelles,* little wild plums. Whatever it was, it was good.

On a rainy Thursday night Au Bascou, which is not famous or in the center of town, was packed with happy diners.

❖ *Au Bascou: outstanding Basque cuisine at fair prices.*

Auberge de Jarente
7 rue de Jarente, 75004 Paris (01.45.51.78.08)
Métro: St. Paul
Tues–Sat noon–2:00 P.M., 7:30 P.M.–10:30 P.M.,
closed in August

Situated on little rue de Jarente in the Marais, this bistro is well named, with the ambiance of an inn conveyed in its dark wood, dark tablecloths, and small-paned windows overlooking a quiet corner. The Basque theme is carried out on the pale walls, with original posters of La Côte Basque, a Spanish wineskin, a copper bedwarmer, and *pelote* bats lending an intriguing informality.

Lunch here is a bargain: a 13-euro menu includes three courses and a quart or quarter-liter of a French vin du pays.

At night, the four-course meal is 22 euros including wine, or 19 without. Ours started with one of their own creations, a Kayola salad, fresh and delicious, a bright plateful of lean, smoked bacon, served warm, with diced yellow peppers, mushrooms, spinach, tomatoes, and parsley on a bed of lettuce. The *timbale de chiperons à l'estragon,* an intriguing cold hors d'oeuvre, was a concoction of tiny squid, served in a little clay pot with onions, lettuce, and pearl barley in a vinaigrette.

A couple in the corner on their way out recommended the *cassoulet:* "Outstanding." So we ordered it and *marmiteko de thon*, fresh tuna cooked in a little clay pot of rich, mostly tomato flavors, with white wine, onions, and garlic to add further flavor. The *cassoulet*, which included a fair amount of duck, sausage, and lean pork, along with the white beans that form its base, was delicious, a memorable dish.

Following the *plat*, a choice of cheese or salad. Our waiter particularly recommended the Brie, which was ripe to perfection and just right with the pleasant *vin du pays*.

Desserts were more than adequate: the *pralinée,* a praline ice cream confection, was made up of layers of praline ice cream separated by toasted almonds, the whole on *crème anglaise*. A *fondant au chocolat* was moist and rich, and the fruit salad a winning combination of fresh nectarines, watermelon, cantaloupe, and apple in their juices.

❖ *Auberge de Jarente: flavorful Basque cuisine in a charming setting.*

Baracane-Bistro de l'Oulette
33 rue des Tournelles, 75004 Paris (01.42.71.43.33)
Métro: Bastille
Mon–Sat noon–2:30 P.M., 7:00 P.M.–midnight

This bistro makes the most of a long, narrow room near the elegant Place des Vosges, by using pale yellow colors, black and white photos, and old brass coathangers.

Two economical lunches here tempt business people in the Marais: a *plat*, or main dish, with a glass of wine for 9 euros, and a choice of hors d'oeuvre or dessert with a main dish and a glass of wine for 14 euros.

The hors d'oeuvre had more refinement and subtlety than many bistro offerings: it was smoked salmon topping a bed of lettuce and red onions garnished with dill in a pleasing mayonnaise with dill and chives.

Following was a fricassée of lamb with thyme, an attractive, generous serving in a tasty broth of tomatoes, carrots, and zucchini, accompanied by the precisely-carved little potatoes that make you wonder if French cooks aren't frustrated artists. The *plats* were well-flavored and filling.

The wine list featured good selections from the South, available for 3 to 4 euros a glass. A half-bottle of Gaillac Château Lascours was a smooth red that went well with lamb.

Our friendly and efficient waitress was fluent in English.

❖ *Baracane de l'Oulette: good value for money.*

Bofinger
5-7 rue de la Bastille, 75004 Paris (01.42.72.87.82)
Metro:Bastille
Open daily noon–3:00 P.M., 6:30 P.M.–1:00 A.M.

Bofinger, near the Bastille, was the first place in Paris to serve draft beer. Started as a small brasserie by Frédéric Bofinger in 1864, it did not appear in its present form until 1919 when new owners enlarged the premises and hired architect Guy Legay and designer Mitdgen.

A lunch *formule* at 19 euros offers *entrée* and *plat* or *plat* and dessert, and wine. It's available from Monday to Friday, except on holidays, and attracts businesss people from the Bastille area as well as camera-laden tourists. If you want to dine at night, a 30-euro *prix fixe* menu includes hors d'oeuvre, *plat*, dessert, and a half bottle of wine.

A common criticism of the Flo Group is that menus tend to remain the same for a long time, so this menu may still be in force when you arrive. The hors d'oeuvres *compôte d'aubergines et mozzarrella* (eggplant and mozzarella), six *huitres creuses de Bretagne* (oysters from Brittany), and gazpacho are followed by *plats filet de merou à la graine de moutard et julienne de légumes* (grouper filet with mustard and slivers of vegetables), or *navarin d'agneau aux olive et courgettes provençales* (lamb stew with olives and zucchini), and ending with *glace* (ice cream) or chocolate mousse.

We started with gazpacho: colorful, with deep, intense tomato flavor, it was dotted with tiny croutons and little bits of cucumber and parsley. A tangy delight, cool and refreshing, almost a meal in itself.

Plats are well presented at Bofinger: the *navarin* of lamb was served on a background of dark sauce, the plate ornamented with small tomatoes, potatoes, and sprigs of parsley. It was a tender lamb stew in a rich gravy. A delicate fish, the *merou* was on a tasty bed of carrots and zucchini in butter, strikingly set off by red tomato, dark -green fresh dill, and a sprinkling of parsley. The sauce had just the right touch of mustard for piquancy.

The little attention we could spare from lunch was irresistibly drawn to Bofinger's stunning decor—a skylight overhead was decorated with fruit and flowers in shades of lilac, pink, and yellow. Enormous mirrors, frilly Victorian-style light fixtures in the shape of flowers, and the old bistro rails above the diners once used to hang the hats that were then in fashion.

❖ *Bofinger: decent, reasonably-priced, if predictable food in a setting of Art Nouveau splendor.*

Brasserie de l'Ile Saint-Louis
55 quai de Bourbon, 75004 Paris (01.43.54.02.59)
Métro: Pont Marie
Mon, Tues, Fri–Sun 12:00 P.M.–1:00 A.M., Thurs 5:00
P.M.–1:00 A.M., closed Wed and in August

The Brasserie is on the top of the Ile Saint Louis, a tiny island in the heart of Paris with some of the most expensive real estate in the city. Though the tables in front overlook the river and Right Bank, most patrons head back to a room which takes you to an old-fashioned restaurant in pre-war Germany, or, in this case, Alsace. Everything about this place, from the casual greeting of the maître d' as he waves you to a table to the food and ambiance, has a Teutonic flavor.

You choose from lots of hot and cold German specialties, to be washed down with Alsatian wines, or, if you prefer, beer. This is hearty, rib-sticking fare—even the hors d'oeuvres lend one ballast, with selections like *salade de frisée et lardons* (bacon and lettuce salad) and *tarte à l'oignon* (onion quiche), all around 7 euros.

The *plats* go on in the same theme: *choucroute garni*

(sauerkraut with sausages and pork), *onglet de boeuf aux échalottes* (flank steak with shallots*), faux filet beurre maître d'hôtel* (sirloin steak with lemon and parsley butter), and others, priced from 14 to 22 euros.

The wine list includes mainly wines of Alsace and some standards, including Rothschild's Mouton Cadet and a number from Georges Duboeuf. Most are reasonably priced from 15 euros a bottle.

Nothing is subtle about the Brasserie de l'Ile: everything speaks of Old Germany on a night of celebration, with the noisy, cheerful, roof-lifting din. Above and around you are turn-of-the-century original posters, some featuring brasseries, mounted heads of small animals and others not so small, and the enormous head of a *sanglier*, or wild boar, complete with tusks, glaring aggressively down. Colors are strong and vibrant: huge, burnished copper pots gleam against dark beams. In some ways the Brasserie may remind you of one of the legendary old taverns frequented by generations of Ivy League students. The waiters, though, are defiantly Parisian, and, like the traditional Parisian waiter, they manage to seem both servile and superior at the same time.

Our three orders, *choucroute garnie, onglet de boeuf,* and *omelette mixte* were good if not subtle. The *choucroute*—sauerkraut—is not as sour as you may be used to, the cabbage slightly crisper and with less of a vinegary flavor, but the portions are huge and the accompanying crisp juicy sausage, pork slices, and smoked bacon were tasty and filling. An *onglet de boeuf,* or flank steak, was flavorful and served with potatoes. The *omelette mixte,* a fluffy, golden ham-and-cheese omelet, was well-made and delicious.

You don't come to the Brasserie de l'Ile Saint-Louis for really sophisticated French cuisine or a quiet, romantic tête à tête, but if you want a time-warp type of experience, a romantic "Sound of Music" pre-war *bierstube* which also has a decent wine list, 55 quai de Bourbon is the place to go.

❖ *Brasserie de l'Ile Saint-Louis: a taste of Alsace.*

Camille
24 rue des Francs-Bourgeois, 75003 Paris (01.42.72.20.50)
Métro: Bastille
Open daily noon–midnight

A cheerful little bistro on the corner of rue des Francs-Bourgeois and rue Elzevir, Camille has the incomparable advantage of being open when you need it. The decor is simple: sponged ochre walls, a few posters, including an impressive original of a circus. But it's a cosy place to go when you want decent food at a price that won't break your budget: a 16 euro lunch *formule* offers *entrée* and *plat* or *plat* and dessert.

Our meal started with *salade de chèvre*, rounds of warm goat cheese on toast topping a salad of mixed greens in a tasty vinaigrette.

We proceeded to the *plats*. The *bar* (European sea bass) was three filets over a mixture of tomatoes with a savory blend of red peppers, lemon juice, and chopped parsley. With this, boiled potatoes. The *rouille d'agneau* was a large center cutlet of grilled lamb, the herbs contributing a Provençal flavor, on a bed of ratatouille—again, the good flavors of the South.

With the *plats* we chose a Pays d'Oc Sauvignon, available in carafes at 4 euros for a small carafe and double that for a demi, or half liter.

At night prices are à la carte, with hors d'oeuvres for 7 to 11 euros, *plats* from 13 to 16 euros. And the choices are excellent: hors d'oeuvres include escargots and foie gras; *plats* are generous and reasonably-priced—a steak with pepper or Béarnaise sauce is 14 euros.

At Camille, the servings are such that a *plat* can be a meal. But if you want to indulge yourself a little further, desserts are 7 euros à la carte. We found the bittersweet chocolate tart an excellent finish.

There's a pleasant informality about this bistro, and we found ourselves chatting with the Breton on our left and a couple who had come all the way from Hong Kong with their small son.

❧ *Camille: an address to remember in the Marais.*

L'Endroit
24 rue des Tournelles, 75004 Paris (01.42.72.03.07)
Métro:Bastille
Mon–Sat lunch and dinner

L'Endroit has an excellent location near the Place des Vosges and the Bastille. It also has a 14-euro menu (11 at noon) that tends to promise more than it delivers.

We were rather taken by the spare, clean, and minimalist decor, the rich, warm colors that recall the South of France. Like most people around us we ordered from the set menu, starting with a *tapenade de légumes*, a little ramekin-shaped mound of tomato, red pepper, zucchini, and carrots, with a touch of lemon. Although a few olives would have given the mixture more zest, we found it a successful hors d'oeuvre, accompanied by the mini-basket of fresh bread. A half bottle of Sancerre from Verdigny-en-Sancerre was a pleasant accompaniment.

Afterward we chose the *émincé de poulet à la vanille* and the *papillotte de saumon*. The fresh-tasting salmon arrived, surprisingly, still in the large nest of aluminium foil where it had cooked with tomatoes. The chicken was perhaps a three-ounce portion—certainly no more—divided into little pieces in a sauce flavored with vanilla. The idea seemed original, but the portion measly. Both dishes were accompanied by small ramekin-shaped mounds of white rice. Now, chicken is not caviar and rice is not expensive, so it's hard to see why the kitchen seemed so stingy.

For dessert, a tiramisù was light and nice, powdered with cocoa, tasting of coffee, classic and successful.

❖ *L'Endroit: the right address if you're on a calorie-restricted diet. With a little more warmth in the welcome, and more generosity in the servings, this could be a good* endroit—*a place to return to.*

La Fontaine Gourmande
11 rue Charlot, 75003 Paris (01.42.78.72.40)
Métro: Filles du Calvaire
Mon-Fri noon–2:30 P.M., 7:00 P.M.–10:30 P.M., Sat dinner
only, closed August

La Fontaine Gourmande is a little bistro that draws from the sophisticated set who live and work in the 3rd arrondissement. It's a neighborhood hangout, in a neighborhood that's gay and artsy with a touch of Greenwich Village about it. The Denise René Gallery, home of puzzling paintings and sculpture, is just down the street, as are the offices of the local Socialist Party. Small workshops abound.

The look inside is of the Basque country, with exposed stone walls, reproductions of old posters, and tiny bouquets of dried flowers on the small tables. A Second-Empire style bar in warm wood is topped with zinc, and a high ceiling gives a feeling of spaciousness.

La Fontaine offers low-priced lunches. For 8 euros you can enjoy a hearty *tartine,* an open-faced sandwich flanked by an abundance of green salad. We tried the *vosgienne,* a large and delicious concoction with three types of cheese— Emmenthal, Conté, and Reblochon—melted on new potatoes with *lardons* (bacon), the whole on *pain poilâne.* One of the two *plats* offered at lunch was *cabillaud* (fresh cod) in a good cream sauce, accompanied by crisp green beans, broccoli, and small boiled potatoes. A small carafe of a fruity white Georges Duboeuf wine for 9 euros made a nice accompaniment.

Predictably, prices go up in the evening, with hors d'oeuvres from 8 to 12, and *plats* from 13 to 18 euros.

❖ *La Fontaine Gourmande: very competent cooking and friendly ambiance.*

Les Fous d'en Face (The Crazy People Across from Us)
3 rue du Bourg-Tibourg, 75004 Paris (01.48.87.03.75)
Métro Hôtel de Ville
Tues–Sat lunch and dinner, closed August

Les Fous is liked by just about everybody and it's no wonder. Here you can have a sophisticated lunch for 14 euros excluding wine.

The noon menu one day offered the usual *formule: plat* with hors d'oeuvres or dessert for 14 euros. Typical noon offerings, written on the blackboard, might be endives *au pamplemousse* (with grapefruit) or *salade de foie de volaille* (salad with chicken livers) to start, followed by a choice of *bavette grillé* (grilled flank steak), *gigot d'agneau* (leg of lamb), or *filet de julienne, sauce basilic* (burbot fish with basil sauce).

A short wine list, also on a blackboard, offered wines mostly from the Loire. We eventually settled on a very satisfactory rosé, a Touraine.

While waiting for our *plats* we glanced around at the clientele—business and professional people, with some government workers from the nearby Hôtel de Ville. We were diverted to hear two well-dressed men next to us grumbling about the investigations for corruption that had been going on. One of them was complaining about lawyers:

"Les avocats, ils sont tous nuls," (Lawyers are all zeros) pronounced a mustachioed gent, his hair in a gray crewcut. "La justice est pourrie." (The courts are rotten).

(We wondered if there were lawyer jokes in France—there must be). Later we were to hear the same man discussing the situation further and using words that do not belong in a family guidebook.

The *gigot,* or leg of lamb, was a hearty meal, a plate of generous slices of flavorful lamb in sauce, with crisp, scalloped potatoes, and *haricots verts*—green beans. The *julienne,* or burbot fish, dotted with flecks of red pepper and basil, was served with a delicious cream sauce, with rice and little circles of cooked zucchini. Both *plats* were good and substantial meals.

At dessert time, we were glad we'd chosen that option. The desserts brought to mind tropical climes and exotic fruits, suitable to the heat wave Paris was experiencing. A colorful mango sherbet, as delicious as it looked, was garnished with tiny slices of peach and strawberry; the *flan de noix de coco*, a delectable creation, half cake, half coconut and Bavarian cream, was served on *crème anglaise* with slices of strawberry and mint leaves for garnish.

❖ *Les Fous d'en Face: the location is superb, and lunch a gourmet bargain.*

Le Grizzli
7 rue Saint-Martin (01.48.87.77.56) 75004 Paris
Métro: Hôtel de Ville
Mon eves, Tues–Fri noon–2:00 P.M., 7:30–11 P.M., Sat eves

At the Grizzli, you'll find yourself in a charming small bistro, with classic dark ochre walls, turn-of-the-century type molding—and bears! Within, in addition to the eight small tables and an unusual marble bar, large framed caricatures of bears on the walls lighten and amuse. Well-placed soft lights are reflected in the mirrors, and the thin, lacy café curtains allow a look at street life outside. The black banquettes along the sides of the room have aluminum rails in a Deco design, probably original.

A menu of unusual interest at 19 euros featured the starters *terrine de canard aux noisettes* (duck terrine with hazelnuts) and *brochette de moules* (mussels on a skewer), then a choice of salmon or free-range chicken, and cheese, ice cream, or sherbet to finish.

Moules en brochette were sticks of breaded mussels, sautéed until golden, with a pot of Béarnaise sauce to accompany them. Delicious, with touches of garlic and butter. The haddock was elegantly arranged against a background of dark beets, the slight saltiness of the fish compensated for by the natural sweetness of the vegetable.

The *plat* was a large salmon steak topped with a sprinkling of sea salt, an effective touch which heightened the flavor of the salmon. Pesto sauce and a bed of well-flavored ratatouille made this a variation from the usual. A carafe of the good house rosé was a refreshing accompaniment.

Desserts from the menu include the classics as well as *tarte au chocolat* (chocolat tart) and *croustade aux pruneaux* (prunes in pastry). With the 19-euro menu is a choice of cheese, glace, or sorbet. Ice creams and sherbets come in intriguing flavors, including *pruneaux armagnac*, the plum-flavored ice cream and the armagnac complementing each other unexpectedly well.

Service is courteous, laid-back but not intrusive. We have, however, been told that there has been a change in ownership.

❖ *Le Grizzli: an old-fashioned Parisian favorite.*

Le Hangar
12 Impasse Berthaud, 75001 Paris (01.42.74.55.44)
Métro: Rambuteau
Mon eves only, Tues–Sat noon–3:00 P.M., 6:30
P.M.–midnight, closed in August
No credit cards

Le Hangar is one of those trendy, contemporary bistros that have been cropping up and attracting a young crowd. The owners have brought a minimalist elegance as well as serious cooking to this backlot commercial area. Le Hangar is attractive, with exposed stone walls, a modern black-and-red façade, pleasant terrace, and Provençal tablecloths. It's well located, only a few steps from the Pompidou Museum.

An interesting and inventive cuisine here: hors d'oeuvres were all between 6 and 8 euros. *Plats* including *fettucine au citron et crevettes roses* (fettucini with shrimp) and *escalope de foie gras de canard* (slice of fattened duck liver), varied between 11 and 20 euros.

We chose the *filet de boeuf aux morilles* and *dos de saumon* from the menu. The steak came in a delicious sauce of morel mushrooms and cream, with a small plate of scalloped potatoes on the side. The *dos de saumon avec courgettes* was less impressive: a small portion of salmon paired with rolled-up zucchini made for a skimpy, uninteresting *plat*, which could have been improved by a slice of lemon or a light sauce.

The real strength of Le Hangar may be its desserts. The *petit gâteau mi-cuit au chocolat* was a partially cooked—*mi cuit*—cake that arrived still warm, the interior of dark chocolate oozing out at a touch, melting onto your spoon. If you don't care for chocolate, Le Hangar typically has possibilities like *clafoutis à la rhubarbe* (rhubarb cake), apple crumble, and *crêpes à l'orange et au Grand Marnier.*

Service was friendly, and the waitresses seemed genuinely to care about customer satisfaction. Thoughtful touches were the *amuse-gueules* at the beginning, *tapenade* with toasted slices of baguette, and a post-dessert plate of tiny mini-desserts, enough to give you a notion of what they can do with lemon tart, macaroons, fudge, and shortbread.

❖ *Le Hangar: results uneven, but they're trying. Not worth a trip across town, but if you're in the neighborhood, you'll like it.*

Lina's Sandwiches
47 rue des Francs-
Bourgeois, 75004 Paris
(01.44.78.95.00)
Métro: Bastille
Open daily to 7:00 P.M.

The Lina's in the Marais has the characteristic cheery, sponged-yellow interior with green accents in the trim. Color, too, is in the bright vegetables prominently displayed that will make up your sandwiches at budget-friendly prices, from 3 euros for *oeuf-mayonnaise* to 8 euros for the club. The sandwiches are good: ours on freshly toasted *pain biologique* were delivered warm to our table. Soup and salad run from 4 euros to 6 euros, and, for the thirsty, Lina's offers coffee for 2 euros and even a glass of wine for 3 euros.

Comfortable chairs, some high metal bar stools around circular metal tables, a green board with the day's selections, a freezer of Häagen-Daz for the homesick Americans—in short, all that you need to settle in and feel at ease. Lina's in the Marais caters to yuppies with children from the neighborhood; many of the clientele seem to know one another.

❖ *Lina's: not a bistro, but a friendly alternative for a quick snack, and a welcoming place for children.*

Le Louis Philippe
66 quai de l'Hôtel de Ville, 75004 Paris (01.42.72.29.42)
Métro: Hôtel de Ville
Open daily noon–3:00 P.M., 7:00–11:00 P.M.

This is a place where time has stood still. Or so you might think, stepping over Florent, the enormous dog that guards the door, and entering this bistro. Whether you go in or not depends on your feeling about dogs and the weather—there is a terrace.

photo © Juliana Spear

Ushered out of the picturesque bar into the restaurant side, we chose a table which gave us a view of the tiny kitchen—but even this table had its compensations. It also gave a good view of an antique sign on the wall, in wonderful Art Nouveau lettering on glass: *Café 20c la tasse.* The sign is right over an antique green coal stove, itself on a cracked-tile floor with the name "Louis Philippe" in mosaic: this place has been here for a while.

Service was swift: the 14-euro lunch offered several possibilities, including *charcuterie* (cold sliced meats and salami), *salade d'endives* (endive salad), and that old standard, *oeuf dur à la mayonnaise* (hard-boiled egg).

To follow, you could have the *plat du jour*, which that day was *agneau* (lamb), or choose *escalope de volaille poêlée citronelle* (sautéed chicken or turkey cutlet with lemon), or perhaps *onglet à l'echalotte* (flank steak with shallots).

Satisfactory hors d'oeuvres: if the *quenelles au brochette* (fish dumplings on a skewer) didn't have much flavor in themselves, the hot cheese sauce surrounding them did. A *salade aux endives* involved chunks of Bleu d'Auvergne and walnuts in a vinaigrette on endives.

The trout was certainly edible if slightly past its first youth, accompanied by a tasty tomato and eggplant sauté; the *onglet à l'échalotte* was rich and filling, the meat in a well-made sauce.

Classic bistro desserts followed and were just right: a rich and satisfying *mousse au chocolat* and a *crème caramel.*

For wine to go with the meal, we chose a pleasant rosé, Côtes de Ventoux, at 11euros. Wine prices were generally fair.

An upstairs dining room offers great views of the surrounding area, the churches of St. Gervais and Notre Dame, along with the experience of the antique staircase, a circular marvel in wrought iron.

❖ *Le Louis Philippe: good value in a popular area.*

Les Philosophes
28 rue Vieille-du-Temple, 75004 Paris (01.48.87.49.64)
Métro: Hôtel de Ville
Open daily to 2:00 A.M.

There are cafés in Paris in which weighty matters are discussed, and there are even some where these conversations are regularly scheduled. This is not the case with Les Philosophes. The only serious matter we heard under discussion was about that lightest of all ideas, the frivolous subject of fashion.

Although it is in the Marais, with all of the strange and exotic flora and fauna swirling by in these narrow streets, Les Philosophes keeps the look of a standard Paris bistro, with an old-fashioned circular staircase near the exposed stone on the far wall. Brown and cream dominate the color scheme, with the large pipes high up on the wall recalling the strange architecture of the Pompidou Museum, a few blocks from here.

Art Deco light fixtures brighten the interior, and you notice that bistro trademark, the *ardoise* with the day's specials noted in chalk, so that tomorrow they can offer something else without fuss.

Menus are at 14, 19, or 22 euros: the 14-euro lunch menu, predictably, offers the hors d'oeuvre or *entrée* and *plat* or *plat* and dessert; the higher-priced menus involving all three and a greater choice. Wine is about 4 euros a glass, but some nice wines from the South are available in small carafes for just a little more.

The *rillettes* of haddock was a nice little fish salad with toast points, along with a classic tomato-and-lettuce salad in a light vinaigrette. The next course varied in quality: one serving of *osso bucco* was tasty and well-flavored, the other disappointingly full of gristle. (At that point we noticed that the regulars were ordering fish). A glass of the pleasant Languedoc reconciled us to the failings of the *plat*, and we finished up with a *tarte Tatin*, not the classic but made with *mangue*, or mango.

A scattering of tourists have also discovered this pleasant

bistro, and we heard the earnest young Frenchman beside us charming a long-haired New Yorker with talk about the fashion industry in both countries.

❖ *Les Philosophes: one of the better choices in the area for a budget lunch.*

Le Réconfort
37 rue de Poitou, 75003 Paris (01.42.76.36.)
Métro: St.Sébastien-Froissart
Mon–Fri lunch and dinner, Sat dinner, closed Sun,
2 weeks in August

Attractions at Le Réconfort are the warm welcome and opulent decor. In a pleasant ambiance that recalls Provence, the colors are soft orange and muted reds, with ochre walls and ceiling—even the beams. You might be in a tale from the Arabian Nights, with *faux* Oriental rugs continuing the reds, oil paintings on the walls, fresh flowers in yellows and oranges on the tables. There are some unusual effects: a chandelier is made up of old bottle caps, the concrete floor has been stained and burnished to look like old leather, and leather armchairs are an invitation to relax.

Upstairs a chest of drawers is covered with old newsprint— probably from *Libération*, a left-wing newspaper. And at least when we were there, the staff was dressed in black, as were a number of the clients. The unisex WC is considered, according to one of the black-costumed workers, to be one of the most artistic of such facilities in Paris. It almost certainly is, now that the space-age loo at the old Café Costes is no more.

Lunch here is easy on the wallet: noon menus or *formules* go for 11 or 14 euros, depending on whether you choose just two of the daily hors d'oeuvres, *plat,* and dessert, or take all three. At Le Réconfort, most wines are available only by the glass or full bottle; we chose one of the rare half bottles, a St. Nicholas de Bourgueil.

A cold cucumber salad was attractively presented, with tomatoes and flat-leafed parsley setting off the cucumbers in a cream sauce with fresh dill. The cucumber, sliced to look like pasta, was cool and refreshing in a portion large enough to share.

An enormous, tender and tasty *entrecôte* steak with *gratin dauphinoise* (scalloped potatoes) kept one of us occupied for some time. The *salade du jour* was attractive enough to merit a photo: it was, like antipasto, made up of several good hors d'oeuvres, with pleasing contrasts of texture and flavor—sardines on toast spread with *tapenade*, a blend of chopped olives and anchovies, mozzarrella on tomatoes, *jambon cru*, thin slices of smoked raw ham on ripe, sweet cantalope, grated carrot and zucchini with a *fromage blanc* and dill dressing.

A la carte, typically hors d'oeuvres and desserts run about 7 euros, with plats from 10 to 16 euros. An advantage of ordering à la carte here would be the chance to try the exotic ice creams: tropical flavors, like mango and ginger carry on the Arabian Nights theme. Our desserts were pleasing: rich slices of cold *fondant au chocolat*, sprinkled with toasted almonds on a swirl of *crème anglaise*, and a *bavarois au fromage blanc*, a light jellied custard, much lighter than cheesecake, served on a base of *coulis aux fruits rouges*, an intensely flavored sauce of crushed fruit, with raspberry and blackberry the dominant flavors.

❖ *Le Réconfort: "Very good, and they're nice there," a local from the area remarked. We agree.*

Le Temps des Cerises
31 rue de la Cerisaie, 75004 Paris (01.42.72.08.63)
Métro: Bastille
Mon–Fri noon–3:00 P.M., 7:30 P.M.–11 P.M., closed August

At the end of the rue de la Cerisaie, this Temps des Cerises is not at all like its rowdy cousin with the same name in the 13th arrondissement. This is a quiet, romantic little hideaway, a picture-perfect version of a neighborhood bistro, with a real zinc bar, attentive and friendly proprietors, walls with historic photos, highly-polished oak tables, and a variety of wines at fair prices.

On the walls a jovial let's-not-take-life-seriously mood is

suggested by the cartoons, sketches, and carvings of the proprietors, some showing the two of them together, others of just Monsieur Vimard. With his smile and his bristling mustache, he's an irristible subject for an artist.

Also, there's a three-course menu written on the *ardoise*. At any weekday lunch you'll find Le Temps wildly, joyously crammed full of the locals who include musicians and journalists enjoying the day's specials. They might start with *oeuf mayonnaise*, (egg with mayonnaise), or *poisson pommes à l'huile* (fish with cold potato salad), and go on to *tendron de veau* (veal rib roast), *émincé d'agneau à la crème d'ail flageolets* (thinly sliced lamb with garlic cream and kidney beans), finishing with *tarte aux abricots* (apricot tart), *crème caramel,* or cheese. With lunch we'd recommend the Réserve Maison, at 5 euros the bottle, 4 euros a half, and 2 for a quarter carafe.

Having enjoyed this Temps des Cerises for years, when we met old friends from Boston who were on a brief visit, we decided to take them here for a long chat. They were enchanted by the ambiance, looking about them in wonder that something which is so authentic is still alive and well and existing in Paris.

❖ *Le Temps des Cerises: a very special bistro with unforgettable ambiance and good* cuisine familiale *at bargain prices.*

La Tartine
24 rue de Rivoli, 75004 Paris (01.42.72.76.85)
Métro: Hôtel de Ville
Open to 10:00 P.M., closed Tues, Wed A.M.,
2 weeks in August

Although La Tartine is actually much older, dating from somewhere in the nineteenth century, your immediate image of it is from one of those famous Brassai photographs of Paris in the 1920s and '30s. The dark, somewhat ominous interior, the stone-faced women well past the first bloom of youth, the moody reflections in old mirrors, the half empty glasses left on wooden tables—it's all here, unchanged in the twenty-first century at La Tartine.

Trotsky came here during his time in Paris before the first World War. Even in his day it would have been thought of as an old wine bar. Here is a triumph of unimproved decor: nothing has been renovated, updated, or desecrated in the name of progress; here is aged molding, the walls and ceilings a smokey dark ochre and burnt sienna so old it looks like cracked leather.

A marble-topped bar is black with Second-Empire details in gold. Dour waitresses preside, wearing put-upon expressions and looking as if they could have emerged from the canvases of Toulouse-Lautrec.

Here is an extraordinary list of wines near the bar, wines available for small prices because they come in small glasses (8 centiliters). If you feel like a normal-sized glass, double the listed price. So the lovely Côteaux de Layon we ordered on a late afternoon was 4 euros, not 2. There's a *plat du jour* at mealtime, or a plate of *charcuterie* or *fromage* available any time.

Over the wine, the buzz of animated conversation—intellectuals from the Marais. A note above the bar announces: Beaujolais Médaille d'Or Concours Générale de Paris. We'll have to go back and try the Beaujolais another day. Young people from the area show up, attracted by the special appeal of this historic wine bar. Some are there for coffee on the *terrasse*, where cane chairs—no garden store plastic, thank you, for the Tartine—are arranged behind the traditional pedestal tables.

The sour-faced maîtresse d' limps out to the terrace to take an order. A young bearded would-be hippie, a living ana-chronism, sips his Coca-Cola at the bar. What a travesty!

The elegant-looking French-Canadian woman on my left announces to her companion: "Je vais aller pisser avant de diner" (I'm going to pee before dinner). One doesn't envy her sweeping toward the downstairs in her long black dress, knowing that La Tartine has what are called Turkish facilities, clean but primitive, probably the same ones used by James Joyce, Trotsky, and others who made this place part of their Paris experiences.

❖ *La Tartine: an extraordinary setting for enjoying a glass of wine.*

Trumilou
84 quai Hôtel-de-Ville, 75004 Paris (01.42.77.63.98)
Métro: Hôtel de Ville
Open daily noon–3:00 P.M., 7:00 P.M.–10:00 P.M.

Although Trumilou is on the banks of the Seine, when you're inside you feel as if you could be far away from Paris in a small country town. Yet it is centrally located. The schedule may make it an old standby, useful if you find yourself with an appetite on a Sunday, a day when many restaurants are closed.

Even on Sundays, the budget-conscious will be pleased to note, Trumilou keeps its country style, with prices still only 13 and 15 euros for the *formules*, the *prix fixe* menus, including the main dish with hors d'oeuvre or dessert, or all three.

Hearty main dishes include choices like *pavé de rumsteak à la bordelaise* (rumpsteak in red wine sauce), *travers de porc rôti au miel* (honey-roasted pork ribs), and simple desserts: *gâteau à l'ananas* (pineapple cake), *crème caramel,* and *fraises au sucre* (strawberries with sugar).

The look at Trumilou seems not to be planned, but something that happened over time. Around us were a hodgepodge of objects relating to farming: a handmade pitchfork, a rake, wooden clogs which might have been worn by some French farm worker, a small model of an oxcart, burnished copper pots, a set of pewter measures, collector's plates as if from a country kitchen, dried sunflower bouquets, a stuffed Mallard duck, the mounted head of a mountain goat. In wild and comic contradiction to all of these rural references are the two large and elaborate crystal chandeliers lighting up the room.

Our hors d'oeuvres came: the eggplant caviar was smooth and tasty with the thin toasted rounds of baguette, on a bed of *frisée* lettuce with chunks of tomato. Marinated salmon was a very successful *entrée*, with good-sized pieces of salmon arranged on greens including spinach and tomatoes. A light, lemony vinaigrette set off the flavor of the salmon. Bread—the ever-present baguette—was fresh.

Our main dishes appeared, and were found acceptable by everyone in the group. *Carrelet,* or plaice, ordered by three in the party, is an unusual flat saltwater fish. The native-born Parisian in our group pointed out its skin, gray with orange spots. It was presented in boneless filets on a large platter with peeled, boiled potatoes and a white sauce delicately flavored with sorrel.

The spareribs were in sauce with a light barbecue flavor, satisfactory and not overly sweet, despite being cooked au miel. The thick beefsteak was well-flavored and chewy, cooked as requested, in a red wine sauce with a quantity of fries on the side.

❖ *Trumilou: substantial food at a reasonable price.*

Le Valet de Carreau
2 rue Dupetit Thouars, 75003 Paris (01.42.72.72.60)
Métro: République
Mon–Fri, Sat eves

On a fine day you can sit and meditate at the small white tables under the trees of the Carreau du Temple, near the République. The noisy traffic of the nearby boulevard could be a million miles away.

Smart people come here for lunch, which at 12 euros for two courses is a good buy. Dinner at night is more romantic and more expensive: interesting hors d'oeuvres (*rillettes de saumon, terrine de canard,* etc.) are around 9 euros, with main dishes about 13 to 16 euros, and desserts all 6 euros if you order à la carte. Otherwise, there's a 28-euro menu which includes wine.

Here the ambiance is delightfully relaxed, more than at many restaurants. At Le Valet women come by themselves or in twos, often wearing flat shoes and looking unfashionably comfortable in this village-like setting, with the old Marché du Temple, a dusty indigo blue, across the street. Inside the restaurant, dark apricot walls set off abstract paintings. A Morris fountain in the square is in the characteristic *vert wagon,* or hunter green of Paris.

A simple hors d'oeuvre was lightly poached eggs on a bed of moussaka-like vegetables: eggplant, tomatoes, and onions. It was a pleasaant way to begin a meal, if not for those concerned about cholerestol.

Plats are generous and filling: we tackled hefty servings of good-flavored *osso bucco* with taggliatelli. A steak was topped with seasoned butter, with good French fries on the side. Desserts are well-prepared—the *moelleux au chocoolat* is elsewhere called a *fondant au chocolat*; no matter, it was delicious. An apricot tart with a sort of shortcake crust had the intense flavor of the fresh fruit.

❖ *Le Valet du Carreau: good* cuisine familiale *in a setting which could be a forgotten square in a small town, away from city stress.*

Les Vins des Pyrenées
25 rue Beautreillis, 75004 Paris (01.42.72.64.94)
Métro: Bastille
Mon–Fri noon–3:00 P.M., 8:00 P.M.–11:30 P.M., Sat eves, closed 2 weeks in August

This simple place calls itself a bistro, a wine bar and a restaurant, but whatever the classification, it's a fine little spot just south of the Marais near another charming part of Paris called the Village of St. Paul.

An eye-catching red façade on quiet little rue Beautreillis, just off rue Saint-Antoine attracted us to the Vin des Pyrenées. Inside, the number of *ardoises* devoted to wines convinced us that here is a place where the grape is taken seriously.

In this old-fashioned bistro, a nineteenth-century cast-iron chandelier still hangs near the door. The original tile floor has not been replaced. In a blending of styles one sees a lot of these days, an historic old icebox acts as a support for the sound system, a computer, and the coffee machine. Small café tables in oak and aluminum front the dark red banquettes. Some surprising touches will appeal to collectors: a spiral staircase, antique hall trees, an old sign advertising wines, a few seats from an oak choir stall.

With this basically good background, there's room for kitsch, and it's here too, in the plaster-of-Paris heads looking like Toby jugs displayed on the wall, the strange-looking old decanters, and several bizarre platters. Still, the ambiance is warm and inviting.

But on this Wednesday afternoon, the customers—mostly local business sorts, the men in suits and the women in casual dresses—were there not for the decor but for lunch: the 13-euro lunch gives a choice of *entrée* and *plat*, or *plat*, glass of wine, and coffee. The *entrée* claimed our attention: to start, a copious salad of *jambon du pays* (cured country ham), with green beans, corn, black olives, and tomato on a bed of lettuce. It was crunchy and delicious, a good contrast of flavors and textures. Hors d'oeuvres available à la carte at 7 euros for lunch or about 8 euros at night might include Scottish salmon, melon and smoked ham, fresh goat cheese salad with smoked ham, and beef *carpaccio.*

Described on the *ardoise* as a *suprême de pintade aux pleurottes*, the *plat* was a large serving of well-flavored guinea hen, with puréed potatoes and pleurotus mushrooms in a rich sauce of cooking juices fortified with red wine. Half a carafe of the house rosé at 8 euros was a suitable accompaniment.

Other intriguing *plats* available for from 10 to 14 euros included *gratin de macaroni au saumon* (cheese-topped macaroni with salmon), *magret de canard rôti au miel et aux épices des Indes* (duck breast roasted with honey and curry spices), and *filets de rascasse* (scorpion fish in parsley cream sauce), *perche* (perch), and *dorade* (John Dory).

Desserts, mostly about 7 euros, included bistro classics and a few surprises; besides the usual, there were fresh mangos, chocolate cake with orange sauce, and green apple sherbet with calvados.

But, satisfied with the good hors d'oeuvres and *plat*, we finished with small cups of strong espresso, served with a chocolate-covered almond. Although it was getting on past 3:00 in the afternoon, the black-clad young waitress did not rush us; she spoke fervently of her upcoming vacation, enough to convince us that she does, indeed, speak English.

❖ *Les Vins des Pyrenées: good food, low prices, and friendly service in a bistro near popular tourist destinations.*

WRITERS' WATERING HOLES: THE 5TH & 6TH ARRONDISSEMENTS

Physically Montparnasse was little more than a gray and dull street holding a broken double row of cafés, but in spirit it was stronger than home or religion...

—Jimmie Charters, *This Must Be the Place*

This is the Paris of our collective memory, of our youthful imagination. This is Henry Miller, James Joyce, Richard Wright, Hemingway and Scott Fitzgerald, Sartre and De Beauvoir. This is the Paris of the famed literary cafés—Le Sélect, Le Café de Flore, La Rotonde, Les Deux Magots. This is the Latin Quarter and the Sorbonne, the puppet shows in the Luxembourg Gardens and the boulevards of St. Germain and St. Michel.

This is still the Paris of the tiny little streets, the smoky basement jazz clubs, the steamy Greek restaurants with their windows stacked with slabs of cooked meat and tomatoes. Young couples clutch in a half embrace and wander down these streets, looking first at one side and then at another.

This is the Latin Quarter, a Paris for night people. During the daylight hours you can see the aged and dirty buildings, the poor and foreign workers, the garbage overflowing the green plastic containers, but at night, this all disappears and the magic of Paris descends.

Montparnasse nights! This was the Paris that crowds of pleasure-seekers chose for their revelry. The sense of escape and abandon that we associate with the Moulin Rouge and the Folies Bergère were once sought in a string of bistros on the Left Bank. Bistros of the 5th, 6th, and 14th arrondissements provided perfect places for the Lost

Generation and for the sophisticates who knew what they were looking for, to lose themselves in hours of pleasure-seeking. Some sought a refuge from Prohibition. Others just wanted a liberating foreign experience. Still others desired an escape from the responsibilities of home, a place to while away the time in the company of friendly compatriots.

This café scene appears in Hemingway's *The Sun Also Rises:*

> Those who work have the greatest contempt for those who don't. The loafers are leading their own lives and it is bad form to mention work. Young painters have contempt for old painters, and that works both ways too. There are contemptuous critics and contemptuous writers. Everybody seems to dislike everybody else. The only happy people are the drunks, and they, after flaming for a period of days or weeks, eventually become depressed.

In a certain stretch of the not-especially-attractive boulevard de Montparnasse runs a series of bistros with names that resonate in history, associated as they are with the great names in literature and the arts.

The two most popular bistros for Americans were singled out for comment by American writer Robert McAlmon. He observed American life in Paris during the 1920s: "The influx of expatriates had begun before this, but now they hung out in Montparnasse at the Dôme and the Rotonde," he wrote.

photo © Juliana Spear

The Dôme won out over the Rotonde because of a cigarette. Jimmie Charters, former boxer and barman at the Dingo, told how this happened. In the early 1920s, the manager of the Rotonde saw a young American girl smoking on the terrace of his bistro. Shocked at this brazen behavior, he asked her to move inside. She refused. He insisted. Finally she rose and left. She marched across the street, over to the Rotonde's main competition, the Dôme, taking much of the English and American clientele with her.

From then on, the Dôme was a focal point for expatriates abroad. As Jimmie Charters remembered:

> In the normal course of events you went there in the morning, or whenever you got up, for a breakfast of croissants and coffee, to read the morning paper, and to rehash with your friends the events of the night before.... But by afternoon you would be back again on the terrace of the Dôme drinking your apéritif, that stimulating forerunner of the night to come.

Many expatriates, while not creative geniuses themselves, were still unforgettable characters. Florence Martin, or Flossie as she was known, a *zaftig* 200-or-so-pound former chorus girl from New York, tended to dominate her favorite bistro, the Dôme. She was popular for her jolly disposition. "Flossie was a dashing bit of color, of the Rubens type. Her orange hair was piled neatly above her clear, baby-smooth skin," noted writer Robert McAlmon. Flossie was not obviously affected by drink, and was rumored to start her day with a breakfast of potatoes and gin. James Joyce found her totally beyond his understanding: "He had difficulty in believing that such a person actually existed," McAlmon observed.

Competition between the bistros could go too far. Hilaire Hiler, a painter who took over the Jockey Bar, found Finnety, a lawyer, about to succumb to a fatal dose of poison in the bar's washroom. With a stomach pump, he managed to save the man's life. Then he learned that Finnety, suffering from a bone disease, still wanted to do away with himself. "Next time go somewhere else," suggested Hiler, adding "The Dôme is my rival, you know." The following night Finnety's dead body was found in the washroom of—of all places—the Dôme.

Farther down the boulevard du Montparnasse, set back today behind a hedge not of lilacs but arborvitae, is the Closerie des Lilas, which Hemingway described as "the nearest good café when we lived over the sawmill." Converted into an "American" bar in the 1920s, the Closerie became a favorite of many writers. There, F. Scott Fitzgerald gave Hemingway the manuscript of his new novel, *The Great Gatsby*, to look at. Hemingway wrote much of his own novel, *The Sun Also Rises*, at the Closerie's bar. He also wrote the short story "Big, Two-Hearted River" there. Some say that the famous writer actually preferred to work standing at the bar, kept on his feet by painful hemorrhoids.

The crash of 1929 and an abrupt change in many people's fortunes caused a sudden exodus of foreign pleasure-seekers from Paris. One who stayed on was perhaps the most poverty-stricken of all, Henry Miller. At first completely destitute, he was rescued by the kindness of acquaintances who would pass on a few francs, an item of clothing, a part-time job. He shared little other than nationality with most of the Americans the French had become used to seeing in their bistros.

In a letter written to Anaïs Nin in 1932, Miller reported that morning for him had taken on a pattern: "Oranges first, and then porridge at the Coupole." Poor as he was, he had to resort to the bistros: "Am writing from a café because the cold drives me out of the room. Am going over the *Tropic of Cancer* with a fine comb. A little dull, here and there, but on the whole good. If anybody had written a preface for it, they might have explained that the book was written on the wing, as it were, between my 25 addresses." Many of those addresses were Left Bank bistros.

Later, during the war, Simone de Beauvoir, the French writer associated with the Existentialist movement, was to give the same reason, the coldness of the hotels, for her own regular patronage of the cafés. She recalled a moment from her first years of acquaintance with philosopher Jean-Paul Sartre:

> As soon as our favorite café, the Closerie des Lilas, opened for the day, we sat down on the *terrasse* with cups of hot chocolate and piles of croissants lined up in front of us. There was still the problem of paying for them though. Sartre left me there as a kind of hostage, got into a taxi, and did not reappear for an hour.

No one was more at ease in the bistros of Montparnasse and St. Germain-des-Prés than de Beauvoir. She told about how she and Sartre set up their "general headquarters" at the Dôme, with German refugees all around. Their conversations didn't distract her, for as she felt, "facing a blank sheet of paper all alone is an austere experience." A few weeks later in the winter of 1938 to 1939, she became seriously ill with an infected lung. During her period of recuperation, Sartre brought her helpings of the *plat du jour* from the Coupole. At night she made do with ham and fruit in her hotel room.

Another friend took her for the first time to the Flore, the café which later came to be most closely identified with de Beauvoir and Sartre. The Deux Magots, when it was mentioned in her journal, was only a second choice: "The Flore is shut, so I sit on the *terrasse* of the Deux Magots," she noted.

But work in her cold little hotel room was impossible, so she would go to the Flore whenever she could. Mornings were very special, and she has left us with an unforgettable picture of Paul Boubal, the proprietor:

> ... I loved the moment when Boubal, a blue apron tied around him, came bustling into the still empty café and began to bring his little world to life again... A pair of bloodshot eyes would blink at one from that tough, solid Auvergne face; for the first hour or two he would remain in a perfectly filthy temper. He would shout out orders, irritably, to the kitchen hand... he would also discuss the previous night's goings-on with the waiters, Jean and Pascal, and send back a cup of ersatz coffee, the same stuff the customers drank without raising an eyebrow, with... the contemptuous comment: "Give them shit, they'd still eat it." He received and got rid of salesmen in the same cantankerous fashion.

Later Boubal was often questioned about his famous clients. Of Sartre, he used to say: "He was my worst customer. He stayed there scribbling for hours from morning to night, in front of him just one drink, never a second one." But Boubal never considered putting the philosopher out or suggesting that he order another drink. Once he confided to a journalist: "Ah! If I had only kept Sartre's scribblings, his rough drafts. They would be worth millions...."

This part of Paris is changing. James Joyce would no longer be able to afford it. A major drugstore has been bulldozed and now Armani has a shop there. A beloved record store has been replaced by Cartier. Well-regarded bookshops are gone and trendy boutiques have taken their place. The historic cafés are still there, most of them, but even these have capitulated to fame. Schoolteachers like Sartre no longer take their morning coffee at Les Deux Magots. Le Dôme serves admittedly good food, but few struggling American writers would feel comfortable there now.

The area where Sartre scribbled and Miller mooched drinks still has worthwhile bistros and brasseries:

Le Balzar
49 rue des Ecoles, 75005 Paris (01.43.54.13.67)
Métro: Odéon
Open daily to midnight

What has happened to the Balzar? Trying to find out was the reason for our visit. Le Balzar, a well-known brasserie at the edge of the Paris university quarter, gathered attention when it was the subject of Adam Gopnik's article in the *New Yorker*. It had been an old-fashioned and well-loved local hangout which was being sold to the Flo Group, a company which owns chains of restaurants. Some feisty and articulate supporters—this was a neighborhood hangout and the neighborhood was, after all, the Sorbonne—organized a group called "Friends of the Balzar" and unsuccessfully attempted to stop the sale of a place which had seemed to be their own. They felt that the brasserie's original character would be desroyed.

The decor of the Balzar is undistinguished but pleasing: you find yourself in a large, attractive room with mirrored sides. Brown banquettes have zinc rails above them. Some posters of current art shows can be seen against the brown paneling, but there's no serious attempt at a studied decor. Most of the color is provided by paintings of the restaurant, one Cubist-influenced, the other more realistic.

This is not a neighborhood hangout of stuffy bankers; we would guess that a large number of the patrons are older Left Wing sorts, *ancien soixante-huitards*, who remember the barricades in May of '68.

The service is friendly, but the headwaiter seemed uptight. At first he tried to steer us to a tiny table near the kitchen. When we protested, we were wedged into a similar-sized one in a better location opposite the door, where we found ourselves between a German couple and three Parisians. A Japanese family was finishing their meal at a window table.

Noticing our scribblings, the headwaiter came back to our table to remark, without a smile, "C'est de l'espionage industrielle?" (Industrial spying?) We cheerfully admitted it, and he backed off.

Hors d'oeuvres, from egg with mayonnaise to Norwegian salmon are from 5 to 12 euros, and main dishes from 16 to 25 euros. Wines are reasonably priced, 8 for a half bottle, with many full bottles at 15 euros. Around the room, people tended to order the same wine, a red Château de Brague, smooth and rich. An *oeuf en gelée* hors d'oeuvre was a little ramekin-shaped aspic on greens, containing a partially cooked egg with ham and a black olive. The aspic had a good flavor of beef broth.

When the *plats* arrived, the fish, *raie* (skate or ray), was floating in butter, covered with capers, and edged with small boiled potatoes. The fish was well-flavored, but the quantity of butter really excessive. A *rumsteak* was a good value, flavorful and reasonably tender. No sauce, but that's how this particular steak is usually served. With it came a mound of French fries that were first-rate by any standards.

For dessert, the Parisians next to us recommended the *millefeuille*. It was light and flakey, with a good *crème pâtissier* and a topping of powdered sugar. Another successful dessert that night was a *tarte au citron*, a tart with a pure and intense lemon flavor, not overly sweet, just the right touch of tartness. Both are made on the premises.

The headwaiter showed up again to question one of the regulars on our left about his dinner, how the veal compared with what was served in the old days. The young Frenchman assumed a dreamy expression: "Jadis, il y avait du croustillant..." (Formerly, there was a crunchiness). We had the distinct impression that he was teasing the headwaiter, that he might himself have been one of the "Friends of Balzar" organized to keep the Groupe Flo from making changes.

The Hotel St. Jacques, the setting for the old Cary Grant–Audrey Hepburn movie *Charade* is just down the street. Probably some of the movie people took their meals here.

❖ *Le Balzar: standard fare in a brasserie favored by the intelligentsia.*

Bistro de la Gare
59 blvd de Montparnasse, 75006 Paris
Métro: Montparnasse
Open daily 11 A.M.–1:00 A.M.

Eating at the Bistro de la Gare is like being invited to dine at the home of a stunningly beautiful woman who can't cook. You realize that looks can be impressive but not everything.

This bistro is surely the prettiest budget restaurant in Paris, with original tiles in which morning glories swirl up trellises in Art Nouveau splendor. Country vistas are rendered in tile, and dark wood loops and swirls around and above mirrors and on ceilings.

And then there's the food—often no better than ordinary cafeteria fare. We were at first rather taken by the possibilities in the 13-euro noon menu. But the descriptions were better than reality. Our meals began in complete contrast: his hors d'oeuvre was a damp slab of gluey pastry with a suggestion of dried tomato and some onions on it, hers rather tasty slices of cold duck on lettuce with wedges of nectarine.

Contrasts continued: She received a plate of tepid, obviously warmed-up salmon with sticky, unappetizing rice, containing bits of mystery vegetables—mystery because there was no perceptible flavor there. He lucked out with a hot, generously sized breaded veal cutlet, with a heaping of flavorful French fries.

The Bistro de la Gare is owned by the Flo Group, but they don't boast about it. In view of the food we received, this is understandable.

❖ *Le Bistro de la Gare: the decor is the best part.*

Le Bistro d'Opio
9 rue Guisarde, 75006 Paris (01.43.29.01.84)
Métro: Mabillon
Open daily lunch and dinner.

A 13-euro *prix fixe* lunch. A student in the Cours Supérieur at the Cordon Bleu recommended this bistro, specializing in Provençal cuisine.

Les Bookinistes
53 quai des Grands-Augustins, 75006 Paris
(01.43.25.45.94)
Métro: St. Michel
Mon–Fri noon–2:30 P.M., 7:00 P.M.–11:00 P.M., Sat. eves

One of the recent trends in the French food world has been the opening of "baby bistros" by famous chefs. One of the better known is Les Bookinistes, a Left Bank bistro opened by Guy Savoy, a well-known, Michelin 3-star chef.

The look here is international elegance: soft pastel walls and ceiling, tall mirrors with intriguing lines of Gustav Klimt-type colors around them, and modern black designer chairs. Serious money was spent here.

At noon, the *menu du marché* offers *entrée, plat,* and dessert for 25 euros or two of them for 22 euros. A la carte, *entrées* run from 11 to 13 euros, *plats* from 14 to 25, and desserts from 9 to 10.

We were first treated to a dish of small red olives in the way of *amuse-gueules.* The *menu du marché* gave two choices for each course. Taking both possibilities, we also chose the *vin du mois,* Saint Chinian Domaine Navarre 1999, an excellent value at 19 euros.

Only the regular menu was translated into English, so to order from the money-saving *menu du marché* it would be useful to have a reading knowledge of French, although we should mention that the servers speak good English. At Les Bookinistes, you feel as if you're being served by a very competent and bilingual wait staff.

An endive hors d'oeuvre was endive stuffed with tuna salad with sprouts and cream. The hors d'oeuvre involving duck was different—we give points for originality here—consisting of slices of duck rolled with olive tapenade, the tapenade contributing an unusual flavor. An accompanying snow pea salad provided a contrast in texture, adding that needed bit of crunch.

Plats came to the table on hot dishes: a small serving of *dorade* resting alone in the center of the too-hot-to-touch plate was complemented by peeled tomatoes, chopped yellow bell peppers, and onions in a separate cast-iron dish. The chicken, served on a hot cast-iron platter, was flavorful and moist.

In midsummer, however, it might be well to reconsider the policy of having dishes reach the table sizzling hot, radiating heat up at the diners. This is also not the best way to treat fish.

Desserts from the regular menu were good: the *fruits rouges au jus de cerises* (red fruit with cherry juice) was pleasantly piquant and without excessive sugar, the red currants still attached to their stems. The *cappucino aux framboises et griottes, glace pistache* (sour blackberry and raspberry soup with pistachio ice cream) was even more successful—intense strawberry, raspberry, and red currant flavors with a topping of pistachio ice cream contributing smoothness and sweetness.

❖ *Les Bookinistes: Disappointing considering the hype, but with satisfactory if not particularly special food. Just across from the* real *bouquinistes (booksellers) by the Seine.*

Bouillon Racine
3 rue Racine, 75006 Paris (01.44.32.15.60)
Métro: Cluny-La Sorbonne
Open daily noon–3:00 P.M., 7:00 P.M.–midnight

The original Parisian *bouillons* were late nineteenth-century restaurants serving inexpensive food to the working poor at low prices. Yet some of these restaurants were quite elaborate if not elegant. Probably the best-known remaining example is Chartier near the Bourse.

The Bouillon Racine is an Art Nouveau dream with its curves, swirls, and fanciful shapes around mirrors that send back even more fanciful reflections. Here it is not Mucha-type women such as the ones that embellish Chez Julien, but sensuous flowers around which the swirling green woodwork curves. The backs of the wrought-iron chairs and bar stools curl about like tendrils of twigs and branches.

Set lunch was a simple 13 and 17-euro menu: the first an entrée and *plat*, or *plat* and dessert, the other including all three. Drinks are extra, starting from about 4 euros.

Belgian cooking is not known for its delicacy and finesse and the Racine is no exception. Even the hors d'oeuvres can be heavy: the *prix fixe* lunch began with a plateful of smoked salmon, garnished with wisps of fresh dill.

We had no sooner tasted a few forkfuls of that than our waiter whisked away our plates and brought the main dish, a *carbonnade de boeuf Flamande*, or Flemish beef stew cooked in beer, served in a deep soup plate with tomatoes, carrots, and parsley, and surrounded by potatoes. As we said before— filling. We were back in good old *cuisine familiale* territory, but the *carbonnade* could have used more garlic and a better quality of dark beer in its background. It was greasy, but would be a sustaining meal for a cold day when you have several hours' worth of manual labor ahead.

Service was brisk and efficient, although not particularly friendly. Jean, our waiter, was efficient to the point of being intrusive. He seemed to be always hovering about, the better to keep things moving and get them over with. No sooner had we ordered than the hors d'oeuvres were slapped down in front of us. Should we show the slightest sign of having finished a course, he would seize the plates and make off with them toward one of the lavishly decorated doors to the kitchen. A lunch which should have taken at least an hour here lasted around 30 minutes.

Jean may be the old régime's answer to McDonald's and the fast food industry. Still, it would have been pleasant to be allowed to relax for a few moments in such a setting.

❖ *Bouillon Racine: great if you have a ravenous appetite, eat fast, and have never quite believed in calories; but a glorious decor.*

Brasserie Lipp
151 blvd St.-Germain, 75006 Paris (01.45.48.53.91)
Métro: St. Germain
Open daily noon–1:00 A.M.

We were ready to dislike the Lipp—over the years it's developed a reputation for being snobbish, expensive, and mediocre. At the top of the menu in red letters and in English is the brusque statement, "No salad as a meal." Some assert that the waiters are cool to foreigners, and Lipp food was said to be variable and overpriced.

It's not just that the Brasserie Lipp doesn't permit its customers to indulge in a salad as a meal. A tendency toward the use of the imperative is continued in other signs, some about pipe smoke (they're against it) and portable phones (not in favor of those either). Still, all reservations aside, this is an entertaining experience for people who are in love with Art Nouveau and literary history or who wish simply to glimpse a famous face. This is the historical landmark that Hemingway remembered: "The beer was very cold and wonderful to drink. The *pommes à l'huile* were firm and marinated and the olive oil delicious."

You enter and are guided past the dazzling main room where people look you over to find out if you're worth a second look, to a smaller, less ostentatious one in the back, with Art Nouveau features but not so many of them. Only the famous, celebrities from show business and the media and VIPs from politics make it into the first *salle*. (The late French president François Mitterrand was a regular). In the second one, where the Lipp tends to place French people of less consequence and foreigners, we heard French, Italian, and English spoken around us.

Once there, we had time to study the menu: hors d'oeuvres à la carte run between 7 and 16 euros, *plats* around 16 euros. On this Monday the daily specials at about 17 euros were *filet de thon poêlé au beurre d'anchois* (sautéed tuna with anchovy butter), *navarin d'agneau printanier* (stew of spring lamb), and *pavé de rumsteak au poivre* (pepper steak), with various cheeses and pastries to follow from 6 to 10 euros.

Looking at the wine list, you could choose the Réserve Lipp at 5 euros a glass, but most wines come by the full and half bottle, from 9 to 65 euros, depending on whether one wants half a bottle of Bordeaux réserve Barthes or a vintage cuvée of Dom Perignon.

Heavy white linen, immense linen napkins, Art Nouveau tiles in a floral theme, an elaborate light fixture above that is mirrored to look like a dozen busy waiters in the traditional black and white, large fresh bouquets of flowers, a ceiling painted to resemble old leather... this is a heady experience.

One of us took *rumsteak*, the other *thon*; when the tuna came, it seemed underdone and was sent back. When finished, it was well flavored and highly satisfactory. The *rumsteak*, a large broiled steak topped with a pat of butter, simple with nothing but its own juices and a touch of pepper was one of the best we've tasted in Paris. The French fries that acompanied it on a large separate plate were moist and slightly crisp, not as dry as many might prefer. Bread was ordinary Paris baguette—some *pain de campagne* or *pain complet* in the basket would have been welcome.

Cheeses included Crottin de Chavignol, Roquefort, and

Brie de Meaux, all around 8 euros. We ordered the Roquefort and found it excellent, served with butter and the accompanying baguette.

Like most brasseries, the Lipp doesn't offer complex French cuisine, but satisfying, simple basics. Service is good-natured. Our waiter suggested a finale: "Café? Cognac?" Our response: "On va aller aux Deux Magots" (threatening to go to their even-more-famous competition accross the street). He made a face and turned away in mock disgust.

❖ *Brasserie Lipp: worth a trip to the 6th arrondissement.*

Le Buisson Ardent
25 rue Jussieu, 75006 Paris (01.43.54.93.02)
Métro Jussieu
Mon–Fri lunch and dinner, closed August

Even if this bistro is right across from one of the ugliest buildings in France—the Jussieu campus of the University of Paris, a modern design that combines the charm of a cattle stockyard with that of an old-fashioned American prison—when the Buisson's wonderfully crunchy, homebaked bread reaches your table, you stop caring about the view.

Just across from the Jussieu campus of the Sorbonne, Le Buisson Ardent has to cope with a setting one has to describe as unpromising. Or, as the English writer John Russell put it in his book *Paris,* "The Sorbonne is ugly beyond belief." And the Jussieu campus is not the best-looking part of the Sorbonne.

But a special effort has been made with this interior: the high ceiling covered with what looks like raw silk, the murals of romantic country scenes, heavy table linens in pale apricot, a bas-relief in Art Moderne style over a doorway. Two large light fixtures are fitted with apricot-colored silk shades, dripping with fringes, along with smaller wall lamps of similar design. There's an elegance about the slender-stemmed table crystal, the linen tablecloths, and apricot-colored café curtains.

A lunch menu is available at 14 euros and a *prix fixe* dinner at 25 euros. Hors d'oeuvres and *plats* show an engaging

inventiveness with a tendency to favor the cuisine of the South and Southwest, and they should: the chef trained with greats Alain Senderens and Jacques Cagna.

We glanced at the moderately-priced wine list—no Cheval Blancs or Latours here. Most wines were sensibly-priced reds from the South or Southwest, with a sprinkling of others. We chose the *vin du jour*, a low-priced but perfectly adequate *vin du pays* from the Tarn in the Massif Central region of southern France.

For starters we chose the *moules* and *roulé de jambon*, and were pleased: the mussels were cold, in a spicy sauce of tomato, red peppers, onions, and even pickles. The *roulé de jambon*—tasty slices of ham rolled around avocado—were arranged around a bright summer salad, with the orange, purple, and green tones of slivers of carrot and red cabbage on a bed of green lettuce.

Along with the hors d'oeuvres came the house wine, a well-flavored red, slightly chilled as a concession to the hot weather, and the best bread we've tasted in Paris this year, possibly because the cook bakes his own.

In deference to the weather, dress was casual for Paris: most men were wearing ties with short-sleeved shirts and slacks. This said, we were awed to notice a white-haired gentleman outside, sitting at a table in the summer sun, clad in full wool suit and tie.

Plats were simple and appealing: a large steak with chives came on a plate with yellow beans and slivers of tomato; a *pintade* or roast guinea hen was served with slivers of zucchini and tomato. No sauces, just the *jus* they came with, but for lunch on a hot day, cream sauces would have been too heavy.

Of the dessert choices, the apple crumble was tart and delicious, Granny Smith apples with a touch of peach. A *mousse au chocolat* was served fluted on the top with a deep, not-too-sweet flavor of chocolate.

Service was friendly and efficient, and we left the Buisson Ardent with the positive feeling of having spent time in a place with people who really care about food and about pleasing their clientele.

❖ *Le Buisson Ardent: worth a trip, even to Jussieu.*

Le Café des Délices
87 rue d'Assas, 75006 Paris (01.43.54.70.00)
Métro Notre-Dame des Champs
Weekdays noon–2:30 P.M., 7:30 P.M.–11:30 P.M.

In a subtly Japanese-influenced interior of the Café des Délices, a feeling of tranquility prevails. Each table has a miniature brown stoneware tea set, the little teapot filled with olive oil, the tiny cups containing spices. Plaintive singing, North African in origin, wafts in from the back. The formal look of the dining room is warmed by subtle colors, café au lait walls, and brown place mats over orange linen.

We were brought an *amuse-gueule* of guacamole with rounds of toast. We chose not to try the 13-euro lunch special of *boudin purée* (veal sausage, mashed potatoes), which included a glass of wine and coffee. Instead, we chose fish from the à la carte menu, *dorade poêlée, cocos aux anchois et piment, nem aux herbes,* (sautéed sea bream, chickpeas, eggroll with herbs), and *dos de lieu jaune, huile de chorizo et de dattes, purée de maïs* (pollock with dates and corn purée). Both choices were pleasing: the *dorade* delicious and crisp in a cardamom-flavored sauce with chickpeas and a crisp eggroll on the side. The *dos de lieu jaune* or pollock was on a purée of potatoes, with a date-and-raisin chutney adding sweetness and spiciness, unusual flavors with fish.

Tiny loaves of warm *pain de campagne* were so good that we asked and found that they are made on the premises. Half a bottle of Bourgogne *blanc* was an ideal accompaniment to lunch.

Desserts at 6 euros included *choco mousse et feuilles* (chocolate mousse and leaves), which we tried. It was a scoop of rich chocolate mousse garnished with leaf-like pieces of crisp *tuiles* (tile cookies), served with strawberries, blackberries, and blueberries on the side. The tartness of the fruit was a perfect foil for the chocolate, and the tuiles provided a nice variation in texture.

❖ *Le Café des Délices: in a peaceful spot, cuisine that's special.*

Aux Charpentiers
10 rue Mabillon, 75006 Paris (01.43.26.30.05)
Métro: Odéon
Open daily lunch and dinner until 11:00 P.M.

If you want to convince friends of your knowledge of the "real" Paris, take them to Aux Charpentiers. You'll lead them into an attractive, old-fashioned bistro, with special touches of its own, appropriate to its past as a gathering-place for a guild of carpenters. You pass a lovely old zinc bar from pre-war days. You tread the planks of an old oak floor on your way to the typical café table. At the windows are white-lace café curtains.

Aux Charpentiers has warm wood featured in its decor. Chairs are not the usual flimsy café variety, but substantial and comfortable, a walnut brown with cherry-colored fabric in the seats and backs. Small dark wooden structures like parts of cages are mounted on the walls. Our waiter explained that they represented individual projects done by workmen, journeymen who were trying to be received as full master carpenters. An impressive wood structure in the window won a bronze medal at the 1889 exposition.

The better-than-average menu has *plats du jour* according to the day of the week: Monday, veal Marengo, Tuesday, *boeuf à la mode* (beef stew), etc., all the way to Sunday, with the traditional lunch of that day, *gigot d'agneau de lait d'Aquitaine* (leg of lamb from Aquitaine). Prices run from 13 euros to a high of 17 euros for the lamb. So you choose your day according to your favorites.

Arriving late for lunch this day, we chose *plats*: he was attracted to the *faux-filet poêlé sauce Roquefort* (sautéed steak with blue cheese sauce) at 17, and I the *caneton rôti sauce olives* (duck with olives) at 14 euros. A house wine, a half of Rouge Charpentiers, was fairly priced at 10 euros.

We dug into our *plats* with relish when they arrived: the *canard aux olives*, large portions of well-cooked duck with many olives in a savory sauce, was served with white boiled potatoes, and was filling and well-flavored. The steak was huge and succulent, as rare as requested, accompanied by rounds of crisp fried potatoes. It was set off by a good Roquefort sauce, the cheese enhancing the flavor of the beef.

At one point during the meal we saw a departing tourist giving the *bise* (kisses) to her waiter. (You and I do not need to go this far in expressing our appreciation, by the way). But we were quietly appreciative, and look forward to returning.

Note: This bistro is appreciated by George and Barbara Bush, who've been seen dining here. Also Jacques Chirac, who celebrated his 60th birthday in the same room. Bush's successor, Bill Clinton, liked L'Ami Louis in the 3rd district—too rich for our budgets.

❖ *Aux Charpentiers: Good value in an attractive setting.*

La Closerie des Lilas
171 blvd du Montparnasse, 75006 Paris (01.43.54.21.68)
Métro: Port Royal
Open daily 11:00 A.M.–1:00 A.M.

La Closerie was described by Hemingway in *A Moveable Feast* as "the nearest good café when we lived in the flat over the sawmill at 113, rue Notre-Dame-des-Champs, and it was one of the best cafés in Paris. It was warm inside in the winter, and in the spring and fall it was very warm outside..."

photo © Juliana Spear

The regulars at this bistro, a remarkable group, included at one time the Russian revolutionary Lenin. La Closerie has a warm, intimate-looking bar in dark wood. If you want to eat, stick to the Brasserie side, where you can eat at a reasonable price with a little care: *plats* of fish and chicken are from about 15 euros, and cheese or dessert for 9 or 10.

❖ *La Closerie des Lilas: literary history in a cozy setting.*

L'Epi Dupin
11 rue Dupin, 75006 Paris (01.42.22.64.56)
Métro: Sèvres-Babylone
Tue–Fri lunch and dinner, Mon dinner, closed weekends,
Mon lunch, 3 weeks in August

The offerings at L'Epi Dupin show a lightness and originality that you do not find elsewhere at twice the price.

Usually when you're surrounded by tourists in a Paris bistro, you're right to be suspicious. In this case it means that there are some very savvy people who've heard of L'Epi Dupin and have booked well in advance to taste extraordinary cuisine at low prices: a 18-euro lunch menu, and a 29-euro *prix fixe* menu at dinner.

Hors d'oeuvres one day included *carpaccio de saumon, millefeuilles de queue de boeuf* (oxtail in puff pastry), and *aubergines à la bordelaise* (eggplant in red wine sauce). Around us, opinions were unanimous: "Very good indeed," remarked the Englishwoman to my right about her *millefeuille de queue de boeuf.* "Exquisite," was the judgment pronounced by a visiting American about his *carpaccio.*

Main dishes promised and delivered originality. *Caille*—quail—was roasted deliciously crisp in a well-seasoned sauce, with whole roasted garlic and tiny mushrooms. My husband could not be induced to part with any of his *filets de rouget grondin au pistou* (red gurnard filets in Provençal sauce), which he pronounced: "Delicious—best fish I've tasted." The San Francisco lawyers on our left, who had requested the help of a little translation to keep them from accidentally ordering something like lambs' brains, had finished up by choosing the *ongle de boeuf* (flank steak). They were calling it exquisite.

The dessert list here displays a fine originality: *poêlée de cerises au coulis de griottes* (sautéed cherries in a tart cherry sauce), *dariole au coulant de chocolat, sauce pistache,* (Chocolat fondant in a cone shape, pistachio sauce)—the list goes on.

Servings are generous and each dessert involves several flavors: one consisted of the nougat-flavored ice cream served on a *coulis,* or fruit sauce, with large *tuiles*—thin, almond-flavored cookies studded with almonds—the whole garnished with mint leaves delicately frosted with powdered sugar. The *poêlée de cerises* looked like an exotic flower, with quantities of red cherries lightly cooked in a sauce surrounded by the leafy garnish.

The only flaw in an otherwise perfect lunch were the house wines, surprisingly rough, the red less successful than the white. (We believe the owner is going to reevaluate his wine list).

At lunch, our end of L'Epi was crowded with tourists, most of them congratulating themselves on having succeeded in getting a reservation. At night it's more difficult—we heard of three-week waits, a particular difficulty in the summer since L'Epi closes on July 24 for the holidays.

Note: we had a wonderful experience there but have recently heard reports of dissatisfied diners.

❖ *L'Epi Dupin: sophisticated food at close to* cuisine familiale *prices, an outstanding value.*

Café de Flore
172 blvd St. Germain, 75006 Paris (01.45.48.55.26)
Métro: St. Germain
Open daily to 1:30 A.M.

Sartre's remark about the ways of liberty passing through the portals of the Flore is repeated on the front of the menu, but what you chiefly note here is their liberty with your money. Drinks in this bistro are outrageously priced: wines by the glass from 7 euros, beers from 7, and cocktails from 11 to 12—double the going rate. (For this you could have lunch somewhere else).

Still, when you're not thinking about your slimming wallet, you can look around and appreciate the understated elegance of the Flore interior: the Deco lighting, the spare clean lines, the tall potted palms, the red banquettes. Large mirrors are edged with brass, and the waiters (efficient but not especially friendly), are in their usual black and white. On this sunny day, the clientele inside looked like old regulars, while tourists confined themselves to the terrace.

There are economical ways of sampling the Flore's atmosphere. Drinks are high but a few foods are not above the usual range in Paris. We chose a ham and cheese omelet, which was presented on a white Café de Flore plate, with an accompanying small basket of French bread and a small carafe of water. The omelet tasted good, if a trifle greasy and not as puffy as we would have liked. Salads, ranging from 6 to 26 euros, are also a reasonable choice at the Flore.

Unusual fan-shaped mosaic tiles are on the floor, framed posters of art shows lead up the stairs to the fabled first floor, still the most "in" part of the Flore, a place where today's intellectuals meet and talk. But the main floor is better to look at, and it is where young Simone de Beauvoir spent hours writing her books and helping Sartre revise his. It is where the two of them met Albert Camus and where Simone first saw Truman Capote, whom she dismissed as "tiny... smaller even than Sartre... looking like a giant mushroom."

Lalique crystal or something very like it conceals the lighting in wonderful Art Deco wall sconces. An enormous bouquet fills much of the window ledge, right in front of the lacy café curtains.

❖ *Café de Flore: go for the ambiance, which is still special, the legend which is still part of this place, not for the so-so food and the over-priced drinks.*

Chez Marcel
7 rue Stanislas, 75006 Paris (01.45.48.29.94)
Métro Notre Dame-des Champs
Mon–Fri noon–2:00 A.M., 7:30 P.M.–10:00 P.M.,
closed August

On a little street off the boulevard Raspail and close to the Alliance Française, Chez Marcel strikes one as a place where everything is done right. The narrow room is warm and welcoming, with wallpaper in subdued tones to set off the rich, gleaming copper pots, posters, and oil paintings that give this the warmth of an old-fashioned dining room in a friend's home. The old bar on your right as you enter has witty ephemera about it, Deco-inspired advertising and old landscapes. Lamps with lacy, beaded lampshades give a warm illumination to the bar area and here and there in the room.

Prices are a pleasant surprise for the expensive 6th arrondissement: a 12-euro lunch menu provides the usual bistro fare with some surprises. A variety of wines are available by the *pichet*, or carafe. We shared a *pichet* of rosé from the Pays d'Oc for less than 8 euros.

We were seated at a little table, one of a line leading to the door. Near us were French businessmen in intense conversation. A nice touch was a large bouquet of pink hydrangeas separating us from their table, like a floral hedge. But it wasn't so effective that it separated us from their witticisms. One must have spilled a little red wine on the table (covered with paper over white linen), and he quipped: "Oh, now I suppose I'll be charged extra for a stain on the *dentelle de Sèvres* (Sèvres lace)."

To start, the *oeuf mayonnaise* was nicely prepared, the homemade mayonnaise piped on eggs, with tomatoes and parsley adding color. A tasty terrine was served on greens, with pickles to pique the appetite. A variety of breads were cut on demand, so came to the table fresh.

Brochette d'agneau (grilled lamb on a skewer) was a large, generous *plat*, the flavor of the lamb enhanced with sautéed onions, red peppers, and zucchini and accompanied by sautéed potatoes. *Quenelles* came in a small cast-iron casserole with little white potatoes. The *sauce à la nantua*, a cheese sauce, provided just the right balance for the light and subtle flavor of the fish *quenelles*.

On the way out, after finishing the good espresso accompanied by a small bittersweet chocolate, we asked the owner-managers who had given us attentive service the eternal question: is Chez Marcel a restaurant or a bistro? "Plutôt bistro," said the gray-haired proprietor. "La service, les plats, la décor—bistro lyonnais" (The service, the food, the decor—Lyon-style bistro). His blond wife interjected, "Non, c'est un restaurant traditionnel." "Non, pour moi c'est bistro," (No, for me it's a bistro) insisted her husband.

You'll have to decide for yourself.

❖ *Chez Marcel: a place you'd love to have in your own neighborhood.*

Paul

77 rue de Buci, 75006 Paris (01.55.42.02.24)
Métro: St. Michel
Open daily, weekdays to 8:00 P.M., Sat to 9:00 P.M.,
Sun to 7:00 P.M.

Paul is not a bistro, but a bakery with a *salon de thé*. Still, it's a treasure in an over-priced district. We first started noticing this chain of bakeries in Lille, when we found some of the nicest coffee and pastries there. Later a friend who lives in Paris year-round alerted us to the presence of a Paul near the big department stores in the 9th arrondissement. This one in the 6th is just as appealing—a large, airy room with chandeliers, a marble fireplace, walls in the palest green with delicate molding around the ceiling. There are oak tables, comfortable armchairs in the style of Louis XIII, and huge windows looking out onto the street.

Added to this are unbeatable prices—a 12-euro lunch, friendly service, and one of the best locations you can imagine. Offerings are described in more detail in the chapter "Romantic Bistros."

❖ *Paul: for low-priced light lunches and snacks in an elegant setting.*

Le Petit Saint-Benoît
4 rue St. Benoit, 75006 Paris (01.42.60.27.92)
Métro: St. Germain
Mon–Sat noon–2:30 P.M., 7:00 P.M.–10:30 P.M.,
closed in August

Nothing could be simpler than finding the Petit St. Benoît. You walk up rue Saint-Benoît, the little street that runs between the most famous cafés in Paris, the Deux Magots, and the Flore. Soon you reach Le Petit Saint Benoît, with all of its old-fashioned charm. A large terrace outside, an old zinc bar, red tablecloths covered with paper in thrifty bistro fashion, dark banquettes, historic red-and-white tile on the floor, brass hat rails, a venerable clock, obscure mirrors, and that vanishing feature, a set of numbered drawers at the end for regulars who used to keep their own cloth napkins there.

Intellectuals from the neighborhood stop by for an apéritif, a before-dinner drink. We noticed a gray-haired individual with piercing eyes who might have stepped out of an historic photograph of the district. History is evident in the old framed photos on the walls, and in framed memorabilia of all sorts: a frontispiece of a famous novel with signed dedication by the author; a cartoon or quick sketch by an artist who patronized the place; a glimpse of a famous face caught when its owner was enjoying a moment on the *terrasse*.

The Petit St-Benoît is easy on the budget: hors d'oeuvres are all 3 euros, plats about 9 euros and desserts 4 to 5 euros.

Our *plats* arrived a little quickly—one had visions of dishes lined up in the kitchen, ready to be whipped out for customers. One of us had selected the salmon and the other the *blanquette de veau*. Salmon was a large filet served on puréed potatoes, with a cream sauce with sorrel for extra flavor. A slice of lemon would have been nice, but to find these prices at this address is so amazing that one can't quarrel with their economies. The *blanquette de veau* (veal stew), a bistro standard, came with rice and was tasty and filling.

Pichets of pleasant house wines are available at 7 or 12

euros depending on the size selected. Our demi of chilled rosé was perfect for a warm summer night.

Service at Le Petit St.-Benoît is swift; they must accomplish several seatings each evening. But that's all right, and it may account for this bistro's survival in an area where the rents have driven out the small booksellers and little businesses, replacing them with the big names in the fashion industry.

❖ *Le Petit St.-Benoît: low-priced* cuisine familiale, *old-fashioned charm and an unbeatable location.*

Le Reminet
3 rue des Grands-Degrés, 75005 Paris (01.44.07.04.24)
Métro: St. Michel
Wed–Sun lunch and dinner, closed 2 weeks in August

With a choice location in the 5th arrondissement, just off Quai Montobello near the edge of the Seine, you would expect Le Reminet to be in the "big splurge" category. After all, Notre Dame is virtually across the way. Yet it's one of the few bistros in Paris to offer luxury food at low prices.

On entering the small dining room we noticed the 13-euro lunch menu scrawled on the typical blackboard, or *ardoise*, giving hors d'oeuvre, main course, and dessert. You could choose between *harengs pommes à l'huile* (herring with potato salad) and *tomate avec mozzarrella* to start, then *sauté de porc* (pork chop) or *sardines aux xeres* (in sherry sauce). For dessert, *poire marinée au vin rouge* (pear marinated in red wine) or *mousse de châtaigne, crème fouettée* (chestnut mousse with whipped cream).

Lunch was outstanding, starting with a small plate of *amuse-gueules* or appetizers including olives and slices of *saucisson*. Soon the herring was served, not with the expected potatoes, but prettily presented with lettuce, carrots, and various other vegetables in a flower-like arrangement. The flavorful tomato was a particular treat for those of us who depend on our local grocery, garnished as it was with slices of mozzarrella. "This is not supermarket mozzarrella," we agreed.

Main dishes were equally successful: the *porc sauté* came in a sauce lightly flavored with orange, and the sardines were crisp and tasty on a bed of slivers of carrot and zucchini. A light and pleasant finish to lunch was provided by chestnut mousse garnished with whipped cream and pears marinated in red wine.

With the food we enjoyed an Alsatian wine, Gewurtztraminer, a white with a touch of sweetness that set off the pork to perfection. The wine list features small producers, especially from the south.

Hugues Gournay, the owner-chef, came to our table to chat. When asked about his cuisine, he spoke not of preparing dishes specifically from his native Normandy but of using "produits très frais—produits du marché," (fresh market produce) with some of his own ideas about herbs and spices. He has succeeded admirably.

❖ *Le Reminet: outstanding food at amazingly reasonable prices.*

Le Sélect
99 blvd du Montparnasse, 75006 Paris (01.42.22.65.27)
Métro: Vavin
Open daily to 3:00 A.M.

Of the American literary cafés of the 1920s, only the Sélect would today look much the same to Hemingway and Fitzgerald. The Dôme has become a horrid example of Atlantic-City glitz combined with Las Vegas flash, though it does have good, if expensive, food. The Coupole might seem somewhat familiar to expatriates from the twenties, although they would shudder at the prices people pay for brasserie offerings. The Rotonde has location but little else: it has acquired all of the romance of a New Jersey diner. The Closerie des Lilas, long lacking the lilacs, has become an expensive French restaurant. Others such as the Jockey have totally vanished.

At Le Sélect, besides the appearance of an historic place, you can get good food at reasonable prices. And if you have something else on your schedule on a given night, you can fit that in too, because the service is brisk and efficient. Like

many other such places, Le Sélect is enjoyable for the banter you hear between waiters and customers: when we heard the distant sound of glasses crashing to the floor for the second time, we asked our waiter what was happening. "Ils boivent trop" (they drink too much), he said seriously, miming someone pulling on a bottle.

We love the Sélect for its ambiance: ochre-colored walls, the original moldings from 1923, fine Lalique-influenced lighting fixtures, wrought iron, the sense that here is a place where time has stood still. Before, we'd always considered it a place for a drink or light snack. The thing to realize is that they also offer real food.

Since it was Sunday, the usual 14-euro menu, which includes a quarter bottle of wine, wasn't available, but we still ate well. We ordered a *pavé grillé sauce roquefort* (steak with Roquefort sauce) and a niçoise salad. Both *plats* were large and generous: the steak, accompanied by sautéed potatoes and tiny *haricots verts*, compared favorably with some we'd been served at much more expensive bistros, and we were really surprised at the attractiveness and size of the plate with all the ingredients of a classic *salade niçoise.*

If we hadn't made those choices, the Sélect offers other salads and classics such as *croque monsieur* and onion soup, as well as the sort of thing that would please a committed "foodie:" smoked salmon salad, foie gras, *côte de veau, magret de canard,* and various cheeses.

A good half bottle of Beaujolais, a Brouilly, for 12 euros was a smooth and suitable accompaniment for our meals.

A lively discussion with our waiter, Philippe, referred to in the menu as Philippe the Barman, made for an interesting finale. We asked if he knew when the infamously tough proprietress of the café who was generally known as Madame Sélect had died. "Il n'y avait pas de Madame Sélect" (There was no Madame Sélect), he maintained. He was adamant about it, not backing down even when we pointed to a framed sketch from the old days with the words "Madame Sélect" beneath the caricature of a lady with strong jaw and upswept hair.

❖ *Le Sélect: a time-warp experience from the Jazz Age.*

AFRICAN-AMERICANS IN PARIS: THE 6TH ARRONDISSEMENT AND BEYOND

...I love this café life, this quiet existence mixed with noise and quick motion which is attached to every large city... In Paris I find everything that appeals to me: lights, noises in the night, places where one has fun according to one's liking, a sympathetic and tolerant world, in sum, a true civilization.

—Countee Cullen

For African-Americans, particularly writers, bistros were fundamental to survival in the strange city. They were meeting-places, outdoor living rooms for people who would otherwise be whiling away solitary hours in cold hotel rooms. The bistros gave writers a chance to observe street life and get to know the city even if they had only rudimentary French. Here was the possibility of meeting people and making friends. Ever since World War I, African-Americans had discovered that the racism which blighted their lives and threatened their safety in the United States did not seem to be such an issue in France. Even now, the social barriers between the races that exist elsewhere seem less important in Paris.

For writer Chester Himes, who left the United States in search of a better life in Paris, this acceptance was to be a crucial part of the city's appeal. Already published in the US, Himes came to be well known as a writer of the *Serie Noire* books, featuring Grave Digger Jones and Coffin Ed. (The best-known book in the series, *Cotton Comes to Harlem*, was later made into a movie). His sometimes raunchy, frequently misognyistic and often rambling autobiography, *The Quality of Hurt* and *My Life of Absurdity* is one of the most entertaining accounts of life abroad written by any expatriate.

For years Himes was frustrated in his efforts to survive as a writer in the United States. France seemed a better alternative; he was attracted by accounts of the City of Light sent by his old friend Richard Wright, already well known for his novels *Black Boy* and *Native Son*. Wright had made a home for himself in Paris and urged his compatriot to follow.

Himes's entry into Paris on April 11, 1953, didn't go as planned. He arrived at the train station and didn't see the people who were supposed to meet him. After waiting for a time, he finally took a taxi and, with difficulty, managed to communicate to the driver Richard Wright's address in the 7th arrondissement. Once deposited in front of the building, Himes dragged his luggage up several flights of stairs. Suddenly the lights gave out and another light appeared from behind curtains. Then, as he told it:

> ... a monster charged forth, the likes of which I had never seen. She looked like some prehistoric species of the human race; obviously female, judging from the huge drooping breasts topping a squarish big-hipped body beneath a flagging purple robe and the things in her hair, and she seemed in a rage....

> 'Allez!' she screamed. 'Allez! Allez! Vite! Vite!'

This was his introduction to Paris and its people.

Not able to communicate with any assurance in French, knowing few people in Paris, and having very little money, he nevertheless quickly became a part of the group that gathered in the café-bistro Le Tournon, on the rue de Tournon in the 6th district. As Himes tells it—and one must allow a little latitude for the male penchant for exaggeration—he had no trouble attracting female companionship for the evenings. He and his friend, cartoonist Ollie Harrington, would get a repartee going of jokes and not-too-serious put-downs, almost a comic routine, and people would crowd near to witness the fun.

Of course, African-Americans who decided to emigrate to France had a variety of reasons for doing so. Not all imagined that life in Paris would be easy. Some might have said with

James Baldwin, "I have never, thank God—and certainly not once I found myself living there—been even remotely romantic about Paris.... My journey, or my flight, had not been to Paris, but simply away from America."

As Baldwin also discovered, "the moment I began living in French hotels I understood the necessity of French cafés." The Deux Magots was part of his first experience of Paris. He went there when he arrived in November, 1948, and was sitting at the Deux Magots when he recognized Richard Wright, who helped him to find a hotel.

The Deux Magots was also where Baldwin and Himes first met. Himes had been visiting Richard Wright when there was a telephone call from Baldwin, who needed a loan. According to Himes, Wright had been annoyed by Baldwin's attacks on him in several articles. Their conversation at the famous bistro led to a heated argument over Baldwin's denunciation of Wright for creating a stereotype in Bigger Thomas, the main character in *Native Son*. Himes saw the situation—Baldwin's needing money—as an occasion for Wright to get his own back:

> Dick accused Baldwin of showing his ingratitude
> for all he had done for him by his scurrilous
> attacks. Baldwin defended himself by saying that
> Dick had written his story and hadn't left him, or
> any other American black writer, anything to write
> about. I confess at this point they lost me... All of
> the women and the majority of the men... took
> Baldwin's side—chiefly, I think, because he looked
> so small and intense and vulnerable....

Sometimes a café experience could turn bad. One turned out very badly for Baldwin. One night in a St. Germain-des-Prés café, Baldwin was, as he says, "discovered" by a tourist he'd met before in New York, adding "only because we found ourselves in Paris we immediately established the illusion that we had been fast friends back in the good old U.S.A." Before the evening was over, Baldwin had promised to find a room in his hotel for his new friend.

The tourist came to Baldwin's hotel, bringing a sheet belonging to the place he'd just left. Baldwin borrowed the sheet, putting his own dirty ones in the hall for the chambermaid. He didn't think any more about it until his new friend was visited by the police. Then the gendarmes went to Baldwin's room and spotted the sheet with, as he described it, "Lettered in the most brilliant scarlet I have ever seen, the name of the hotel from which it had been stolen." Baldwin found himself under arrest.

Days of misery followed. As he remembered: "For once, locked in, divested of shoelaces, belt, watch, money, papers, nail file, in a freezing cell in which both the window and the toilet were broken, with six other adventurers, the story I told of *l'affaire du drap de lit* (the case of the sheet) elicited only the wildest amusement or the most suspicious disbelief."

Added to the physical discomfort was the mental agony of not knowing what was going to happen. A French boy who'd stolen a sweater from Monoprix would, everyone agreed, receive a six-month sentence. And, Baldwin added:

> ... my cellmates had been amusing themselves with
> me by telling terrible stories about the inefficiency
> of French prisons, an inefficiency so extreme that it
> had often happened that someone who was
> supposed to be taken out and tried found himself
> on the wrong line and was guillotined instead...

> though I knew they were teasing me, it was simply
> not possible for me to totally disbelieve them.

What did happen was that a kindly prisoner who was due to be released offered to take out messages for anyone in the cell. At first Baldwin refused; then he thought of someone who might be able to help, a former employer. This man came to see him and found him a lawyer. When Baldwin came to trial, the case against him was dismissed with general laughter at the absurd situation that had caused the arrest in the first place.

> *Blues in the rue Pigalle. Black and laughing, heart-breaking blues in the Paris dawn, pounding like a pulse-beat, moving like the Mississippi!*
>
> —Langston Hughes

Some African-American writers, members of the Harlem Renaissance movement, had tried life in Paris years before Wright, Himes, and Baldwin. Langston Hughes reached Paris in February 1924 with only seven dollars in his pocket. He lived in a garret near the Place de Clichy and survived by working at odd jobs—doorman at a small nightclub on the rue Fontaine, dishwasher at the Grand Duc Cabaret at 48 rue Nollet in the 17th district—and wrote poetry when he could. About his life in Paris, he wrote:

> The room was right out of a book . . . I guess dreams do come true and sometimes life makes its own books. Because here I am, living in a Paris garret, writing poems and having champagne for breakfast (because champagne is what we had with our breakfast at the Grand Duc from the half-empty bottles left by unsuspecting guests).

Despite this romantic picture of the poet's life abroad, Hughes found reality tough enough that he would warn friends: "Stay home!.... Jobs in Paris are like needles in haystacks for everybody and especially for English-speaking foreigners."

Sometimes the available jobs became too challenging even for a starving poet. His first job as a *chasseur* (doorman) at a nightclub on the rue Fontaine ended when he discovered he was also supposed to be the *videur* (bouncer) and stop fights. "I didn't like the task of fight-stopping, because the first fight

I saw there was between ladies, who shattered champagne glasses on the edge of the table, then slashed at each other with the jagged stems," he wrote. After that incident, a job as dishwasher at the Grand Duc looked good. But the experience of life in Montmartre was not lost on Hughes, who incorporated the rhythms of the jazz all around him into poems like "Jazz Band in a Parisian Cabaret."

When he got back to the United States, Hughes had to adjust to the segregation in the nation's capital. He wrote: "I felt very bad in Washington last winter, so I wrote a great many poems. (I wrote only a few poems in Paris, because I had had such a good time there)."

An African-American who founded an important cabaret in Montmartre was Ada Smith du Conge, commonly known as "Bricktop." Her club, on the rue Fontaine, became a hangout for the famous and the socially prominent.

She had left New York because she was offered a job at the Grand Duc. Her start in Paris was not promising, however. Seasick on the way over, she reached the city and found the Grand Duc not the impressive nightclub she'd imagined, but a tiny little bar. She was tempted to say something inappropriate, but a handsome young Negro came out of the kitchen and offered her something to eat, getting her away from the club owner. Later she recalled that the young man had been Langston Hughes.

Countee Cullen spent a few days in Paris in 1926 as part of a trip with his stepfather. Cullen travelled to France with many more advantages than Hughes had had, including an M.A. from Harvard. Returning later with a Guggenheim grant to study, he evaluated Paris as "a peerless city. Liberty, equality, fraternity are not only words. They express the spirit of which Paris is made." While he lived there, however, most of his contacts were not French but American. Cullen's relative prosperity contrasted with Hughes's poverty and gave opposing impressions to Americans in the United States of the ease of life in Paris.

Poet Claude McKay had no illusions about the French, but could perceive advantages to the bistros: "Paris, away from Montmartre and Montparnasse, seemed to me to be the perfect city of modern civilization. It was the only city I knew which provided quiet and comfortable clubs in the form of cafés for all its citizens of every class."

"I sat at my first sidewalk café last night and fell in love with Paris on the corner of Place de l'Opéra and Boulevard des Capucines," wrote Arna Bontemps. Also part of the Harlem Renaissance, Bontemps was not able to visit Paris until 1960, almost 40 years after his friends became acquainted with the city. During this visit Bontemps was guided around the city by Richard Wright and Ollie Harrington.

> *The French adopted me immediately. They all went to the beaches to get dark like Josephine Baker... I felt liberated in Paris. People didn't stare at me. [But] I was afraid to go into prominent restaurants in Paris. Once, I dined in a certain restaurant with friends. An American lady looked at our table and called the waiter. "Tell her to get out," the lady said. "In my country she is belonging only in the kitchen." The French management asked the American lady to leave.*

—Josephine Baker

When Josephine Baker first went to Paris in 1925 as a dancer in the Revue Nègre troup, she expected to be just another member of the chorus. That was not how it worked out. French artist Paul Colin had something to do with Josephine's startling debut. Colin had been commissioned to design a poster to publicize the Revue Nègre, which was to appear at the Théâtre des Champs-Elysées. He needed a striking model for his poster, and, looking at the leading lady, felt discouraged: "Maude de Forest looked like a washerwoman." Spotting a beautiful girl in the chorus, he thought: "What a pity she's not the star."

The show was reworked, the beautiful chorus girl whom Colin featured in his poster became the focus of attention, and Josephine Baker was on her way. At first, Baker's shyness was a problem. "In spite of her magnificent body, she was extremely modest," commented Colin. "I couldn't seem to make her understand that I wanted her to pose *nude!*"

Janet Flanner, who reported on Paris for the *New Yorker*, remembered Baker on her opening night:

> She made her entry entirely nude except for a pink flamingo feather between her limbs; she was being carried upside down and doing the split on the shoulder of a black giant.... She was an unforgettable black ebony statue. A scream of salutation spread through the theater.... Within half an hour of the final curtain on opening night, the news and meaning of her arrival had spread by the grapevine up to the cafés on the Champs-Elysées, where the witnesses of her triumph sat over their drinks excitedly repeating their report of what they had just seen.... She was the established new American star for Europe.

Suddenly the toast of Paris, Josephine went on to make her life in France.

She would courageously work for the French Resistance during World War II, eventually receiving the Légion d'Honneur in recognition. She continued to work as a dancer long after most dancers abandon such a grueling profession. When the costs of supporting her adopted children at her chateau in the Dordogne became too great, she made a final comeback. Benny Luke, former dancer and manager at Haynes, remembers her triumph at the Bobino Music Hall in the 14th district on March 14, 1975. Baker had been unwell, but managed to glide about an enormous stage, putting on a performance that gave no sign of what the effort must have cost. At the end of the show, "She held up her arms and we all cheered." Days later she died and was given a great state funeral at the Madeleine.

Duke Ellington recalled later how touched he felt about something that happened during his first engagement in Paris. During the intermission of his band's performance at the Salle Pleyel there was a reception backstage. It turned out that a duchess lost a valuable diamond ring. Everybody, including musicians and guests, started looking for it, but the duchess soon called off the search, saying,"I can always get diamonds, but how often can I get a Duke Ellington?"

Years later, novelist Maya Angelou had her chance to experience Paris as part of a tour of Europe. She was hired to sing and dance with a touring company presenting *Porgy and Bess*. In Paris they appeared at the Théâtre Wagram. Opening night went well, and soon African-Americans who lived in the city took her around. She recalled:

> We went to the Left Bank, and he showed me where F. Scott Fitzgerald and Hemingway did some flamboyant talking and serious drinking. The bareness of the bar surprised me. I expected a more luxurious room with swatches of velvet.... High up over the facade hung a canvas awning on which was stenciled the romantic name DEUX MAGOTS.

Later she saw L'Abbaye, a bar owned by Gordon Heath, a black American, and the Rose Rouge, which, she wrote, was "closer to my idea of a Parisian night club. It had velour drapes and a uniformed doorman; the waiters were haughty and the customers well-dressed." After appearing in *Porgy and Bess*, she would sing a midnight show at the Mars Club, then take a cab to the Rose Rouge to finish the evening with another appearance there.

Friends urged her to leave the company and take up residence in Paris, and for a while Angelou seriously considered it. Then a telling incident occurred that made her question how tolerant the French really were. Hired to sing at a fund-raising event, Angelou arrived with two Senegalese friends. When the Parisian hostess found out that the men were from Africa, not America, her smile disappeared. Angelou never saw her again.

Similar stories are told by African-Americans who live in Paris today. Singer and professor Almeta Speaks, originally from North Carolina, has made her life in Paris. She says that the French have a mythology about themselves as rescuers of blacks. But, she says, "If I go down the street, I'll be treated as an African. When I open my mouth and they find out that I'm American, it's all different." The African-American community in Paris, she says, is not as cohesive or as small as it once was. People are more transient these days." Still, she concludes, "There is a freedom here, and writers have written about that freedom."

Janet McDonald, dynamic author of *Project Girl* and *Spellbound,* discussed life in Paris for African-Americans and her first visit to Paris in 1995:

> It's infinitely easier than in the US. There's all the difference in the world.... I felt like I could actually live there.... I don't know what it is about the French—they seem to like us. There's a different kind of racial dynamic—there is racism in France, but we are not the recipients of it. For an African-American [life] feels pretty comfortable, and it feels different in the U.S.

There are no present-day equivalents to the Café Tournon in its heyday as a bistro for expatriate African-Americans. But the question of how to choose a good bistro was addressed by Richard Wright in an article written in 1953. Wright outlined some of the inadequacies of many Parisian hangouts. He emphasized that one shouldn't give up too easily, that the perfect place might be just around the corner:

> In my search for a café I strayed into the Deux Magots, the Flore, the Montana, the Reine Blanche, Lipps, the Royal St. Germain.... It was no go—too many tourists, too many tense characters on the make.... One could not sit a quarter of an hour without somebody violating that most sacred rule of café life: leave your neighbor alone.... I finally found my favorite bistro by straying one day into the Monaco, just off the Carrefour de l'Odéon.

Restaurants of historical importance to African-Americans in Paris include:

Brasserie Lipp
151 blvd St.-Germain 75006 Paris (01.45.48.53.91)
Métro: St.Germain
Open daily noon to 1:00 A.M.

Frequented by James Baldwin, who mentions the Lipp in his last novel, *Just Above My Head*. Richard Wright also patronized this brasserie. Described in detail on pages 63–65.

Café de Flore
172 blvd St. Germain, 75006 Paris (01.45.48.55.26)
Métro: St. Germain
Open daily 7:00 A.M.–1:00 A.M.

James Baldwin often went to the Flore, where he wrote *Crying Holy* and worked on *Go Tell It on the Mountain*. At the time, the upstairs room was a hangout for gay men. Incidentally, *Go Tell It on the Mountain* saved him from trouble with the French police. One evening when they were checking papers, Baldwin had forgotten his *carte de séjour*, but was carrying a copy of the novel. It had a large photograph of the author on the dust jacket. When he showed his book as a makeshift proof of identity to the policeman, he was surprised at the respectful reaction he received: "Vous êtes écrivain, Monsieur!" (You're a writer, Sir!)

Much of his writing was done in the rather plain upstairs room, now a favorite of French journalists.

❖ *Café de Flore: over-priced, but worth a look because of its importance as a literary café.*

Haynes
3 rue Clauzel, 75009 Paris (01.48.78.40.63)
Métro: St-Georges
Tue–Sat 7:00 P.M.–12.30 A.M., closed in August

If you ever tire of French cooking, good as it is, and feel like quietly snuggling into a truly American place in Paris, you

might want to drop in at Haynes, the historic landmark bistro and gathering spot of the African-American community since 1949.

When Haynes was started by Leroy Haynes, a G.I. who settled in Paris after World War II, it quickly became a favorite stop for almost every African-American writer and jazz musician who visited or resided in Paris during the postwar years. Richard Wright used to come here. So did James Baldwin. Dozens of slightly askew, framed photographs of famous people, most of them signed, cover the stucco walls.

Haynes is probably the closest thing Paris has now to a gathering place for African-Americans, serving, as it does, food reminiscent of the American South, and having a considerable history involving expatriate Black Americans.

Service at Haynes is part of the fun: the bar is presided over by Benny Luke, well-known for his career as a dancer and actor (he was Jakob in the original *Cage Aux Folles*, both on stage and in the movie). Benny runs things with cheerfulness and charm, while other personnel hurry about with plates, drinks, and whatever is needed. The small room with ten or so tables fills up fast, so reserving ahead is a good idea. There was a 7-euro entertainment charge the night we were there. The cost may vary according to the entertainment; it was a remarkable value on this Saturday night.

While waiting, we were served a chili mixture in little ramekins with thin, crisp baguette slices as an *amuse-gueule*. We had time to admire the stuccoed wall with framed photographs of great stars and entertainers who have been here. Taylor and Burton, in their youthful and beauteous stage, are the ones that stand out.

When our *plats* arrived, we were struck by the size of the servings: each plate was loaded with food. The New Orleans-style shrimp gumbo was delicious with a Creole sauce. The fried chicken, red beans, and rice platter, while less successful, was still acceptable. We dug in, found the food tasty and savory, and the house wine drinkable and fairly priced.

After the set, we took a moment to chat with Benny Luke about the two leading actors in *Cage aux Folles*. "What were they like to work with?" we wondered. "I didn't know Ugo—he was an Italian I'd never met before, but the actor who played Zaza was a friend; we'd been playing the roles on stage for years before they made the movie," he said.

We finally left, exhilarated with our evening chez Haynes. Many diners paused on their way out to write raves in the *Livre d'Or* (guest book) by the door.

❖ *Haynes: a significant part of African-American history in Paris.*

Polidor
41 rue Monsieur le Prince 75006 Paris (01.43.26.95.34)
Métro: Odéon
Mon–Sat noon–2:00 P.M., 7:00 P.M.–midnight

Richard Wright liked the Polidor, which is not far from the five-room apartment at 14 rue Monsieur-le-Prince where he lived from 1948 to 1959. The Polidor is an historic bistro from the turn of the century, with traditional French paneling in dark cream, a venerable tiled floor, oilcloth- and paper-covered tables which you'll be sharing if you go there for one of their bustling, crowded lunches. The convivial atmosphere is greatly enhanced by the motherly waitresses who whisk about getting and delivering orders. Featured are the old standards of bistro cuisine, with a main dish depending on the day of the week. On Wednesdays it's *hachis parmentier*, similar to meat loaf with mashed potatoes.

There's dark wainscotting, elegant old plate glass mirrors, some with the *vin du mois* (wine of the month) and other available vintages handwritten on them. A cheerful bistro feeling pervades in this place. Mostly business people lunch here, but a few longhaired Left Bank intellectuals can be seen. The maîtresse d', a hefty, buxom blonde, bounds about the restaurant, greeting, shifting a place mat here and there, and showing people where to go.

photo © Juliana Spear

We started with fresh *crudités* and *oeuf mayonnaise* along with good bread. The main dish was an old reliable, puffy and golden *hachis parmentier*, meat loaf crowned with good mashed potatoes. It's good, stick-to-the-ribs *cuisine de grand-mère*.

The service, although cheerful, was rather negligent; one of us received our *plat* several minutes earlier than the other, so we sat and nibbled from one plate.

For dessert, at extra cost, there were some interesting possibilities including *bavarois au cassis* and *fondant au chocolat,* etc. at prices ranging from 3 to 7 euros. The *baba au rhum* is the characteristic doughnut-shaped cake in a *crème anglaise* heavily fortified with rum, a delicious if intoxicating dessert. The ice cream, two intense-flavored scoops of chocolate and coffee, may well be *fait maison* (made on the premises) as the menu claims.

❖ *Polidor: good value in an expensive area.*

Le Sélect
99 blvd du Montparnasse, 75006 Paris (01.42.22.65.27)
Metro: Vavin
Open daily 8:00 A.M.–3:00 A.M.

Le Sélect is the best preserved of any of the historic cafés. Here in 1957 Chester Himes worked on *A Jealous Man Can't Win*, part of his *Série Noire* novels for Marcel Duhamel, a director at Gallimard.

❖ *Le Sélect: worth a visit. Described in detail on page 78–80.*

Le Tournon
17 rue de Tournon 75006 Paris (01.43.26.16.16)
RER: Luxembourg
Mon–Fri 7:00 A.M.–8:00 P.M., closed August

Near the Senate behind the Jardin du Luxembourg, Le Tournon is an unremarkable little bistro, with nothing about it to indicate its importance in African-American life in the 1950s and '60s. Even so, we've heard French people

praise this café for its welcoming ambiance. A circular, copper bar has rounds of white neon above, but the café tables in this simple place are not marble, but formica. Tan banquettes line the walls, and the floor tiles are in a crazy-quilt pattern. A large pinball machine—possibly the same one Richard Wright used to play—blocks a view of handsome buildings across the way. An amiable-looking, middle-aged French couple tend bar.

There's a good range of possibilities here outside regular lunch and dinner hours: large salads, sandwiches with *pain poilâne*, tasty cold plates of *jambon de Paris* (ham) or *rosbif* (cold roast beef) with salad offer a substantial mid-afternoon meal. Prices are reasonable: sandwiches are from 3 euros and if made from *pain poilâne*, from 4 euros, omelets from 4, complicated salads and cold plates about 8, standard bistro desserts (open-faced apple pie, crème caramel) about 4 euros. A hot *spécialité du jour* is available at mealtimes for 9 euros. Wines by the glass or a quarter, half or whole carafe, range from 2 to 12 euros. A Côtes du Rhône went well with our light lunches.

Our friend enjoyed her *rôti de porc* (roast pork) with *salade verte*. "It's a wonderful salad: the dressing is very mustardy and the pork is good," was her comment.

Regulars include a few retired people, businessmen from the area, an occasional politican from the Senate.

❖ *Le Tournon: an historic bistro that's worth a stop.*

MOVERS AND SHAKERS: THE 7TH & 8TH ARRONDISSEMENTS

> *People come to Paris, to the capital, to give their lives a sense of belonging, of an almost mythical participation in society.*
>
> —Marguerite Duras

T he glamorous seventh, the imposing eighth: their importance is declared in the monuments around you, monuments like the Eiffel Tower, the Arc de Triomphe and the golden-domed Invalides. Like a ribbon through the center is the Champs-Elysées, splendid boulevard of trees and shopfronts dedicated to luxury or power, where citizens of the world come to promenade and take in an extraordinary vista stretching from the Arc to the Place de la Concorde.

What has not happened here? What could not happen in the future? The air is alive with possibilities.

This was F. Scott Fitzgerald's Paris. When he got to France, with a best seller behind him, in a sense he'd already "made it." No putting up in a squalid writer's garret on the Left Bank for him. To a friend he wrote," We have taken an appartment [*sic*] in the Rue de Tillsit near the Etoile for 8 months and I have taken a studio near by to write in. We're glad to leave Italy and Paris in the Spring is no easy place to settle down to work. In fact most of our time is taken up in dodging our friends, most of whom seem to be over here."

Going out to see his friends was essential, however, for James Joyce: "After I have worked all day, the thought of eating at home becomes unbearable. I want to see people, I want to get away from the work.... One is free. It is wonderful to let go, to chat without reservations," he explained to a friend. To escape the monotony of home, Joyce frequented Fouquet's, on the Champs-Elysées. There he ordered oysters, chicken, mushrooms or asparagus, usually leaving them untasted. Instead he would concentrate his attention on the carafes of white wine that he consumed nightly. Once he told about meeting Proust. In the course of their conversation the great French writer had spoken about nothing but duchesses. "I was far more interested in their maids," Joyce recalled.

Here in the 7th arrondissement are concentrated the centers of power: the National Assembly and the ministries of Defense, Education, Industry, and Commerce. The 7th is the seat of the French government, an all-encompassing entity. The Eiffel Tower is here; so is the Musée d'Orsay, a favorite for most tourists. Much of the aristocratic "old money" lives here, discreetly. Cole Porter had a large apartment in the 7th during the 1930s; his elaborate gilt Steinway is now tucked away in a corner of the American Cathedral parish hall. Celebrities like Alain Delon, the French counterpart of Marlon Brando, have apartments overlooking the river.

If the 6th arrondissement was the cradle of creativity for the young and the not-so-young who went to Paris to make something of themselves, the 7th and 8th are the domain of those who have already arrived. This part of the city is expensive and fashionable, with much of the sophisticated sparkle of the Upper East Side of New York. This is the world of the fashion-setters, the "in" crowd, the people everybody loves to imitate.

The 8th, lying directly north across the river from the 7th, houses much of the opulence and flamboyance of Paris. Many of the great fashion houses are here. Givenchy is on the avenue George-V, as is the luxury hotel of that name. Across the street is the Crazy Horse, the world's most famous—and expensive—strip club. Fouquet's, the legendary café that's a favorite of Arab princes and movie starlets, is on the corner of the Champs-Elysées. Avenue Montaigne, lined with the shops of fashion houses, used to be the home of Marlene Dietrich. If you see a red Ferrari or

a yellow Lamborghini parked outside a building in Paris, it will almost certainly be here.

For real, old-fashioned glamor, what our generation (which advertising has taught the use of superlatives) refers to as "superstars," look above you. What could be loftier than the Jules Verne, on the second level of the Eiffel Tower, with a view over the most beautiful city in the world? Here, if you're ever going to spot them, come celebrities, people like Sylvester Stallone, Arnold Schwartznegger, and Madonna.

In the 8th arrondissement are some of what the French call *temples de gastronomie*: Lucas Carton on the Place de la Madeleine, Taillevent on the rue Lamennais, and, on the vast sweep of the Place de la Concorde, Les Ambassadeurs. Situated in the Hotel de Crillon, Les Ambassadeurs is an example of old Paris at its most exuberant, with more than a touch of decadence in the eighteenth-century molding curving decorously over long mirrors. We heard recently from someone who'd enjoyed dinner in that lavish setting: "The service there was like a ballet," he said.

But the 8th arrondissement has been known as much for its stars and brilliant débuts as for any refinements of cuisine. At the Théâtre des Champs-Elyées, 13 to 15 avenue Montaigne, Josephine Baker and La Revue Nègre opened in

1925 and stunned the audience, many of whom were artists themselves, like Fernand Léger and Robert Desnos.

Near the Théâtre des Champs-Elysées is a bistro open to all: the Bar des Théâtres at 6 avenue Montaigne in the 8th district does not require that you belong to the world of fashion and the theater to sip coffee or wine at its bar or partake of substantial food in the restaurant section. There you can rub shoulders with a glamorous set: fashion models, actors, actresses, and others from the theater and film world including the theater across the street.

The Place de la Madeleine is not a bad beginning for a gourmet, with Fauchon on the northeast corner. The splendid interior is the closest French equivalent to Fortnum and Mason in London, a lavish, extravagant display of good things. Whether or not you have needs or desires, it is good to stop here for the visual delight of it all. Across the way, on the opposite side of the Place is Fauchon's rival, Hédiard. Different colors, of course—Hédiard packages in dramatic scarlet and black.

Although we started out with Fauchon, where we first learned the sublime possibilities of a French *sorbet*, in recent years we've come to spend more time at Hédiard. Somewhat smaller than its rival, less crowded, Hédiard seems less of a tourist attraction and more of a serious source.

If you're not naturally a shopper, and the thought of spending hours under the gaze of Parisian *vendeuses* fills you with horror, you'll still enjoy going from the Place de la Madeleine to the Place de la Concorde to window shop, looking at the splendid *vitrines* along the way.

Leave Hédiard and the Place de la Madeleine, and walk toward the Concorde. You are on the rue Royale, and one of the most impressive delights is still ahead. Forget monuments for a moment. A block to the right, on the rue du faubourg St.-Honoré is Hermès, with windows that are extraordinary in their color and originality. Inside, the sales assistants are courteous and expertly snap open glowing squares of silk for browsing shoppers.

Some dining possibilities in this exclusive area:

Altitude 95
Eiffel Tower, 75007 Paris (01.45.55.20.04)
Métro: Champ de Mars or Trocadero
Open daily noon–3:00 P.M., 7:00 P.M.–11 P.M.
Elevator ticket: 4 euros

By the time we managed to get up to Altitude 95 in the Eiffel, we felt we'd helped to construct the famous tower—it was that difficult. You have to get a "lift" ticket, and you have to find the right ticket window, or *guichet*, to get one. Near the north *pilier* is a kiosk with the sign "Restaurant" above it. Here we went, only to see a notice "Fermé" (Closed). We waited, the ticket-seller did come back, and the two very necessary tickets were ours.

After that, it was easy—just a matter of hiking briskly around and in front of the hundreds of grim-faced tourists who'd been waiting for the lift in the ordinary queues, getting to the north *pilier*, and waiting again for the elevator that would take us to the restaurant.

Once you make it to Altitude 95, you're in a child's heaven, an Erector Set-inspired room. It's pretty in a Star Wars way, all sleek and polished aluminium with silver rivets that remind one of early airliners or Airstream travel trailers. We sat at a small table that was silver and metal, with the comfortable club chairs drawn up to it, also in metal and gray, the design outlined in rivets along the seams. We looked up at a metal ceiling with domino-shaped holes and metal struts like those one observes in the Tower itself.

It's quite relaxed and friendly, in part because this is one of the few places in Paris where you'll see lots of children munching *frites* and sipping Coca-Cola from the 8-euro children's menu. Their parents, some in T-shirts and baseball caps, will be tackling substantial fare, possibly the 17-euro menu, like a heavy winter meal: cauliflower soup, roast loin of pork or salmon, and Camembert or *île flottante*. The 26-euro *menu du chef* not available, we chose *plats* à la carte: salmon with tomatoes and red bell peppers for 15, and chicken in a garlic and cream sauce for 20 euros.

We were impressed by the quality of the house wine: a carafe of 50 centilitres, adequate for two, was only 8 euros; 25 centilitres, a quart, available for about half of that. The white wine was very drinkable, better than many house wines we've tasted closer to the ground.

The *plats* were also better than expected, the chicken well-flavored in a cream sauce with a subdued flavor of garlic, and the salmon hot, with the flavors of the South—tomato, bell pepper, and zucchini.

Desserts à la carte are 8 euros. We chose the *palet*, a multi-layered chocolate confection, with a base of vanilla-flavored *génoise*, topped with bittersweet chocolate and a layer of coffee bavarian. All in a *coulis de framboise*—raspberry sauce. A special conclusion to a very palatable meal.

❖ *Altitude 95: fair prices in an extraordinary setting. For the tourist, a way to avoid the long lines for the ride up the Eiffel Tower.*

L'Atelier Renault
53 Champs-Elysées, 75008 Paris (01.49.53.70.70)
Métro: George V
Open daily to 2:00 A.M.

This is an elegant designer café where people come to eat, drink, and watch the action on the Champs-Elysées. The other day there was more action than usual, as we watched Lance Armstrong in the Tour de France bicycle race from a privileged lookout on the second floor (first floor to Europeans) of the Atelier Renault.

L'Atelier Renault is a showplace for the car manufacturer, and no expense has been spared. In a sleek gray and silver interior you sit on designer chairs and admire the Champs-Elysées. Like more ordinary cafés, Atelier Renault allows you to order just a drink. And since it was a warm day, we, and most of the people around us, also requested a *carafe d'eau* (ordinary Paris tap water) which came chilled.

There's usually a lunch special: this time it was pasta (penne), ice cream or tiramisù, and a glass of wine for 18 euros. We were content with club sandwiches with salad and mustardy mayonnaise on the side. Larger *plats*, including cod, slices of beef with tagliatelli, and Moroccan-style glazed lamb were all around 14 euros.

And we had the thrill of watching the cyclists, as well as the company nearby of a winsome quintet of United Airlines stewardesses, some of whom couldn't resist shouting encouragements to their favorite—"Go Lance!"—to the consternation of the serious-looking French people nearby.

❖ *Atelier Renault: a well-located designer café.*

Au Babylone
13 rue de Babylone 75007 Paris (01.45.48.72.13)
Métro: Sèvres-Babylone
Mon–Sat lunch, closed August
No credit cards

There's no doubt about it—Au Babylone is the real thing. The skylight from before electric lighting, the square little walls not painted for many years—this is not one of the new pseudo-bistros. The room for the customers may be nineteenth-century, but when you peer around the corner, you can see that the kitchen is all white and stainless steel.

It's a buzzing, smoky, alive little bistro crowded with people, even toward the end of the regular lunch period. This is a no-nonsense, old-fashioned place, right next to the Bon Marché department store.

A good regular bistro menu: hors d'oeuvres with items like *mousse de canard au porto* (duck mousse with port) go for 4 euros. Free-range chicken with potatoes and roast beef, for example, are about 9 euros. After that you can have salad, cheese, and desserts like *clafoutis cerises* (cherry cake) and *glaces* (ice cream) for 4 euros each. Two or three wines are available by the bottle, with house wines at 2 at the glass and 4 the *pichet.*

There is, however, a dearth of choices for the *prix fixe* menu at lunch. "Rosbif ou poisson?" (Beef or fish) asked the waitress—this did simplify life.

The hors d'oeuvres looked rather wilted by the time they reached our table, and the house wine turned out to be a sour red—regular habitués were taking the Beaujolais. But the *plat* pleased us both. A generous portion of *julienne*, a firm-fleshed white fish in *beurre blanc* (white butter sauce) was well-flavored, accompanied by potatoes with parsley.

The house pastry long gone, we chose *glaces* (ice cream) and were delighted with the not-too-sweet French version of this dessert, in bitter chocolate, intense coffee, and pistachio flavors.

The owner-chef, a pleasant-looking, dark-haired young man, emerged from the hot kitchen after all the clients were served. Switching into English, he told us about the beginnings of Au

Babylone, which has always been a family business. His father came from Italy years ago, and when he'd discovered that the French at that time weren't receptive to any cuisine but their own, he had started this, as a French restaurant.

❖ *Au Babylone: authentic, with a character of its own. Completely unlike the slick, shiny, anonymous establishments we noticed on our way.*

Bistro de Paris
33 rue de Lille, 75007 Paris (01.42.61.16.83)
Métro: rue du Bac
Open daily noon–2:30 P.M., 7:00 P.M.–10:30 P.M.

This bistro is convenient to the Musée d'Orsay, a former train station and now a museum, once used by Orson Welles as a movie set. If you're in the 7th district, you may want to try this shiny, mirrored bistro. A small room is transformed with mirrors which give the illusion of an infinite number of tables extending out into the distance. The design suggests elegance and formality.

The headwaiter, a rather theatrical-looking man with a bristling handlebar mustache, could have stepped out of a turn-of-the-century photo. His young waiters seemed serious and a bit nervous, but the service they gave was minimal; only after repeated requests did we manage to obtain a *carafe d'eau*, ordinary water, and our empty bread basket went unnoticed.

The 15-euro *formule* (set lunch) includes a bistro salad, main dish, and glass of wine. Starters à la carte are varied and interesting, including items like red pepper with avocado and smoked ham, artichokes with goat cheese and thyme, and *carpaccio* of red tuna and small salad. A cold purée of eggplant topped with mixed greens in a dressing with olive oil started off the set lunch. Tasty but heavy.

For main dishes we chose fish and braised veal. Portions were ample, the *rascasse* (a Mediterranean fish used in bouillabaisse) hot and attractive on a bed of penne, with tomatoes and parsley giving color. The *fricassée de veau* (braised veal in wine sauce) was similarly garnished. The flavor of the veal was enhanced by a rich tomato base which included chunks of cooked artichoke. Le Bistro de Paris shows a strong Provençal influence, using a lot of tomato, olive oil, olives, eggplant, and zucchini.

Desserts here are creative: soup of summer fruits, green apple sherbet with calvados, bittersweet chocolate dessert with raspberries, as well as traditionals like *crème brûlée*.

❖ *Le Bistro de Paris: reasonable prices in an expensive area.*

Le Café du Musée Jacquemart-André
158 blvd Haussmann, 75008 Paris (01.45.62.04.44)
Métro: Miromesnil
Open daily, 11:00 A.M.–6 P.M.
(Museum admission not necessary to visit café).

Would lunch in a fabulous chateau appeal to you? Then we can't think of a better place to go than the Musée Jacquemart-André, a private museum on the boulevard Haussmann. The museum café used to be the dining room of the millionaire who built this extraordinary home in 1875 for himself and his wife. Before Madame Jacquemart-André died in 1912, she willed the mansion to become a private museum, open to the public.

When we went to the café we found ourselves in a palatial room. The walls are soft yellow, the ceilings high, the molding elaborate. Bas-reliefs around the edge of the ceiling recalling stories from mythology border a fresco in the center which was brought from a villa near Venice. Tapestries soften the whole effect, and elaborate red-shaded lamps, with lights emerging from leafy shapes in gold, give warmth and intimacy.

Too late for lunch, we ordered tea and pastry. For 8 euros you have tea and your choice of pastries. Choosing a pastry was difficult, but we settled on a *framboisier*, an elaborate confection of *génoise*, pastry cream, fresh raspberries, and whipped cream, and a *truffée au chocolat*, a cake like a dense chocolate mousse, with a luscious rich flavor. With this there's a pot of the tea of your choice.

If we'd arrived earlier, salads would have been an option: they are large, fresh, and range in price from 9 to 14 euros, from chicken salad to the popular *vigée*, a seafood salad.

On a Sunday, a return visit, we heard a Parisienne mutter "Formidable!" as she stood on the magnificent stone terrace viewing the formal French garden with its colorful beds of wax begonias.

Either the regular lunch menu or brunch is available on Sundays. Brunch, at 23 euros, starts with a basket of *viennoiserie* (pastries)—a croissant, *pain au chocolat*, sesame-seed rolls and bread with butter and jam, and a large glass of freshly squeezed juices. With the breads you have all of the strong French coffee you can drink, and a plate of smoked salmon, a green salad, potato salad, and a warm poached egg topped with *fromage blanc* and chives. After all this there's fresh fruit salad or pastry.

❖ *Le Café du Musée Jacquemart-André: budget prices in palatial elegance.*

Le Café du Marché
38 rue Cler, 75007 Paris (01.47.05.51.27)
Métro: Ecole Militaire
Mon–Sat 7:00 A.M.–midnight, Sun to 4:30 P.M.

In the chic 7th arrondissement, would you expect to find a restaurant with an attractive terrace and cheerful service, offering enormous helpings of family-style food? If such a place existed it would be mobbed—and so it is. Rain was sprinkling a glossy finish on the paved street as we walked up from the Ecole Militaire métro.

At Le Café du Marché, we found ourselves waiting in line, glad finally to get a small table wedged in between others on the plastic awning-covered terrace. Inside and out, the café was wild and noisy, full of energetic young twenty-somethings and their older compatriots. Most of the patrons

were disguised, dressed-down yuppies from the area, what the French call "branché," but their avant-garde eyeglass frames gave them away. The elegant young men had the currently-fashionable short sculptured haircuts and sometimes hints of beards; their girls were probably more Calvin Klein than Gucci. We were not surprised to see a Woody Allen lookalike in one corner, discussing, most likely, post-structural film theory with his animated white-haired friend. But most of the crowd was young.

The salads served at Café du Marché are large and attractive—but it being chilly, we chose hot *plats*, the duck and the steak. Both came on huge plates with more than enough rounds of rather greasy fried potatoes. Both were good, and served in portions that would meet the approval of a hungry Arkansas truck driver. A demi-carafe of St. Pourçain red was fairly priced at 8 euros, but was served inappropriately chilled. A detail, considering the value we were receiving for our money.

Around us *steak tartare* was popular, the young Frenchmen who'd ordered it dousing the raw ground beef with Heinz ketchup and Tabasco sauce. Others were munching club sandwiches.

We could (and should) have done without dessert, but the curvacious young waitress particularly recommended the *moelleux au chocolat*, at 6 euros. It was a partially-cooked chocolat cake, oozing warm bittersweet chocolate at the touch of a fork. One serving with the accompanying pot of *crème fraîche* was ample for the two of us. Other desserts included *profiteroles*, *crème brûlée*, and *tarte tatin*.

❖ *Le Café du Marché: a high-density, high-energy place with noise levels to match. Simple meat-and-potatoes cooking. Great fun.*

Le Clos des Gourmets
16 avenue Rapp, 75007 Paris
Métro: Alma-Marceau
Tues–Sat lunch and dinner, closed in August

Le Clos des Gourmets has a creative menu and an elegant setting near the Eiffel Tower. Upon entering, we found ourselves in a bright room, the interior attractive in yellow tones, with scumbled blue on the molding. The Irish artist in our party remarked on the beautifully finished decor.

Service is friendly at Le Clos, and the head waitress speaks fluent English. One is required to make hors d'oeuvre, main course, and dessert choices at the beginning of the meal, and with the complicated menu, that involves some fast reading.

The *carpaccio* of duck ordered from the 29-euro menu looked like a flower on the plate, with lamb's lettuce and thin wafers of parmesan cheese for contrast and flavor. Duck pâté was presented in two slices of aspic, very flavorful with the good baguette and butter that accompanied them. Goat cheese-filled ravioli was served warm, topped with chopped tomato and parsley. A subtle and unusual starter with the warm olive oil and balsamic vinegar dressing.

A main dish, the *thon*, or tuna, was served in pie-shaped wedges. It came cooked just as requested, delicious with a crisp coating of sesame seeds with a warm vinaigrette on the greens and cooked tomatoes. The *foie de veau* (calf's liver) was in a rich beef sauce, again with just a hint of balsamic vinegar to add a slight sweetness. The Guigal red Côtes du Rhône at 23 euros was an enjoyable accompaniment to everyone's meal.

Desserts again showed that touch of ingenuity that sets a restaurant apart. The *millefeuille*, the chocolate dessert *feuillantine au chocolat Guanja*, and the sherbets we ordered so delighted our group that our friends—an engaged couple—had devoured theirs before they considered giving each other a sample! *Millefeuille* was crisp puff pastry of outstanding lightness with a delicious filling of lemon cream.

❖ *Le Clos des Gourmets: for an evening out with well-to-do Parisians.*

Florès

25 rue Royale, Cité Berryer, 75008 Paris (01.40.17.02.19)
Métro: Madeleine
Mon–Sat 8:30 A.M.–7:00 P.M.

Just after leaving the Place de la Madeleine, look for the tiny pedestrian street Cité Berryer on your right. It is a splendid little private enclave, special enough to be worth a search, shut off from the noise of the rue Royale. On this little pedestrian street that reminds one of narrow streets in the very select parts of central London is a *salon de thé* that's worth remembering.

Florès describes itself variously as a brasserie, *salon de thé*, and restaurant. Here in a setting of unusual charm you can lunch on low-priced sandwiches and salads. The *plats*, typically quiches with salad, go for 8 to 10 euros. Excellent tarts and other pastries are available to sample with the tea for 5 euros or with the espresso at half that price.

There are two ends to this little street: a graceful arch at one end opens on to rue Royale, and at the other near a wineshop is the rue du faubourg St-Honoré. One doesn't get much more exclusive than that.

Colors, soft and intense by turns, warm this little passageway. Across the street from Florès is the light periwinkle blue of a boutique that specializes in crystal. Beside it is the *vert wagon*—hunter green—of a clothing store, competing with the deep cobalt blue of Aquascutum.

❖ *Florès: a charming stop on an almost hidden street. Go, but don't tell too many of your friends.*

La Fontaine de Mars
129 rue St-Dominique, Paris 75007 (01.47.05.46.44)
Métro: Ecole Militaire
Open daily noon–2:30 P.M., 7:30 P.M.–11:00 P.M.

Here even the table linens give one the feeling of being in a special place, topping the tables in red and white, with the words "La Fontaine de Mars" worked into the jacquard pattern. Framed posters and old photographs

decorate the dark cream walls, along with old crockery jars, gleaming copper pots, and antique Victrolas. A sense of intimacy here is enhanced by the warm color and the red-and-cream ging- ham curtains at the windows. Outside is the real fountain, la Fontaine de Mars.

A basket of rough- textured, tasty *pain de campagne* was the right accompaniment for a terrine of lettuce with pickles, part of the 14-euro set lunch. An extra crock of pickles was put on the table. Our friend enjoyed a *salade de lapin* (rabbit salad) with preserved lemon, romaine lettuce, tomatoes, and red bell peppers, in a lemon and olive oil dressing.

Most wines are 17 euros and up—a half-bottle carafe is 10 euros. We chose the house red, a Brouilly, lighter than the Cahors which was the *vin du jour.*

The salmon was a large, perfectly-cooked portion with a small portion of white rice, on sizzlingly hot plates. Sauce Béarnaise, passed in a separate dish, was a simple and effective accompaniment.

We studied the dessert menu: cheese was 5 euros and most desserts range from 7 to 8 euros. We decided to forgo dessert after all, and walked outside to see the fountain and stone arches of the Place St. Dominique.

❖ *La Fontaine de Mars: deservedly popular, an old-fashioned bistro in a lovely setting.*

Au Pied de Fouet
45 rue Babylone, 75007 Paris (01.47.05.12.27)
Métro: Sèvres-Babylone
Mon–Fri noon–2:30 P.M., 7:00 P.M.–9:45 P.M., Sat noon–2:30 P.M. closed August
No credit cards

Alain Passard, the legendary chef at L'Arpège, one of Paris' great restaurants, was asked, "Where do you like to eat when you're not at work?" One place he mentioned was Au Pied de Fouet, where Jean Cocteau, the artist and film director, was also a regular.

Au Pied de Fouet is one of the smallest, most old-fashioned bistros we've ever seen—and certainly the most popular. This combination of circumstances led to the sort of situation that a friend recalls: "It used to be mobbed. I remember Andrée (the former proprietress) yelling to everybody to get up and have their coffee at the bar, so somebody else could have their place."

It's still mobbed. Over the years, this tiny hole-in-the-wall on the rue Babylone has maintained its popularity. Au Pied is highly original, and at lunch is crowded with "suits" and with people who know food.

The emphasis here is clearly on the cuisine, but the decor is memorable too: the zinc bar, the red-and-white checked tablecloths and curtains, postcards from all over thumbtacked to the rafters, colorful enamel teapots, mostly fire-engine red, hanging above the bar, and, to at least partly justify the name, an old cartwheel, a horse's harness, and other bits of farm memorabilia displayed on a high shelf.

As you enter, if you know the elegant, gray-haired maîtresse d' (and most people do), you're greeted as if you were an old friend. You take your cloth napkin out of its pigeonhole in the curious cupboard especially constructed for napkins, and you stand at the bar while awaiting a table.

There is only room for fourteen at the tables in this little hideaway. On our first visit we were lucky to arrive when a space was already free. Edging into the tiny spot by the window, we were able to sit down and study the menu.

Au Pied de Fouet gives fourteen to sixteen hors d'oeuvre choices, at around 4 euros each, and several *plats*, most at about 9 euros. It's typical bistro fare: *oeuf dur mayonnaise, crudités, assiette de charcuterie*, and so on. There's a *vin de la semaine*—in this case, a very drinkable Gamay Marionnet, which we ordered while we were trying to make decisions about hors d'oeuvres and *plat*.

The food here is surprisingly well-flavored: the fish (*grenadier*, a delicate-flavored sea fish) in a delicious cream sauce was accompanied by white rice, the *faux-filet* (steak) good-sized with an accompanying purée of potatoes. There's not a major effort at presentation, but nobody cares about such frills when a meal tastes this good.

Afterwards, we shared one of the trademark desserts, *tarte aux amandes sauce chocolat*, finding the bittersweet chocolate of the sauce a good contrast with the sweetness of the almond tart.

The clientele are French, mostly regulars, including a number of cigarette-smoking, longhaired, intellectual-looking types.

❖ *Au Pied de Fouet: a delightfully old-fashioned little retreat, not to be missed*

Le Monttessuy
4 rue de Monttessuy, 75007 Paris (01.45.55.01.90)
Métro: Alma-Marceau
Mon–Fri noon–2:00 P.M., 7:00 P.M.–10:30 P.M.,
Sat eves only

Le Monttessuy is a bistro with a look of the early part of the century, with long windows in an old-fashioned façade. It's cheerful and popular with business people—one hears French and "American" spoken there. Inside are the requisite red-checked tablecloths, prudently covered by white paper.

Once seated, we could take in the old-fashioned look of the sponged ochre walls, framed pictures of the Paris of yesterday, the antique stove with a crazy stovepipe angling its way across the ceiling. Also appealing was the 15-euro lunch menu, very reasonable for this area.

Most successful were the hors d'oeuvres: the *caillette* (pork and vegetable sausage) warm, in a good-tasting mustard sauce, the *salade de fruits de mer* a flavorful composition of mussels and fresh tomato in mayonnaise, with watercress and lettuce to set it off.

With the main dishes that followed, there was not quite as much choice as we would have liked: most of the *lieu* (pollock) was gone, but one of us got to sample it, well-seasoned in a light cream sauce, and the rest took *coquelet rôti*, competently done if not special, with overdone peas more of the school lunch variety than the *petits pois à la parisienne* on the menu.

But when you're not concentrating on the food, Le Monttessuy charms you by its location—with a view of the Eiffel Tower down the street—and romantic look. A soft light came from the back window covered with curling vines. A couple near us kissed across a table.

None of us was overly impressed by the dessert, banana tart on a custard base, again rather like cafeteria fare, heavy and flavorless. The one remaining portion of *tarte aux pêches* was enjoyed by our guest. Still, despite the uneven quality of the food, this little bistro might be worth a try for its pleasing ambiance.

❖ *Le Monttessuy: a reasonable choice for a low-priced lunch.*

La Petite Chaise
36-38 rue de Grenelle, 75007 Paris (01.42.22.13.35)
Métro: Rue du Bac
Open daily noon–2:00 P.M., 7:00 P.M.–11:00 P.M.

When does a monument become a tourist trap? At least that's what we think has happened to La Petite Chaise. Impressed by what we'd heard about its 19-euro-with-wine menu, we went there on a Saturday night and discovered menus without wine for 24 and 29 euros.

First, the historical monument part: founded as an inn in 1680, la Petite Chaise claims to be the oldest restaurant in Paris. George Sand and Toulouse-Lautrec went there in the nineteenth century, and more recently Colette, Gide, and Giraudoux. The menu related that François Mitterrand was

photo © Juliana Spear

a regular in his student days. (After tasting the food, we began to understand why he later moved upward to the Brasserie Lipp).

The *formule* at 24 euros allows an hors d'oeuvre and main dish, or main dish and dessert; for 29 euros you get all three.

The best part of our meals was the hors d'oeuvre: six little snails, served with garlicky butter, were hot and tasty. From there it was all downhill: the *parmentier de poisson* tasted as if it were 75 percent potatoes, with very little fish involved, accompanied by a side salad that was competent without being interesting. The *cuisse de canard à l'orange* came with scalloped potatoes. Both potatoes and duck were barely warm, served on cold plates, and there was no waiter in sight to listen to comments. We had the distinct impression that duck and sauce had been inadequately reheated after being cooked earlier in the day.

Accompanying the meal was a basket of ordinary Paris *baguette*, and a quite drinkable white wine from Touraine at 13 euros, a fair price. Around us were tourists delving into the old standards with gusto—favorites were the onion soup and the *escargots*.

For dessert we chose the *entremet fruit de la passion*, a dish our waiter described as similar to a bavarian cream. A thin slice of jellied passion fruit nectar was served in a *coulis* of red fruits. Fair enough, but the flavor of exotic fruit was obscured by sugar. It was cloyingly sweet, the most sugary bavarian cream we've ever consumed, completely contrary to the current trend in desserts described by Chef Yannick Alleno of Hotel Scribe. Speaking at the Cordon Bleu, Chef Alleno stated that people are requesting less sugar in desserts these days because they don't want to feel uncomfortably full.

That's unlikely to happen at La Petite Chaise, as servings there tend to be skimpy, but at least the servers were friendly—even if they were rarely around—and the setting attractive if you like gold brocade.

❖ *La Petite Chaise: cuisine fair-to-middling, with nothing very special.*

Chez Savy
23 rue Bayard, 75008 Paris (01.47.23.46.98)
Métro Franklin D. Roosevelt
Mon–Fri noon–3:00 P.M., 7:30 P.M.–11:00 P.M.

Chez Savy has an immediate charm for lovers of Art Deco. There's a wonderful old train car feeling about this place—a train car preserved from the Jazz Age. This is true Deco. The mirrors that line the place are dimmed by age. Under them are bars and rails of aluminum at Deco right angles, and there are Deco fan shapes in the molding around the ceiling. Little lamps on Deco mounts shed a warm light. At odds with the stylish interior is the huge mounted head of a wild boar, glaring down from over the door leading into the back dining room.

Little booths and little tables cramp the back of the first *salle*; still, French businessmen and women crowd in here for lunch and the air is punctuated by their staccato speech and animated gestures.

For 17 euros there's the starter and *plat*, or *plat* and dessert, and for 21 euros you get all three. On the regular menu, Chez Savy provides hors d'oeuvres like *oeufs pochés à la crème de ciboulette* (poached eggs with chives) or salads for about 6 euros all the way up to *foie gras de canard* for 15 euros. *Charcuterie* is a house speciality, as is beef from the Avignon, and we saw people around us with large steaks.

Small slip-ups in the service didn't mar our enjoyment of Chez Savy. We waited half an hour before our request for "un carafe d'eau" was heard. And later the waiter made what we are sure was an unintentional error, charging for a salad that was part of a fixed-price menu.

We started with a raw mushroom salad with an olive oil and chive dressing. It was crisp and different, with bits of tomato to add color. The bread provided was darker and more flavorful than the usual baguette. A *carpaccio de boeuf* was paper-thin slices of cured raw beef arranged over a plate with half a lemon and a sprinkling of mint. A side salad of fresh basil complemented the flavor of the beef.

The *steak-frites* was more sophisticated than at the Lipp the previous day, topped by fried shallots and accompanied by *pommes allumettes*, matchstick-sized fried potatoes, light and not greasy.

Dessert was a scrumptious *tarte aux pêches*, obviously made on the premises with very fresh peaches.

❖ *Chez Savy: good value in a high-priced area.*

Le Square
31 rue St-Dominique, 75007 Paris (01.45.51.09.03)
Métro: Latour-Maubourg
Mon–Sat to 10:45 P.M., closed Sat in August

The lesson everyone learns when traveling is to be flexible. We learned this again the other night when we were going to another bistro, Thoumieux. A look at the menu displayed outside was sufficient to discourage us. Imagine a 27-euro fixed price menu featuring *boudin* (blood sausage)! We felt we could do better. So we walked farther along the rue St. Dominique and discovered Le Square.

Le Square is full of "squares"—conservatively dressed people from a wealthy district who expect value for their money. And they're getting it here. The printed menu lists hors d'oeuvres for 8 euros that include *salade d'écrevisses* (crawfish salad), *carpaccio de truite de mer* (trout *carpaccio*) and *assiette de légumes* (vegetable plate). After that there are the *plats*, in separate categories according to price. Some at 9 euros include *carpaccio de saumon* (salmon *carpaccio*), and *tarte fine à la tomate, basilic et parmesan* (tomato, basil, and cheese tart). At 12 euros there's *cuisse de lapin au gingembre* (rabbit thigh with ginger), *raviolis au quatre fromages* (ravioli with four cheeses), and *pavé de rumsteak au poivre* (rump steak with pepper sauce).

In a hurry, we skipped the entrée and took two *plats*, duck with figs and rumpsteak, and were very satisfied. The duck was served in generous quantity and with delicious ripe figs in a dark, well-seasoned sauce, tasting of the sweetness of the fig and the rich meatiness of the duck. The beef was a good amount of sliced steak, arranged around the plate in an effective peppery sauce. A few vegetables on the side would have been welcome with each *plat*, but we couldn't complain about the size of our portions or the quality of the meat.

Desserts at 6 euros included apple tart, *moelleux au chocolat* (half-cooked chocolate cake) and *vacherin fraise, coulis de fraises rouges*. We chose the latter, a meringue in a rich strawberry sauce, with whipped cream and a scoop of strawberry ice cream. Delicious!

❖ *Le Square: outstanding value in a coveted location near the National Assembly and Les Invalides. You'll need to reserve ahead.*

PARIS WITH A PAST: THE 9TH & 10TH ARRONDISSEMENTS

In Paris one should have everything or nothing. We often had nothing, and that had a special charm, because Paris more than any other city has pleasures available to the poor.

—Eleanor Perényi, *More Was Lost*

While the 7th and 8th arrondissements exude a feeling of privilege, the 9th and 10th bring us back to earth with a bump. They suggest life's realities—hard work and the struggle to get by, sometimes by dubious means.

Even the Opera came into being because somebody tried to kill Napoleon III. On his way to the opera in 1858, he narrowly missed death in an explosion. One hundred and fifty Parisians and the horses pulling the emperor's carriage were killed. Napoleon was determined not to let anything like that happen again. He had the whole area redone, taking out some of the little narrow streets that could shelter future attackers, and replacing them with l'Avenue de l'Opéra.

He also commissioned a new opera building. Charles Garnier won the competition and designed what is now the old Opera, splendid in the ruffles and flourishes of its mid-19th-century decor.

Just north on the boulevard Haussmann are the department stores. Galeries Lafayette and Au Printemps bring in the crowds and make the 9th a major shopping district. The most striking part of each grand *magasin* is its oldest store, which you will find here. In the middle of the original Galeries Lafayette on the ground floor is a center from which you can see all around you the different levels or galleries, each edged by elaborate railing, circling around and up toward a brilliant, multicolored dome at the top. Au Printemps has an even larger dome of fabulous stained glass.

To get a feeling for the 9th arrondissement, leave the contrived atmosphere of the department stores and take the bus or métro to the métro stop rue Montmartre. Walk up the rue du faubourg Montmartre, stopping at Chartier, number 7, located at the end of a courtyard. An old-fashioned *bouillon* from the Belle Epoque, Chartier was originally founded to give working-class people a place whre they could afford to eat simple low-priced meals, often soup, hence the name. High ceilings and elegant but not especially elaborate moldings give a turn-of-the-century flavor that belies the modesty of Chartier's origins.

The seedy side of the 9th runs along its edges, particularly the western side bordering the Gare St. Lazare. Garish streetwalkers strut in front of the shopfronts dominating a short stretch near the rue d'Amsterdam. Farther north, where the 9th arrondissement meets the 18th, the boulevard de Clichy and the Places Blanche and Pigalle are infested with sexshops and associated activity.

This is Henry Miller's Paris. He worked briefly for the *Chicago Tribune* at 5 rue Lamartine in the 9th. His friend Alfred Perlès, who was working as a proofreader, got Miller a job doing the same thing. They would work at night, stopping after work to eat at a nearby bistro. Other customers at the bistro included pimps, prostitutes, and newspapermen. Miller relished the café atmosphere, which he described in a letter to Anaïs Nin:

> It's like the monkey house... And such a noise! Laughter from the bar, like shrieks from the madhouse. I don't know of any café in Paris where there is such a diversity of types. It's foul—but exhilarating. And you can get a *casse-croûte* at all hours.

The street of Notre-Dame de Lorette, running through the center of the 9th, was named after the church. "Lorettes" was the name given to young girls who came up to Paris from the countryside intending to make a living in the capital, and who were often lured into the oldest profession. Emile Zola gives us a view of that life in his novel *Nana*:

> There, until two o'clock in the morning, the lights of the restaurants, the brasseries and the pork butchers, blazed away, whilst a swarm of women hung about the doors of the cafés.

The poverty of this area, the cheap rents, and the notoriety kept out the bourgeoisie, but it did not deter writers from making the Notre-Dame de Lorette district their home. Thackeray, De Maupassant, Dumas, and Hugo all lived around here.

During the nineteenth century the rue Pigalle, now scruffy and disreputable, was home to artists and writers: Edouard Vuillard and Pierre Bonnard lived at number 28, George Sand and Frédéric Chopin at number 16. Victor Hugo was home at number 55 and Charles Baudelaire at number 60.

If you continue north from Chartier on the rue du faubourg Montmartre, going up the street and to the right when you get to the rue Richer, you will see the Folies Bergère. A surprising sight, the Folies doesn't seem to belong where it's situated. The façade is an Art Deco masterpiece, out of place among the dark little streets, kosher delis, and small shops, an island of illusion in an otherwise dilapidated district. Here Josephine Baker made a famous appearance in 1926. Clad in little more than a string of bananas, she was a triumph. Charlie Chaplin and the novelist Colette are among the other legendary names who appeared here.

Nowadays, the show at the Folies Bergère is still entertaining and tame enough that tourists who are not offended by bare-breasted dancers sometimes take their children along to enjoy the show. A former male dancer at the Folies told us about the reality behind the glamorous show. His memories of the place are not particularly positive: "They expected us to do an incredible amount of work for little money. Two shows a day. We finally had to go on strike."

It is hard to believe now that the Grands Boulevards running on the southern edge of the 9th and 10th arrondissements were ever anything more than they seem today, noisy, polluted, and dominated by the traffic. John

Russell has written that the boulevards today have lost the "wayward, improvisatory quality" that we most value in Paris. Yet soon after their creation by Haussmann in the mid-nineteenth century, they were the place to be, the Paris equivalent of Fifth Avenue in New York or Oxford Street in London. Fashionable people met their friends in the cafés on the boulevard des Italiens, particularly at the Café de Paris, Tortoni's, the Café Riche, and the Café Anglais. You would need an introduction to be accepted by the well-to-do habitués of what would seem to us like private clubs.

> *Not every visitor, however, is an enthusiast of the Railway Quarter. The clifflike tenements, the Alsatian restaurants, the disquieting glass-roofed passages, and the submarine smells that drift from the shellfish stalls along the Rue Saint-Lazare—these are not for every taste....*

> —John Russell *Paris*

Farther east in the 10th arrondissement are the two railway stations, the Gare du Nord and the Gare de l'Est, their great fan-shaped roofs beloved of Impressionist painters and filmmakers.

But the neighborhoods around the great railway stations tend to be drab and dilapidated. Not exactly prime territory for bistros. No one expects to sit out on a terrace with the soot and grime that go along with railway stations, and half the fun of a Parisian café or bistro is the chance to sit on a terrace and observe street life. Yet striking exceptions to the dreary conventional bistros are scattered here and there in the 9th and 10th districts. One of them is the Brasserie Terminus Nord, across the street, now owned by the Groupe Flo, splendid with its mirrors and long curving bar.

When we think of the 10th arrondissement, the name Strasbourg-St. Denis comes to mind. Strasbourg-St. Denis is one of the major *ponts de change*, or métro changing stations in Paris. From there, a multitude of possibilities. The neighborhood above the métro has brightened up, become somewhat safer than it used to be, but one should still be cautious about walking there at night.

Is there anything romantic about the 10th arrondissement? Yes there is if you go to the Canal Saint-Martin, angling down from the north. This canal is the site of the French movie named after the Hôtel du Nord on its bank. Arletty, the celebrated and controversial French actress, star of Marcel Carné's great films *Les Enfants du Paradis* and *Hotel du Nord*, lived in an apartment overlooking the canal. Romantic little bistros and wine bars are dotted here and there along the quays, and in the evenings, intense young couples wander hand-in-hand beside the water.

An anomaly in the 9th district, the Café de la Paix is something you'll see just as surely as you will view the Eiffel Tower and Notre Dame. Situated at 5 Place de l'Opéra, this has been one of the watering-places of the great and famous. The menu boasts of habitués that included King Edward VIII, Enrico Caruso, Oscar Wilde, Maurice Chevalier, Josephine Baker... the list goes on and on. Wilde is said to have glimpsed an angel fluttering on the pavement here. In our own time, John Travolta, Shirley MacLaine, and Placido Domingo have dropped by to sample the high-priced cuisine. Almost 5 euros for a cup of coffee!

But for serious bistro fare, try one of these:

Restaurant de Bourgogne
26 rue des Vinaigriers, 75010 Paris (01.46.07.07.91)
Métro: Jacques Bonsergent
Mon–Fri lunch and dinner, Sat lunch closed
mid-July–August 21

A gentle giant from Lorraine presides over Le Bourgogne, and he has named the bistro Chez Maurice, after himself. There are black-and-white photos of him in an earlier incarnation on the walls. To get to Chez Maurice you go down an obscure street off the Canal Saint-Martin, a few blocks from the République, and find a storybook-style bistro, with low ceilings, red-and-white tablecloths, and a happy buzz from the many who jam it to bursting.

Diners do not go to Chez Maurice to sample cutting-edge cuisine or to mingle with the beautiful people. You'll go expecting and finding inexpensive, tasty fare served in generous portions, country cooking that the typical French grandmother might have done. Big containers of salt, pepper, and mustard are ready on the tables, and when one of our group requested ketchup, the waitress cheerfully produced a bottle of Heinz 57.

Blackboards hanging at crazy angles give you the wine list (unchanging) and the three-course menu (changes daily). Wines are mostly unknown reds in the 6- to 12-euro price range, but the Côtes du Rhône we chose turned out to be a remarkably good value.

Traditional bistro fare awaits you here for prices which would seem like a joke somewhere else: set menus for 9 to 10 euros in the evening? We could hardly believe it ourselves. Hors d'oeuvres included the classics: *charcuterie* (cold cured meats) and *oeufs à la mayonnaise* (hard-boiled egg with mayonnaise). Salads were abundant and very fresh, as if prepared minutes beforehand. I remember looking at my large plate of *crudités* and thinking that this would be enough by itself.

Afterward you could select from a list that includes dishes like *boeuf flamand* (beef braised in beer) and *filet de merlue à la portugaise* (hake, a type of codfish). All came with accompaniments of *frites, pommes vapeur* (steamed potatoes), or *pois et carottes*, and each was pronounced "Bon" or "Très bon" by our French friends who had ordered them.

The third course was a choice of cheese or dessert. Everyone in our group of five opted for the sweet finish. Desserts included *tarte aux pommes à l'alsacienne* (apple pie), judged rather too sweet, and the *crème caramel* which was praised.

❖ *Le Bourgogne: low prices, generous servings, outstanding value.*

Café Flo
6th floor Au Printemps main store, 64 blvd Haussmann
(01.42.82.50.00)
Métro: Havre-Caumartin
Open store hours, Mon–Sat 9:35 A.M.–7:00 P.M.,
Thurs to 10:00 P.M.

This café dazzles with its multicolored dome, a sight that would be a national monument anywhere but in Paris. Created by master glassmaker Brière, the dome dates from 1923. It was dismantled and stored in 1939, and forgotten for decades after the war. Finally it was reassembled in 1973 by the grandson of the original glassmaker.

In our experience, the food here is not up to the level of the average bistro, but closer to cafeteria quality. A possible choice for breakfast if you're in the area when the Au Printemps department store opens at 9:30 A.M. Enjoy a *café-crème* at 3 euros and a croissant at 1.

❖ *Café Flo: go for the setting, not the food. One of the sights of Paris.*

La Grille
80 rue du faubourg Poissonière, 75010 Paris
(01.47.70.89.73)
Métro: Poissonière
Open weekdays, closed August 15–31

Years from now, when you dream about your days in France, the wonderful meals at old-fashioned bistros like La Grille will be among the experiences you'll relive with the greatest pleasure. Even if your grandmothers were French and from the country, you'd be lucky to remember their cooking as having been as good as that served here. Happily, it's also one of the friendliest bistros in Paris. The Cullères have run this place for nearly three decades, and they bring to it the warmth of a favorite aunt and uncle.

La Grille is a proudly traditional, old-fashioned place set in two old rooms with woodwork and rooms obviously repainted many times with that special Burgundy shade of shiny enamel so popular in Paris. There are traditional lace curtains everywhere; there are also fresh flowers, an old birdcage, old oval mirrors, framed certificates, a large brass hatrack, huge plates of fruit and cheese, and even a large Boxer dog guarding the door to decide if you're worthy to come in. He always does.

La Grille is a small bistro with only nine tables serving eighteen people, so reservations might be wise. Everything here is à la carte, but the prices are moderate considering the quality of the food.

Cooking is traditional and very good. We started by sharing an entrée of a large and very fresh salad (*frisée aux lardons*, 8 euros), which harbored long strips of smoked bacon. Classic country dishes like *boeuf bourguignon* (15 euros) were on the menu, and the man next to us who'd ordered that seemed pleased, but we both ordered the house specialty, *turbot grillé beurre blanc,* a delicate white fish with a rich butter sauce. It's a dish served only for two (at 59 euros) with probably high caloric and cholesterol levels, but you can share your guilt as well as your pleasure and assure each other it's well worth the risk. Our wine was the 21-euro Menetou-Salon Domaine de Chatenoy, a luscious white from the Loire, recommended by the patron.

At the end, a dessert of fresh berries with mango and small figs along with a small pitcher of cassis (blackcurrant) syrup was a perfect finish.

❖ *La Grille: a charming, country-style bistro with high quality at fair prices. One of the best.*

Chez Michel
10 rue de Belzunce, 75010 Paris (01.44.53.06.20)
Métro Gare du Nord
Tues–Sat noon–2:00 P.M., 7:00 P.M.–midnight,
closed August

Chez Michel is just off the grimy boulevard Magenta near the Gare du Nord, on a relatively pleasant little street. The train station seems far away when you enter this serious restaurant, where the 19-euro menu turns out to be an excellent buy, and where the creativity of a chef whose experience at the Crillon and the Tour d'Argent shows up in his ideas, as well as in their execution.

Dinner there recently started with an unusual *amuse-gueule.* Before we ordered we were able to sample a dish of *bigorneaux,* or winkles, served in their shells accompanied by a small pot of mustard-flavored mayonnaise. We were given pins with which to retrieve the snail-shaped little creatures, and the hunt was worth the effort: they were delicious.

Hors d'oeuvres were of an interest and generosity one seldom sees. The crunchy Breton cakes with wild greens on top were actually little rounds of toast, still warm, with *chèvre*—goat cheese—and greens in a warm vinaigrette, all serving to accentuate the flavors. The tasty oxtail pâté would be a great hors d'oeuvre if you arrived famished; the large jar of pâté was enough for two or three people, with accompanying pickles and mustard and good *pain de campagne* to go with it.

Between courses there was time to take in the interior, which is like an old Norman farmhouse with beams and plaster. A central column with shelves built around it holds wine bottles and blackboards with the day's selections, and servers were informally dressed. Occasionally they seemed a little confused. But the service was friendly and prompt, and that was what counted.

The *dorade* (sea bass) came to the table hot on a warm plate with a topping of lamb's lettuce and little flakes of white cheddar for contrast. It was light and crisp with a flavorful purée of garlic potatoes. Very fresh and appetizing, the tuna was served on a bed of puréed zucchini.

For dessert, we chose the "Paris-Brest" and the coffee jelly. Paris-Brest was a pastry confection of two cream puffs stacked with a coffee cream filling, light and tasty, and the coffee jelly a delectable dessert of several layers, with coffee, cream, and chocolate serving as admirable foils for each other.

❖ *Chez Michel: outstanding value. You'll need a reservation.*

Restaurant Julien
16 rue du faubourg St-Denis, 75010 Paris (01.47.70.12.06)
Métro: Strasbourg-St.Denis
Open daily to 1:00 A.M.

For many years the Julien was quite likely the cheapest and almost certainly the worst restaurant in Paris. We would go there to admire the extraordinary Art Nouveau interior, which the Flo Group restored to its original splendor when it bought the place 30 or so years ago. But we seldom dared to eat much.

When you enter this brasserie, you want to rub your eyes and wonder if you're in a peculiarly baroque sort of dream. For the Julien can't be real—but it is. Not an easy place to

describe, because all you want to do is look, and look some more, at the dazzling excesses of the most extravagant Art Nouveau decor we have ever seen.

It's not just the panels of glorious, sensual women who could have walked out of a Mucha painting; it's the molding, the bas-reliefs of beneficent goddesses, smiling down at us from above the floral-shaped lights. They in turn are surrounded by bas-reliefs of fruit, flowers, the harvest, and everything in the curves and swirls that suggests ripeness, fecundity, abundance.

But the food—ah yes, there is the food. This is *cuisine*

industrielle, unvarying from day to day, but surprisingly satisfying. The *menu Julien* is 29 euros, but after 10:00 P.M. the more limited 21-euro menu is available, and, judging by the din, many were enjoying it.

The Julien has set menus which rarely change: the *menu Julien* offered *foie gras, soupe de melon au sauternes*, (melon soup with sauterne), *tartare de saumon frais et fumé* (fresh and smoked salmon), and *salade d'herbes fraîches* (green salad with herbs) for hors d'oeuvres. These could be followed by *magret de canard aux pêches* (duck breast with peaches) or *filet de sandre aux épices tandoori* (pickerel filet with tandoori spices).

The menu also offers a *demi* of a Côteaux d'Aix, the *menu Faim de nuit* giving a little less in the way of wine, a quarter bottle or a house white or red.

One of us started with the *soupe de melon*, little melon or cantaloupe balls with grapefruit wedges and a touch of sauterne with a mint garnish: delicious, unusual and refreshing on a hot night. The other chose the *carpaccio de saumon*, a mixture of chopped fresh and smoked salmon with olive oil and chives. Flanked by a salad of romaine lettuce in a well-flavored vinaigrette, it was quite satisfactory, with the accompanying crusty rolls of *pain de campagne*.

Then the main course: the *magret de canard*, slices of duck breast, brown outside and red within, artfully arranged on the plate. With it an effective and unusual sauce tasting of white and yellow peaches. Served with crisp, brown *pommes sautées*, this was delicous. The *jambonnet de volaille*, a plump chicken thigh in a Creole sauce with parsleyed rice was more predictable but still successful.

Desserts, so often neglected in bistros and brasseries, were good. One of the specialties was a *granité de pommes au vieux Calvados*, a tart green apple sherbet, cool and intense, its flavor only emphasized by the generous slosh of sweet applejack liqueur that our obliging waiter spilled over it. A *fondant au chocolat* was lighter-textured than most, the chocolate complemented by coffee-flavored *crème anglaise*.

❖ *Restaurant Julien: opulent and romantic, a sentimental favorite; also air conditioned, something not all that common in Paris.*

La Marine
55 bis quai de Valmy, 75010 Paris (01.42.39.69.81)
Métro: République
Mon–Sat 8:30 A.M.–midnight

At lunch, La Marine vibrates with the energy of a young, artistic clientele. The bar covered with grass matting, the green hammocks suspended above, fake zebra hide, and African sculpture and masks give one the sense that faced with deciding how to decorate with a marine theme, the owners decided for some reason to forget all about it and go African.

This crowded and cheerful turn-of-the-century little bistro has the old standards chalked up for its daily specials: *salade de pêcheur* (fish salad), *saumon mariné* (marinated salmon), *foie de veau* (calf's liver), *brandade de poisson* (fish cakes), and the usual bistro desserts: *crème caramel* and *mousse au chocolat*.

Wines, including Corbières, Côtes de Bordeaux, Brouilly, Sancerre rouge, and Lussac St. Emilion are available by the glass or quarter or half carafe, with most glasses 3 euros and up.

A large plate of *brandade de poisson* is served by the young waitress. The good fish in potato purée with spinach and a hint of nutmeg is filling yet subtle.

Time to choose dessert: the *serveuse* repeats the list and assures us, "Tout est fait à la maison" (everything is made here). We finish by going for decadence, with *gâteau au chocolat*. The cake is rich and heavy—a little *crème anglaise* on the side would have helped.

Service is informal, perhaps too much so: the young waitress starts spraying the next table with Windex while we're still dealing with dessert. Next to us, two young artists discuss an upcoming exposition in San Francisco. (It's surprising how often one hears French people talking about the United States.)

❖ *La Marine: on Canal St. Martin, a stop for an artistic "in" crowd.*

Le Parmentier
12 rue Arthur Groussier, 75010 Paris (01.42.40.74.75)
Métro: Goncourt
Mon–Fri lunch and dinner, Sat dinner, closed August

It's a short walk from the canal and the Place de la République is the closest large square, but Le Parmentier's air of quiet refinement, its tasteful yet spare decor make this little restaurant seem a world away from the noisy, beer-dispensing eateries directly on the Place.

A generous lunch menu is only 13 euros, giving you an hors d'oeuvre and *plat*, or *plat* and dessert. Although at these prices it could be considered a budget restaurant, we were pleased to notice touches of luxury that would go with a much higher-priced establishment: flowers and an *amuse-gueule* of *tapenade aux olives* with toasted slices of baguette, to engage our attention while we awaited our hors d'oeuvres.

Ravioli stuffed with cheese in a delicately-flavored cream sauce with a touch of nutmeg provided an unusual hors d'oeuvre. The house bread is not the usual Parisian baguette, but a good *pain de mie*, soft-crusted white bread.

Wines, mostly under 18 euros, include the recent years of small vintners. A carafe of Pays d'Oc in red, white, or rosé, large enough for two, was very drinkable at a modest 6 euros. The *dorade*, or sea bream, on a bed of fennel garnished with lime,was well-flavored, a pleasant and tasty light lunch. The *daube de boeuf*, a stew cooked in red wine and accompanied by potatoes, provided a hearty and substantial meal.

The emphasis at Parmentier is on flavor rather than presentation, and the artistic-appearing patrons who drift in from the untouristy 10th arrondissement look as if they wouldn't have it any other way.

At Le Parmentier the *fondant au chocolat* is what other bistros call a *moelleux au chocolat*, an undercooked chocolate cake, with the rich dark chocolate center oozing past the crust with a touch of the fork. Cold *crème anglaise* (custard sauce) provides a nice contrast. Tiny post-meal desserts—

candied orange slices and miniature lemon tarts—go well with coffee to round out the experience.

❖ *Le Parmentier: excellent value in a setting with charm.*

Chez Prune
36 rue Beaurepaire, 75010 Paris (01.42.41.30.47)
Métro: Jacques Bonsergent
Open daily to 2:00 A.M.

The best way of describing this old Paris neighborhood now evolving into a fashionably artistic part of the city might be "shabby chic." Chez Prune is one of the most popular bistros in the neighborhood, a hot spot for young people. On warm summer nights, the crowds, mostly habitués in their twenties, line up almost onto the street trying for an evening here. Here you're facing the Canal St. Martin and if you walk a few hundred yards down the canal, you find the Hôtel du Nord, the setting for the classic film of that name.

If you can't get into Chez Prune any other time, breakfast or lunch are good in this hangout with its yellow walls bordered with handpainted plums and their foliage, a crazy-quilt tile pattern on the floor. The shabby-chic theme is carried on in the mismatched tables and chairs, wildly inappropriate halogen lighting, and a general studied scruffiness. The young professionals who come here love it.

This is a good place to stop for a drink, given the considerable variety of wines, the futuristic bar stools, and the lively ambiance. A typical menu offers promising possibilities: one day hors d'oeuvres included *potage du Bercy* (fish soup), *petite quiche au fromage et crevettes* (cheese and shrimp quiche), or *croquant de poireaux* (zucchini cake) for 5 euros. For a main dish one could choose from *gratin de poisson à l'estragon* (fish gratin with tarragon), *carré d'agneau aux échalottes* (lamb with shallots), or *salade auvergnate* (Auvergne salad), all for about 9 euros.

❖ *Chez Prune: an in-place for a lively, young, and artistic crowd.*

Au Rendez-Vous des Belges
23 rue Dunkerque, 75010 Paris (01.42.82.04.72)
Métro: Gare du Nord
Open daily, Sun–Wed 5:30 A.M.–2:00 A.M.,
Thurs–Sat to 4:00 A.M.

Just opposite the Gare du Nord, the Rendez-Vous des Belges is a little railroad car of a café that's open almost around the clock and offers a great variety of Belgian beers on tap. While awaiting a train you may want to stop here for a simple meal: *steak-frites* (steak and French fries) for 8 euros, *boeuf haché-frites* (hamburger and fries) for 7, *saucisson* (dry salami) or *omelette-frites* for 7.

There's a coin-operated telephone in the back, useful if you haven't yet purchased a telephone card at a Tabac or post office.

The Rendez-Vous is modern and slick in its small way, yet it gives a nod to the Art Nouveau period with an imitation Mucha mural on the end wall and reproduction Art Nouveau lights over the bar. A pinball machine, not fitting in with any of this, is obviously, noisily, there.

Train conductors pop in here for a coffee before their shifts start, and some of them have a word with the barman in Flemish.

❖ *Au Rendez-Vous des Belges: for a quick snack before you board your train to London.*

Le Sainte Marthe
32 rue Sainte-Marthe, 75010 Paris (01.44.84.36.96)
Métro: Belleville
Mon–Sat 10:00 A.M.–2:00 A.M., Sun noon–8:00 P.M.
No credit cards

If you want to escape the usual tourist rounds in search of Parisian authenticity, go to the rue Sainte-Marthe, near the Belleville métro station in the 10th arrondissement. Belleville is the district of the poor and the hardworking, the ethnics who come from everywhere hoping to sink their roots in

Paris. You get off at the Belleville métro station and walk through some scruffy but not dangerous areas. We passed a sweatshop where young Chinese men, stripped to the waist, were pressing clothing possibly for sale in an expensive boutique. We heard several languages which were neither French nor English.

Some of the concrete apartment buildings making up the square are painted in pastels, an uncommon sight in northern France. These are not expensively-constructed buildings with stone carved facades, but functional and cheap accommodations for the poor. You may notice laundry hanging from windows. The dogs here are not pedigreed and a parked car may lack a hubcap. It all seems very Latin, very Mediterranean, and the ambiance is local, relaxed and still wildly animated. The huge *terrasse* was overflowing on a summer night, with new arrivals reluctantly having to leave the tree-shaded square and move to the hot colors of the interior.

At Le Sainte Marthe, wines are from 5 to 6 euros for a quarter *pichet*, 9 to 11 euros for a half, and 12 to 21 for a full bottle, with a selection of less-known regions, a Côtes du Tarn, for example, and a Vaucluse. We were pleased with the white we chose, a Domaine de Tarriquet.

We arrived too late to eat, but noted that hors d'oeuvres were mostly around 6, and substantial-looking *plats* from 10 to 16 euros. One of our neighbors on the little park chairs beside the green metal tables enjoyed an impressive-looking smoked salmon salad, the large topping of salmon on greens, with watercress, avocado, and mayonnaise.

❖ *Le Sainte-Marthe: currently a hot spot with young Parisians, but still the closest thing in Paris to a small town in Provence.*

MOVING UP IN THE WORLD: THE 11ᵀᴴ & 12ᵀᴴ ARRONDISSEMENTS

That poor boulevard Richard-Lenoir! What on earth has given it that bad reputation! All right, so it does end at the Bastille. Okay, so it is surrounded by miserable slummy little streets. The whole section is full of workshops and warehouses.... Too bad for those who despise the Boulevard Richard-Lenoir.

—Georges Simenon, *Maigret's Special Murder*

The 11th and 12th arrondissements of Paris always remind us of the lower East Side of New York. Tough, authentic, direct, sometimes a little devious, maybe even cruel, they are packed with the old smells and sounds of a dozen countries. The 11th and 12th arrondissements have never been *quartiers* of choice, but places that people escaped from. Now, though, this section has become, if not a home, at least an inspiration to some of the best creative young minds in France.

The 11th district, for years snubbed by snobs and avoided by the well-to-do, has made a comeback. Stretching from the Place de la Bastille to the République, up to the rue du faubourg du Temple, and east to the boulevard Ménilmontant, the 11th has no monuments to boast of, no palaces, no scenic parks.

But it has a past. Walking down the boulevard du Temple, going from the Place de la République toward the Bastille, you pass the Cirque d'Hiver, or Winter Circus. Hemingway sparred a few rounds here with some of his friends who could be persuaded to join him in boxing. Here Fellini filmed part of *The Clowns*. And who would have thought that this neglected monument, with its bas-reliefs of horses and

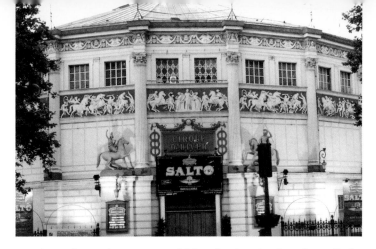

warriors along the top, would be the inspiration for a little boy who would become an international star?

To Maurice Chevalier, the Cirque d'Hiver was, quite simply, paradise. He was growing up in a one-parent family in the working-class suburb of Ménilmontant when he went to the circus for the first time. His mother bought the family the cheap, standing-room tickets which were all she could afford, and they climbed up behind the top seats and clung to the ceiling. To ten-year-old Maurice the circus and the performers were the most exciting thing he'd ever seen:

> [T]he show unfolded before us like a magic spell, an enchantment.... But it was the star tumbling act that thrilled me the most. Here a boy exactly my own age... was catapulted into the air and then caught in a perfect sitting position, hurled once more into a double somersault and caught again... The crowd would go crazy...

Later the Chevaliers waited to see the circus stars coming out onto the rue de Crussol in their ordinary street clothes. The Chevalier family followed them on foot as far as they could, thrilled to be close to such extraordinary people. Then the performers went to a nearby tavern (possibly the Clown Bar) after the evening show, and the Chevaliers walked all the way back to Ménilmontant.

Dazzled by the performances he had seen, young Chevalier decided to become an acrobat. Not especially agile, and "without the strength of a kitten in my little legs," he nevertheless kept practicing with his brother. A fall, a bloody nose, and swollen face, and he had to promise his mother he'd renounce the dream.

With acrobatics an impossibility, Chevalier started to

think about other options. Perhaps he could sing for a living. Show business seemed to him his only hope for avoiding the inevitable for a poor boy from Ménilmontant, a boring life as an ordinary workman. As he wrote in *My Paris*, "The reason I became a music-hall performer is that I did not have enough skill to be an acrobat!"

Half a century earlier, Victor Hugo, author of *Les Misérables*, became involved in a real-life drama on the rue de la Roquette near the Bastille. Then as now, this street was dotted with cafés and bars. During the 1848 revolution, some revolutionaries met in cafés. The proprietor of a café on the rue de la Roquette was a man named Auguste. In June Hugo managed to save him and three of his friends from being executed for having fought on the barricades. "If ever you need me, for whatever purpose, come," said the grateful café owner. Afterward, Hugo had to take Auguste up on his promise to hide him. As a member of the outlawed National Assembly, Hugo had become a wanted man himself.

Today the rue de la Roquette is still lively and raucous at night, its tiny bistros, bars, and boutiques drawing people from the more sedate parts of the city.

Writer Ted Morgan started life in France as Sanche de Gramont, a member of the French nobility. He was charmed when a young American tourist asked him to show her the Bastille. He explained that he'd like to but couldn't, since the famous prison had been demolished almost 200 years before. He went on to get to know the young woman and eventually made her his wife. The moral of the story is that ignorance is not always a bad thing.

The Gare de Lyon is just south of the Place de la Bastille. In this particular *gare* or train station, there is a sense of enticing possibilities. Here is a quick escape from the often gray, rainy North to the South—four and a half hours on the TGV, and you're in Marseille looking at the Mediterranean.

Much of the 12th is given over to the unglamorous but necessary in life: hospitals and transportation. The hospital Quinze-Vingts, specializing in eye problems, is next to the Place de la Bastille and behind the Opera. Just behind them lie a tangle of railway lines and broad thoroughfares.

Untouristy though they seem, these arrondissements, particularly the 11th, account for a sizeable proportion of our recommendations. The reason is the rent. For the 11th district a change started in 1994 to 1995, when a few bold bistro owners decided to take a chance. Their revolution started on the rue Oberkampf with the renovation of the Café Charbon, still the most attractive bistro in the district. Renewal has now spread to the rues Saint-Maur and Ménilmontant.

This area has great bistros—funky little bistros, late night cafés, dark little clubs featuring Caribbean music. If you ever find an old man with an accordion serenading you in a restaurant, it will most certainly be here. The area east and north of the Marais is vibrant with life, almost a new Marais, overrun with stylish shops and with-it cafés. Low rents encourage people who've had the dream that someday they'd like to open a modest bistro. A surprising number of the most talked-about addresses in the city are here, livening up a district that used to be very serious, dedicated to the small industries, workshops, and ateliers. When the smart young Parisian wants a night out, he won't take his girl to the Champs-Elysées or the Latin Quarter; they'll come to the 11th or possibly the 12th arrondissements.

Astier
44 rue J-P. Timbaud, 75011 Paris (01.43.57.16.35)
Métro: Oberkampf
Mon–Fri noon–2:00 P.M., 7:00 P.M.–11:00 P.M.,
closed August

We expected to like Astier. We first heard about the restaurant from a talkative cab driver a few years ago. He recommended it, and so do most of the guidebooks. Our feelings are mixed and, in this case, we're in the minority.

We can't fault the length of the 22-page menu or the wine list (although the best bistros are those which do a few things and do them well), but a lack of flavor throughout and dishes that were insipid when they should have been tasty.

Hors d'oeuvres came to the table glowing with promise, as the presentation at Astier is outstanding; but both the *crème de moules* and the *terrine de poissons*, which turned out to be salmon and other fish layered in aspic on a *coulis* of fresh tomato, were sadly lacking in flavor.

It was the same with main courses: *haddock à l'anglais* was salty to the point of being inedible, but impossible to send back as no waiter was in sight for some time. *Calamars à l'américaine* were a little more successful. Throughout the evening, the staff was overwhelmed by Astier's popularity; they were rushing about in a frantic effort to serve the young crowd.

Despite having reserved a table, we found ourselves stuck in a corner of the smoking room, a small, very confined space. There was nowhere for the smoky air to go with an air conditioner that didn't seem to be working. We had to wait fifteen minutes before receiving the water we'd requested, the wine list was whisked away before we had a chance to peruse it, and the wrong hors d'oeuvres served to the table on our left.

The most impressive course was cheese, consisting of twelve or more attractive cheeses arranged on an elaborate tray. It was dumped abruptly on our tiny table without explanation.

Desserts were attractive without being particularly good-tasting: the *quenelles de fromage blanc au coulis de fruits rouges*, slices of light, fluffy, sweetened, and jelled *fromage blanc* were served in a strawberry sauce with little relationship to fruit, as artificial tasting as if it had just come from a can. The *cassoulette des abricots tièdes, glace au miel*, was little better; warm, stewed apricots with honey ice cream, the ice cream melting as if all had been put together and heated at once.

We were seated next to a young French couple who seemed quite interested in us. As we were about to leave, the girl said to her boyfriend, "You spent a year in Texas. What were they saying?"

How to explain Astier's ongoing popularity? The servers are friendly when you see them. Helpings are large, and presented with real flair. The only thing really lacking is good flavor.

❖ *Astier: so-so food, negligible service, but a great cheese course. Is that enough? We think not.*

La Biche au Bois
45 ave. Ledru-Rollin, 75012 Paris (01.43.43.34.38)
Métro: Gare de Lyon
Mon–Fri lunch and dinner until 10:00 P.M.,
closed mid-July–mid-August, and between Christmas
and New Year's Day

If you have ever had doubts about service in French restaurants, imagining waiters with a cold, superior manner, La Biche au Bois may put an end to such concerns. Good value for money and outstanding service keep the largely business set crowding in here. The clientele are French people in their middle years. Many are regulars, and all are greeted warmly by the proprietors, Monique and Gérard Mettler. Inside, white table linens, large mirrors, William Morris-inspired curtains, and brown banquettes, with tables crowded together. Mirrors are placed on opposite walls, so that when you enter, you see what seems to be hunderds of people lifting theirs knives and forks at the same time.

There is a wide array of choices in the 20-euro menu, some conservative, others more evocative of the bistro's theme—wild game and the outdoors. *Champignons à la grecque* (cold marinated mushrooms), while not so filling, were a tasty beginning. We chose solid bistro fare, *coq au vin*. To accompany this on a warm evening, a rosé de Tavel was just the thing.

The waiter brought a plate of tuna by mistake, and after we'd tasted our *plat* we wished we'd seized it from him. The *coq au vin* turned out to be surprisingly bland. Attractively presented in a flame-orange Le Creuset-type casserole dish, it was bubbling in a heavy brown sauce that seemed to have little to do with the flavors of either chicken or wine. Still, superb cheeses followed, and there was a range of desserts, from the classic *crème caramel, mousse au chocolat,* and *île flottante* to fresh fruit in season and a selection of ice creams and sherbets.

❖ *La Biche au Bois: honest and authentic—we'll return.*

Au Camelot
50 rue Amelot, 75011 Paris (01.43.55.54.04)
Métro: St.-Sébastien-Froissart
Tues–Sat noon–2:30 P.M., 7:30 P.M.–midnight

Nobody goes to Au Camelot for a romantic evening. It's a long, bare, narrow room, with little tables capable of seating only 22 diners jammed together inside. Long lace curtains on the windows shield you from the street. (The rue Amelot, although one of the oldest in this part of the city, does not look like the Paris of legend.)

Two young people preside behind the bar, right next to the door. They polish glasses, pour drinks, seat customers, and keep tabs on what's happening. At this bar, surmounted by a curious-looking lamp with a Deco base, the *serveuse* carefully poured a *kir royal* for one customer and, with the same flourish, produced a chilled bottle of Coca-Cola for another. That, and a bunch of sweet peas arranged in a vase on the bar, lent a homey touch.

Carrying on a conversation is a challenge at Au Camelot because of the noise created by the curious acoustics of a miniscule, lozenge-shaped room, but you hear the happy buzz of satisfied diners.

There was originally a 25-euro menu in which the only

course where you had a choice was dessert. Now the menu is 28 euros and there are choices for every course. A few wines by the glass cost 4 or 5 euros, with most bottles ranging from 16 to 31 euros. We chose a white Châteauneuf du Pape, which was about as macho as a white can get. Also available were various well-chosen smaller wines, mainly reds from Burgundy, Bordeaux, and the southwest.

After you made your crucial decision about dessert, a five-course meal follows: on one Saturday night, ours opened with a huge terrine of cool and refreshing gazpacho, followed by a *poêlée de girolles* (sautéed wild mushrooms) in a *mousselline d'oeuf brouillé* (scrambled egg in sauce). The gazpacho was among the best we've tasted, with a deep, luscious flavor of home-grown tomatoes. The next dish had a base of lightly scrambled egg, with sautéed mushrooms and parsley in a cream sauce, a nice contrast of flavors and textures. Slightly salty for our tastes, but flavorful.

Then the *plat*: home-made lasagna, with a filling of *queue de boeuf* (oxtail), like falling-off-the-bone braised beef, and caramelized onion adding depth to the sauce. A light *plat*, totally appropriate after the two hors d'oeuvres.

The cheese of the day was Camembert, and we each received a generous-sized wedge, good with the bread.

Desserts, which we'd chosen earlier, were light and flavorful: raspberries in a delicate warm custard; strawberries—a more typical presentation—cold with vanilla ice cream between sheets of puff pastry.

❖ *Au Camelot: excellent food without the responsibility of many choices.*

La Cheminée
7 rue J-P.Timbaud, 75011 Paris (01.49.23.06.76)
Métro: République
Mon–Fri noon–2:30 P.M., 7:30 P.M.–11:00 P.M., Sat dinner

Somewhere in this great city, you think, I'll find a quaint little restaurant on a quiet street. The people will be friendly, the food will be good, the atmosphere will make me think of a quiet country inn, and the prices will be those of 10 or 15 years ago.

We have found such a place: La Cheminée. It's worth making a detour to go to this small restaurant near the République, away from the fast-food chains which have taken over that historic square.

At first glance, La Cheminée may seem to lack charm. This is just a first impression. Walk through the front room to the second room. You see old-world charm in the high ceiling, the dark beams against the white plaster, the historic stone walls, and massive fireplace, or *cheminée*. A wild boar's head dominates a far corner, and on the same wall is an oil painting with a view of windmills that looks like old Holland. A wild grapevine curls overhead. Fanciful but effective light fixtures on the sides resemble large flowers, the shades providing metallic petals and bulbs the center, silver-tipped to prevent glare. Elsewhere, the look is of warm earth tones and green, the terra cotta-colored floor tiles set off by green potted plants and green tablecloths.

Hors d'oeuvres at La Cheminée are from 3 to 4 euros, including *poireaux* (leeks), *crudités* (raw vegetables), *salade de foie de volaille* (chicken liver salad), and a hard-to-find luxury like snails at 4 euros for 6, double that amount for a dozen. *Plats*—and this was at night—were from 6 to 8 euros, including such possibilities as *sole meunière, rouget au beurre blanc*, steak, etc.

The service is deftly handled by friendly young waitresses in black and white. One also helps out in the kitchen. While we were waiting to order, we heard her say to a customer, "Ça a été?" (Was it all right?) and his response: "Super—je ne sais pas comment vous faites ça" (Great—I don't know how you do it).

Our hors d'oeuvre snails were hot, plump, and succulent in the delicious garlic and parsley butter, along with the fresh bread.

The food was worth the wait: the *faux filet paysanne* was a large steak with home-fried potatoes, potatoes that had been sautéed with bacon and mushrooms and were crisp, brown, and delicious. *Sole meunière* was hot and lemony, served with stewed tomatoes breaded and flavored with lemon and parsley, and white rice.

Desserts run from 3 to 5 euros, from the *crème caramel* and *pâtisserie maison* at 3 euros to complicated ice cream desserts at 5 euros. Most desserts are made on the premises.

This particular night the *pâtisserie maison* at 3 euros was everyone's idea of a good dessert, the *Opéra*, a multilayered chocolate fantasy. La Cheminée's *Opéra* was served with *crème anglaise* and little puffs of whipped cream on the corners. The chocolate in it could have been more bittersweet, but we're quibbling. We can't remember when we've had a similar dessert at the price.

We learned that the owner-chef was on vacation but being competently replaced by his son, David, who won the title "Meilleur Apprenti de France" (Best Apprentice in France) for his studies in cuisine. A young man with a promising future.

❖ *La Cheminée: one of the better values in* cuisine familiale, *in a charming setting.*

Café Charbon
109 rue Oberkampf, 75011 Paris (01.43.57.55.13)
Métro: Parmentier
Open daily 9:00 A.M.–2:00 A.M.

Artistic, young, and what used to be called hip, with a vague whiff of a counterculture—these were our first impressions of Café Charbon, the granddaddy of the currently fashionable places in the Ménilmontant area of Paris. When Maurice Chevalier grew up not far from here, this would never have been thought of as an "in" area—now it is. The people who come here are of all ages, although everyone looks at the young, slender, and deeply tanned girls wearing similar skimpy black dresses. Alas, they all smoke.

Café Charbon looks as if it has been sitting here dispensing coffee for hundreds of years, all the while sinking into an artistic decadence. It's only been here a few years, although the building that houses it is genuinely old. Quite wisely the owners did not try to modernize the interior of what was originally a turn-of-the-century dance hall. If anything, they played up the antique features of the room:

the high ceiling in an old-fashioned shade of brown and the venerable tall mirrors reflecting light from a number of old, ineffective chandeliers.

"C'est un brunch typiquement parisien" (A typically Parisian brunch), said the friend of a Parisian friend, who stopped his bicycle to greet us and offer suggestions. So we decided to give it a try. Also, Café Charbon is open Sundays and in August— no small consideration in a city where everything seems to shut up tight in the eighth month of the year.

What is a "Parisian" brunch? At the Charbon, we learned that on Saturday or Sunday, you can have coffee or tea, *oeufs brouillés, saucisse,* bacon, *salade, fromage blanc aux herbes, jus d'orange,* and pancakes or *salade de fruits.* In other words, scrambled eggs, sausage, bacon, salad, white cheese with herbs, orange juice, and pancakes or fruit salad. All for 13 euros—a bargain in the Paris of today.

This turn-of-the-century interior retains a Belle Epoque feeling, with its lofty ceilings, old-fashioned light fixtures, mirrors, and murals in keeping with the period. To lighten things up there are plants and a happy buzz from a crowd of regulars. Most of the people you see here are young, with a few gray hairs and bald heads. I noticed one head deliberately bald—à la Jesse Ventura—a sleek-looking, muscular young man who works for the café.

Two beautiful African waitresses gave friendly if occasionally slow service, but there's a lot of space for them to cover in the cavernous Charbon.

Brunch, while not especially American, was a good deal for the ravenous: a huge and delicious baked potato in silver foil, with a sour cream and chive topping; beside it, a ramekin of scrambled eggs, topped with Canadian bacon and a split, grilled sausage. Next to that, a salad of romaine lettuce and tomato. A small round of *fromage blanc* completed the picture. We had asked for wine when our young waitress offered the choice: "Jus d'orange ou vin?" A glass of a very drinkable, chilled house wine went well with the brunch. If one wishes for more, wine is available by the glass for 2 euros and up.

The friend's friend who'd recommended brunch at the Charbon had said, "Il y a les garçons de la presse là" (journalists go there), so when you do go, you may find yourself sharing a banquette with a savvy group of *intellos*—intellectuals from the area. Or possibly with people who just like the ambiance, which is very special.

What was perhaps most American at this brunch was the music. Strains of Ella Fitzgerald and "How High the Moon," drifted over us when we first came in. Toward the end, the scrubbing of the zinc bar and the crashing of glass obscured the good jazz coming from the hi-fi system.

❖ *Café Charbon: good value in a fashionable place.*

Chardenoux
1 rue Jules Vallès, 75011 Paris (01.43.71.49.52)
Metro: Charonne
Mon–Fri noon-2:30 P.M., 8:00 P.M.–10:30 P.M.,
Sat eves, closed August

Chardenoux is one of those incredibly romantic little bistros that have somehow survived the vagaries of fashion to retain the charm they originally possessed. Seated in the first room, we were well placed to study the old bar with its intricate patterns of variously-colored slabs of marble and topped with the original zinc. The dark high ceilings, in colors that suggest old worn leather, had curves and turn-of-the-century swirls around the edges. Large windows opening onto the street were covered with delicate lace. An old-fashioned wood screen with frosted glass separated the barroom from the more formal second dining room.

The wine list will please any oenophile, being a serious collection of recent vintages, many from the Loire.

Competent service is provided by two women who wait tables, open bottles, and decide where to place a table to accommodate an extra diner. Chardenoux attracts a range of people: the occasional tourist, young marrieds with children, retired gourmets from the neighborhood.

Hors d'oeuvres are from 7 to 10 euros and *plats* 13 to 19 euros. An hors d'oeuvre of boiled fennel was served cold in a

cream dressing that tasted of orange, along with tiny crisp *haricots verts*, sprinkled with orange zest and chives. Different and good.

The *plats* claimed our full attention, the *magret de canard* being the most generous portion we've seen, a large piece of roast duck that looked like a small slab of beef, with scalloped potatoes and cooked red bell peppers. It had a rich, roasted flavor, very effective with no sauce except for its own juices and a little butter. *Morue* (salt cod) was in a separate casserole dish, sizzling hot, in a spinach and cream—*florentine*—sauce. With its potatoes and a light *gratin*, or cheese topping, it was scrumptious, a happy marriage of cream, white wine, cod, and the spinach. Both *plats* had an unusual intensity of flavor.

Dessert wasn't really necessary after such a feast, but we chose one anyway, the *fondant au chocolat et aux marrons*, a very dense, creamy, cold chocolate dessert with a consistency similar to cream cheese and an intriguing undertone of *marrons*—chestnuts. With it was a sauce of *crème anglaise,* just right to temper the chocolate flavor.

❖ *Chardenoux: outstanding food in an extraordinary setting. A place not to be missed.*

Chez Paul
13 rue de Charonne, 75011 Paris (01.47.00.34.57)
Métro: Bastille
Open daily noon–2:30 P.M., 7:30 P.M.–12:30 A.M.

Go to Chez Paul and you find yourself with other people who are looking to find a piece of old Paris, the kind you might associate with beloved old movies, with gutteral-voiced intellectuals sitting late into the night making predictions about the problems of the world. (None of their angst seems to have the slightest effect on their appetites.)

There's a venerable zinc bar and walls in faded ochre. Other customers there at the same time as ourselves included an *ancien soixante-huitard* (superannuated hippie, an original from '68), his long hair silver-streaked by the years, his companion, still with almost Rapunzel-length tresses talking on and on with zest.

As the slender young waitress pointed out, there were the "grands classiques." We elected *oeuf à la mayonnaise,* which arrived with the egg slathered with too much mayonnaise, but let that pass. The modest little Rhône in a carafe was just right to go with a *pièce de boeuf* (steak with Béarnaise sauce).

My salmon was excellent, as was my companion's beef—he'd ordered medium, it turned out rare, but was succulent nonetheless. Portions were generous, the staff young and friendly. "Ça vous a plu?" our waitress asked at the end. A runny Brie de Meaux on red leaf lettuce was a fine accompaniment with the Rhône wine we'd chosen.

If you don't get a reservation for Chez Paul, your only hope is to arrive early. We heard the personnel begin turning people away at 8:15.

❖ *Chez Paul: popular and crowded for good reasons.*

Le Clown Bar
114 rue Amelot, 75011 Paris (01.43.55.87.35)
Métro: République
Mon–Sat noon–3:00 P.M., 7:30 P.M.–1:00 A.M., Sun 7:00
P.M.–1:00 A.M., closed Sun lunch, 1 week in August
No credit cards

The Clown Bar has joie de vivre and then some. The walls of this listed historic place are covered with bright original tiles depicting clowns in absurd and funny postures—one shows a diminutive clown perched on the prominent paunch of another. It is this caricature-like pose that the Clown Bar has chosen as its trademark.

Colorful and rare circus-related memorabilia, from clown lighting fixtures to authentic turn-of-the-century posters of clowns, brighten an already happy interior.

Prices are reasonable: hors d'oeuvres from 6 to 9 euros include *terrine maison* (homemade meatloaf), *saucisson* (dry salami), *charcuterie* (cooked cured meats), and *rillettes d'oie* (chopped goose, cooked to a paste). *Plats*, or main dishes, go for 12 to 13 euros, and you could make a meal of one of these. *Onglet de boeuf* (flank steak), *mignon de porc* (sautéed pork filet), and *pavé de morue* (salt cod) were some of the choices.

Desserts are generous here and show a little more initiative than in many bistros and wine bars. Besides old favorites like *crème brûlée* and *gâteau au chocolat*, there was *délice au café*, a plate with small dishes of coffee mousse, cappuccino ice cream, and a *florentin*—a large, crisp, caramel-flavored wafer, a good finish for a confirmed coffee lover.

Every day there's the *plat du jour,* as well as a cheese and dessert *du jour.*

A good if not extraordinary wine list focuses on fairly-priced wines from around the country—the South, Southwest, a Bordeaux, a Beaujolais, a Loire. Wines by the glass are in the 3-euro range, with a few wines available in a *demi*, or two-thirds of a bottle, for about 9 euros.

❖ *Le Clown Bar: a romantic setting, a national treasure.*

Dame Jeanne
60 rue de Charonne, 75011 Paris (01.47.00.37.40)
Métro: Ledru-Rollin
Tue–Fri lunch and dinner, Sat eves, closed August

At first sight Dame Jeanne might not attract one as much as some of its neighbors on the rue de Charonne. It's not remarkable in appearance: wide white umbrellas shade a small terrace, a few plants form a little hedge. Yet the cuisine here is what the French call *raffinée*—refined, special, with the skilled touches that only a serious chef can give. A team of servers attended to us. All were courteous and friendly; still, service here is relaxed, possibly a little on the slow side.

A 19-euro menu provides a three-course meal with no choices, with, for example, tagliatelli as the only *plat* on the day we visited. It might be better to go with the regular 23- or 28-euro menu, the price depending on whether you choose the *plat* with hors d'oeuvre, with dessert, or with both to get substance and variety.

The *effeuillé de raie* was a warm hors d'oeuvre that looked a little like a rectangular French pastry, the strips of skate or rayfish on a bed of sautéed minced onions and colorful red cabbage. Some raw cauliflower contributed texture, and the tangy balsamic vinegar dressing had none of the usual sweetness of this type of vinegar.

Plats were generous and well-flavored: an enormous *magret de canard* came with a topping of sautéed onion and parsley, on a bed of spinach with succulent, tiny mushrooms, and in a simple sauce of just the cooking juices with butter. On the side, an individual pot of purée of potatoes, with butter, was enough to share.

The other *plat*, the tender and delicious breast of veal stuffed with herbs, rosemary, and parsley, was a lighter but still substantial meal. We noticed it was also popular with the Parisiennes near us on the terrace.

Desserts are a particular forte of Dame Jeanne, well-made, beautifully presented, and delicious. A *feuille crème citron, sauce chocolat*, turned out to be a dessert cleverly concealed in two crisp, light gold, perfectly round crêpes, with an intensely flavored lemon filling topped with honey and vanilla ice cream. The dessert *du jour* involved a circle of thin, caramelized sugar, topping two scoops of dark chocolate mousse, the mousse concealing several perfect raspberries.

Dame Jeanne will appeal to people who like good wines at reasonable prices. Here the restaurateurs have taken the time to find little-known growers in the South and Southwest, to provide a list of smooth and drinkable wines for its patrons at affordable prices. So a half-bottle at 8 euros or a whole bottle at 14 buys you some very drinkable wine. "Comparable à une bouteille à 200 francs"(Comparable to a 200-franc bottle), remarked a French lady near us.

❖ *Dame Jeanne: cuisine of creativity and finesse.*

L'Encrier
55 rue Traversière, 75012 Paris (01.44.68.08.16)
Métro: Gare de Lyon
Mon–Fri noon–2:15 P.M., 7:15 P.M.–11:00 P.M., Sat eves
only, closed August

L'Encrier has been in its present incarnation as a bistro for only about five years. But the building dates back to about 1850, so there has been time for change. The look here is black, white, and historic. Extraordinary lights on modern wrought-iron constructions surge from the wall above the kitchen. Fan-shaped lights in a Deco style brighten the stone wall opposite.

As you enter you see a large white-tiled kitchen, open to view, where four men are working energetically, including the friendly, white-haired, jeans-and-T-shirt-clad gentleman

who greeted us and was obviously in charge. We were seated at an old round oak table, reminiscent of many a farmhouse kitchen. Overhead was the warm wood of exposed beams and beside us an historic-looking exposed brick wall.

The best thing about this historic space near the Gare de Lyon is its value. For 10 euros (12 in the evenings), you can enjoy a three-course meal in a bright, attractive setting, with an honestly priced wine to go with it.

Standards from the regular menu show the creativity of the chef, and if you want to try something à la carte, *plats* are a reasonable 8 euros. The wine prices are an especially nice feature of L'Encrier: a *vins du pays* Catalan is 3 euros for a quarter liter and only 5 for a *demi*.

Our hors d'oeuvres were a warm *salade au gésiers* (chicken gizzard salad), tasty on a bed of romaine lettuce, with tomatoes and tiny bits of carrot for color, and a smooth and cool *fromage blanc* (white cottage-type cheese) with *fines herbes*, a savory start.

Next, perch, a large serving in a *sauce duglère*. Light and flavorful, with lemon and white and wild rice on the side. The steaks came with the crisp, thin rounds of fried potatoes that are an Encrier trademark. Unless specified otherwise, steak is served rather rare; you may want to say "bien cuit" if you want it thoroughly cooked.

The *tarte aux abricots* was pleasant and not too sweet, with a custard base and a crisp crust. *Gâteau au chocolat*, while tasty, was on the dry side, but a good *coulis de framboises* (raspberry sauce) and *crème anglaise* helped. A delicious fruit salad included black cherries, oranges, melon, apricots, almond syrup, and a touch of mint.

❖ *L'Encrier: great value close to the Gare de Lyon.*

Jacques Melac, Bistro à Vins
42 rue Léon Frot, 75011 Paris (01. 43.70.59.27)
Métro: Charonne
Mon 9:00 A.M.–5:00 P.M., Tue–Sat 9:00 A.M.–midnight,
closed August

There is a real Jacques Melac, a well-known character with a signature mustache, who always seems to be in the country when we visit his winebar. Yet with or without the proprietor, and in spite of its hard-to-find location deep in the 11th district, this *bistro à vins* has become one of the most popular in the city.

After you've glanced over the lengthy list of wines available at this unique wine bar, you come to the nonalcoholic drinks. A warning is expressed before they list mineral water: "L'eau— sur présentation d'une ordonnance médicale" (water only by medical prescription). That sums up the jocular attitude here, where waiters wear black T-shirts with warnings against water, a suggestive remark about what fish do in it, and their trademark comment that it's only fit for cooking potatoes.

Sitting at the large bar, we saw old beams above us and almost equally impressive massive slabs of cheese in front of us. Light and delicate lace curtains separate drinkers inside from the world outside. Long doors with glass insets give a good view of the leafy foliage trailing along and down from the roof, these plants being Jacques Melac's own vines.

Most wines are about 4 euros a glass. When you order one, you notice that not only is the proprietor's name etched on it, but also his mustache, curving up like a smile. One side of the establishment is more of a restaurant, with long, heavy wood tables that have to be shared when it gets crowded—all the better for striking up an acquaintance with another wine lover.

Our barman spoke English fluently, having spent some months in Chicago, which he'd loved. Between waiting on customers he took time to flirt with a parting blonde.

❖ *Jacques Melac: although it's out near métro Charonne, the selection of wines and the joie de vivre will keep us coming back.*

Le Petit Keller
13 bis rue Keller, 75011 Paris (01.47.00.12.97)
Métro: Ledru-Rollin
Tue–Sat 11:30–1:30 A.M., closed mid-July–mid August

Located just off crowded, popular rue de la Roquette, Le Petit Keller is an appealing little bistro of the type you might find in the French countryside. Brown banquettes, yellow walls, framed paintings that owe some of their inspiration to the works of Picasso and Dali, and a large circular mirror define the main room.

When we entered around 1:00 P.M., most of the regulars— clerical and other workers from the area—had finished lunch and were calling for their *additions.*

While the decor could not be called exciting, this is a little bistro that does *cuisine familiale* (home cooking) competently at a modest price, with a 9-euro lunch menu that rises to 12 euros at dinner. One of us chose *faux-filet,* a small steak in a mustard and pepper sauce with a baked potato garnished with sour cream; the other, stuffed peppers in salad. Both *plats* were tasty and filling. Before the main course, we enjoyed salads livened up by blue cheese, a Bleu d'Auvergne.

What impressed us most about this bistro was something that happened just as we were leaving. It was 2:00 P.M., the end of the lunch period, and the staff must have been tired. An elderly French couple came in, and we heard the gentleman inquire, "Could you find something to eat for Madame?" explaining that he'd already eaten but that his wife, who'd just come in by train, had not. "Yes, of course," responded the waiter, who could have mentioned the time and the end of lunch. Instead he immediately served them drinks and disappeared down the circular staircase to see what could still be rustled up from the kitchen.

❖ *Le Petit Keller: good everyday food of the type most French people are used to, at very affordable prices.*

Le 80
80 blvd Richard-Lenoir, 75011 Paris (01.48.05.07.73)
Métro: Richard-Lenoir
Mon–Sat 9:00 A.M.–2:00 P.M.
No credit cards

Le 80 doesn't accept credit cards. Nor is there much about the interior to win your affection, unless you happen to like large nets suspended above, with fake flowers, old straw hats, and giant plastic butterflies dangling from them, or have a special feeling for windows defaced with plastic coatings of scenes in hot pink and magenta.

But the daily specials on the blackboards all over this rather strange-looking interior are enough to divert any serious foodie from the decor: hors d'oeuvres like a *demi melon et son verre de porto* (melon with port), *gaspacho andalouse et ses croutons,* and *salade d'endives aux noix, pommes et roquefort* (endive salad with nuts, apples, and blue cheese) each going for about 6 euros. The *plats* of the day were equally diverting and fairly priced from 12 to 17 euros.

There was evidence of a masterful touch in the kitchen: the *rascasse* (scorpion fish) we ordered was hot, lightly breaded and in a flavorful saffron sauce tasting of mussels and cream along with rice. An *escalope jurasienne gratinée* was veal which had been topped with a thin layer of ham and then coated with melted Swiss cheese, the saltiness of the ham giving zest to the veal. Both of us were more than satisfied. Portions were ample, and a *plat* at Le 80 provides a meal.

Half a bottle of Comte de Belot Buzet was rich and flavorful, going well with the veal and not overwhelming the *rascasse.*

Desserts were outstanding. The chef specializes in flaming desserts with *Calvados* (*tarte tatin*) or heating sugar to create crisp caramel toppings. We shared a *gratin de fraises,* strawberries in a pleasant cool *crème anglaise,* with a crisp, hot, caramelized sugar coating.

❖ *Le 80: a restaurant of merit in an unlikely setting.*

Le Square Trousseau
1 rue Antoine-Vollon 75012 Paris (01.43.43.06.00)
Métro: Ledru-Rollin
Open daily to 10:30 P.M. except for 3 weeks in August

When you walk into the Square Trousseau, you feel as if you've finally found the ultimate bistro. Here are floor-to-ceiling doors and windows in front, and high ceilings with elaborate moldings in buttery ochre. Through lace curtains of unusual delicacy you glimpse the Square Trousseau, the park which gives this bistro its name. As we were glancing about, orienting ourselves to the place, two businessmen were finishing up their *crème brûlée.* "Excellent," we heard one murmur.

From the conversations around us, we gathered that some of our neighbors were recognizing other customers: "Il y a des gens de la télévision ici" (people from television are here).

Lunch specials are written on *ardoises* (blackboards). Main dishes are all between 13 and 18 euros. We elected to try the *crème de concombre à la menthe,* a delicious cold soup of cucumber with mint, and a *croustillant de chèvre aux quatre épices,* a sautéed square of goat cheese, served hot and presented on a bed of red leaf lettuce. This was followed by a *brandade de morue Benedictine,* a fish-and-potato mixture garnished with tomato sauce, and *poulet mariné au citron et coriandre* (chicken marinated in lemon juice with cilantro). Flavors were subtle and intriguing, the *brandade de morue* a light, satisfying meal.

Not quiet enough for an intimate lunch with your favorite person, Le Square Trousseau is just the sort of bistro where you'd like to invite friends. And it's full of the planners, the movers and shakers, the people who make Paris what it is. A couple near us were discussing an international conference they were attending, organized by the World Bank and the French government. Jean Paul Gaultier is said to be a regular.

❖ *Le Square Trousseau: "Vous ne serez pas déçu," (you won't be disappointed), said a departing Parisian when we sat down. He was right.*

Le Viaduc Café
43 rue Daumesnil, 75012 Paris (01.44.74.70.70)
Métro: Ledru-Rollin
Open daily 9:00 A.M.–4:00 A.M.

If only the food were as lovely as the girls serving the drinks, the Viaduc Café would be heavenly. Unfortunately it's not—most people find the fare rather ordinary. Of course, what's ordinary in Paris might be quite exciting in Amarillo.

Still, this is perhaps the most attractive café we've ever seen near a large railway station. It's smartly designed, *branché*, or hip, and attracting a crowd of beautiful people. About two blocks from the Gare de Lyon, the viaduc transports you into another world, that of the arts. When you go to the Viaduc you feel as if you could be in a design studio, with the immense ceilings formed by the viaduct overhead, the exposed stone on the walls, and the charming wood bar with Second-Empire lines. You sink into one of the old-style sofas or armchairs in cherry-colored wood and admire the view onto the terrace outside.

A great deal of attention has been paid to style here, but none of it gets in the way of your pleasure: the seating has been selected for comfort as well as attractiveness, the staff are young, friendly, and attractive, flitting about like birds.

You can enjoy a light meal here at fair prices—hors d'oeuvres like gazpacho, melon, or vegetable salad from 6 to 7 euros, substantial *plats* like *cabillaud* (fresh cod), *filet de boeuf* (beef filet), and *magret de canard* (duck breast) from 12 to 15 euros, with cheeses and desserts about 6 euros.

There's a good wine list, with most offered in full bottles or by the glass for from 3 to 4 euros.

❖ *Le Viaduc Café: a good place for awaiting a train trip or any time. Quite unlike the grubby cafés usually found near railroad stations.*

Le Villaret
13 rue Ternaux, 75011 Paris (01.43.57.89.76)
Métro: Parmentier
Mon–Fri noon–2:00 P.M., 7:30 P.M.–midnight,
Sat 7:30 P.M.–1:00 A.M.; closed August

If you're a serious admirer of French cuisine, the classics interpreted with untraditional flair, you should make a trip deep into the 11th arrondissement. The rue Ternaux is a street that houses African-owned secondhand stores, a dark-looking laundromat, and forlorn little cafés. Go past them to Le Villaret.

There's nothing remarkable about Le Villaret's decor—a stone wall behind the bar, pleasantly muted earth tones elsewhere in the interior, fan-shaped lighting on the walls. But the food is special. The day we were there with a friend, we went for lunch. At 20 or 24 euros, depending on whether one chooses two or three courses, the lunch offerings at Villaret are a bargain—at dinner it's all à la carte, except for the 46-euro tasting menu. Hors d'oeuvres available included *crème fraîche de rougets et petits croutons* (red mullet cream soup), *tartare de saumon fumé* (minced smoked salmon), and *compôte de jeune lapin à la vieille prune* (rabbit pâté with plum brandy). Then we had a choice of *calamars frais à la crème* (fresh calamar or squid soup), *l'andouillette de pieds de porc panée* (pig's foot sausage), and *poulet fermier de Gers au vin de Loire* (free-range chicken with white wine sauce).

The wine list is serious and expensive with important bottles heading up into the hundreds of euros, but a nice half-liter of Chablis in a *pichet* at 15 euros is just about right for two. The cheapest red, at 16 euros, is a hearty wine from the Languedoc.

The *crème fraiche de rougets et petits croutons* was an intensely-flavored fish soup, reminiscent of some we've consumed with relish much closer to the Mediterranean. Our Parisian friend's *tartare de saumon fumé* was smoked salmon in a ramekin shape, served with a crisp wafer tasting of potato and cheese, a rose-like tomato, and sprinklings of chives. She pressed samples upon us: "The smoked salmon is really good." Tasting it, we concurred.

Following were *calamars à la crème*, well-seasoned in a rich sauce, a generous helping on a bed of white rice. The roast chicken came with green beans and was served with a scrumptious cream sauce flavored with a choice Loire wine. A carafe of Chablis at 14 euros provided a suitable accompaniment.

Servings at Le Villaret are so generous that only one of us had enough appetite left for an interesting and unusual dessert, the *poêlée de cerises*, cherries lightly sautéed with port and served with gingerbread-flavored ice cream and a sprig of mint.

"There's a real chef in that kitchen" we agreed as we left Le Villaret, each of us separately plotting return visits.

❖ *Le Villaret:* cuisine raffinée—*a taste treat for the gourmet, deep in the 11th arrondissement.*

LEFT BANK SOUTH:
THE 13ᵀᴴ & 14ᵀᴴ
ARRONDISSEMENTS

The Dôme soon expanded from a bistro to a big, garish café with rows and rows of tables… toward evening it was impossible to find a seat…. Around you people milled in a slow-moving stream. They were a motley crowd—tall, raw-boned Swedes, sleek Russians and Spaniards, noisy Americans, self-conscious English, anxious or portly French, all intent on their own affairs…. Women dressed in the height of fashion rubbed elbows with shabby models or gaudy prostitutes….

—Jimmie Charters, *This Must Be The Place*

If the 6th arrondissement is the quarter of artists and writers, then the 14th cannot be far behind. The 13th and 14th arrondissements run directly south and under the more famous 5th and 6th districts on the map of Paris, but they do not have the same spirit about them. In the 5th and 6th, you have the feeling that these neighborhoods, however reluctantly, are hosting a perennial fair. People jostle one another along narrow, twisted streets, peer at the street performers giving spontaneous concerts, toss coins to streetside beggars as they make their way to museums by day, to theaters and cafés by night. More sedate in its nature, the 14th, dividing up the boulevard du Montparnasse with the 6th district, still retains some of the famous bistros which lined that street during the Jazz Age.

The so-called "American cafés," which started in the 1920s, are part of every book about the bistros of Paris. With the 6th and the 14th joined at the boulevard like Siamese twins, you have La Rotonde and Le Sélect in the 6th district, and their competition across the street, La Coupole and Le

Dôme in the 14th. Since these bistros were just across from one another, people would go from one arrondissement to the other in their nightly search for entertainment.

Ernest Hemingway wrote about how it used to be. He was sitting at the Dôme when he described to Sherwood Anderson a night in December 1921:

> We sit outside the Dôme Café opposite the Rotonde that's being redecorated... and it's so damned cold outside.... And when it's a cold night in the streets of Paris and we're walking home down the Rue Bonaparte we think of the way the wolves used to slink into the city and François Villon and the gallows at Montfauçon. What a town.

photo © Juliana Spear

It was easy to get caught up in the bistro routine. Canadian writer Morley Callaghan, in *That Summer in Paris,* described the summer of 1929 and his friendships with Hemingway and Fitzgerald. Starting in the 14th arrondissement, Callaghan and his wife would move on to bistros in the 6th and even across the river in the 8th and 9th districts: "We would... walk slowly over to the Coupole, have a little lunch on the terrace, then go across the river to the American Express to inquire for mail. Sometimes we loafed around the Right Bank for hours, having a drink at some café by the Opéra, or the Madeleine."

Now the bistros on the boulevard are quieter than they were, the 13th and 14th arrondissements—the 13th with the Gobelins, the 14th with the catacombs at Denfert-Rochereau—relatively peaceful. There's a cluster of hospitals at the northern edge of the 14th and a cemetery, the Cimetière de Montparnasse, nearer its center. Probably the most famous among the hospitals is La Pitié-Salpetrière, at 47-83 boulevard de l'Hôpital, in the 13th district. Founded as a workhouse for orphans, it became a center specializing in the treatment of mental illness. Freud himself spent six months observing and working there.

Below Denfert-Rochereau is the Cité Universitaire, founded in the 1920s to provide students with reasonable lodgings. Serveral of the pavilions were designed by noted architects, the Swiss and Brazilian ones by Le Corbusier. A stay at the Maison des Etats-Unis years ago gave us an idea of what the Cité is like: comfortable housing, but with an oppressive feeling of sterility and isolation, so far from the center.

In some ways those Parisians who live in the 13th and 14th districts are fortunate. Although their quarters may look desolate in places, they are out of the noisy hubbub and crowds of the Latin Quarter. They have the jewel-shaped park, the Jardin du Luxembourg, stretching down toward them. And they have low rents and some of the most notable bistros in today's Paris.

Some of these bistros are:

L'Avant-Goût
26 rue Bobillot, 75013 Paris (01.53.80.24.00)
Métro: Place d'Italie
Tue–Sat noon–2:00 P.M., 8:00 P.M.–11:00 P.M.,
closed August

Near the Place d'Italie, L'Avant-Goût attracts people who love food and can dismiss from their minds the room they're sitting in. You will not travel there for the setting, nor for the welcome, which was correct but not warm. Conditions may change, but on our first visit the background, or *cadre* as the French say was decidedly off-putting, with coral walls clashing wildly with deep red banquettes and tables. Little lights suspended awkwardly from wires wound around the edges of the room. Tablecloths were economically covered with paper, and napkins were a durable paper too.

If you want dinner here you'll have to reserve; we saw a gentleman being turned away and it was only 8:30 P.M. The 23-euro menu suggested why enthusiastic diners were crowding in: good variety, with *champignons à la grecque* (mushrooms stewed in olive oil with tomato and lemon), *langue d'agneau* (lamb's tongue), *bouillon de pot au feu au cochon* (pork bouillon) offered as starters, followed by possibilities like *maigre bar poelé, risotto aux crustacés* (lean sautéed European bass and risotto with seafood), *cocotte de caille* (quail in casserole), and *filet de canard griotté aux poivrons* (duck filet with sour cherries and peppers).

A Côte du Rhône 1999 from Domaine Rabasse was a sturdy accompaniment to the food. The soups we chose were both light and flavorful, one a fish broth with croutons of *rouille* (garlic and olive oil mayonnaise) and tapenade, the other a savory pork. Both were garnished with watercress and olives.

Service was competent without being particularly friendly. Dress is relatively informal: a teenager at a nearby table was in T-shirt and jeans, the universal costume at McDonald's. Being at l'Avant-Goût and being French, he knowledgeably ordered *langue d'agneau rôtie compôte de tomates* (roast lamb's tongue) and downed it with relish.

If more than one diner orders the *pot-au-feu* (beef stew), it comes to the table in a cast-iron casserole, the stew garnished with new potatoes and olives.

A large portion of *bar* with a crisp cake of fried rice was dramatically displayed on what looked like squid or octopus ink. The *magret de canard* was rich and flavorful on a bed of peppers and tomatoes with a light cream sauce.

A largely BCBG (bon chic bon genre) crowd near the door puffed away on their cigarettes all evening, but we were spared by the good ventilation system.

Intriguing choices at the end of the meal included cheeses, *soupe de melon sorbet à l'estragon* (melon soup, tarragon sherbet), *fraises façon tiramisù* (strawberries tiramisù style), and *chaud-froid moelleux de chocolat* (hot-cold chocolate dessert). The *fraises* and *moelleux* were a tasty and satisfying finish, with the *moelleux* a partly-cooked cake with melting, warm bittersweet chocolate in the center and vanilla ice cream lending it a cold aspect.

❖ *L'Avant-Goût: exceptional cuisine in an unlikely setting.*

Chez Gladines
30 rue des Cinq-Diamants, 75013 Paris (01.45.80.70.10)
Métro: Corvisart
Open daily noon–3:00 P.M., 7:00 P.M.–midnight,
closed August
No credit cards

It's a slice of old Paris begging to be remembered in black and white. It's an old corner bistro dating from the early twentieth century, half-heartedly modernized, with some crazy Deco trim from the 1930s, topped off with a formica bar after World War II and then essentially unchanged. You might not manage to see much of this, however, since Chez Gladines was packed tighter than any place we've ever seen.

Chez Gladines could be the younger sister of Chez Denise, la Tour de Montlhéry, in what's left of Les Halles. We found this bistro blocked by young people when we elbowed our way in, not expecting to get a table. In minutes, we were seated at one of the long tables covered with faded red-and-white checkered oilcloth, rather like an old farmhouse kitchen. We were elbow-to-elbow with young students, many of them wolfing down salads from dishes of a size customarily used as mixing bowls. Service was a bit primitive but charming, and provided by a hardworking girl with a diamond in her nose.

It's a colorful place: there was a ring of people two or three deep by the bar, a bar of pure 1950s formica with a metal top. There's a soft yellow ceiling with Deco moldings. Other decorations suggest the Basque country: black-and-white framed photographs, a pelote bat, and a large leather winesack over the door, evidently handed down by some Basque with a prodigious appetite for the grape.

Huge salads start at 5 euros for the *foie de volaille* (chicken liver) to 9 euros for the popular and enormous *cinq diamants* salad of potatoes, eggs, tomatoes, two cheeses, liver, gizzard, bacon, and, of course, greens. There are also reasonably-priced plates of cold cuts and cheese.

Chez Gladines bills itself as a Basque restaurant, specializing in a cuisine of simple and hearty food. The wine is also basic and uncomplicated. Basque specialties are the main event: the chicken, *poulet basquaise*, for 9 euros, *piments piquellos à la morue* (peppers with cod) for 10, eggs in the *piperade* and *omelette Basque*, for 7, and *thon à la Basquaise* (Basque-style tuna) for 11 euros. If you're not feeling especially adventuresome, there's grilled steak with herbs at 10 euros and several duck *plats*.

We tried a dozen *escargots* as an hors d'oeuvre, and they were hot and flavorsome in parsleyed butter. Following that there was *pavé de canard sauce roquefort* (duck in Roquefort sauce) and *cassoulet*, both at 11 euros and both delicious, although the duck was overcooked. It was accompanied by a huge serving of greasy, fried potatoes. *Cassoulet* filled a hot, heavy iron casserole with generous amounts of duck, sausage, and bacon, classic *cassoulet* ingredients along with the white beans. A farmhouse version of the dish but very satisfactory. We had wisely chosen a half-liter of the house Madiran, a big macho red from the South which balanced the *cassoulet*.

In any case it was difficult to concentrate on food with so many young people around joyously celebrating—what? It wasn't the end of the week. Possibly they'd passed their exams. The feeling of Chez Gladine was happy, exuberant, crazy, and crowded with young life. The hormones were running wild, the flirting was outrageous, and, except for us, there wasn't anyone there over the age of 25.

A young man who could have been actor Gérard Départieu's younger brother asked to borrow our pen. (So that he could write a check and pay his *addition*, we realized.) This happened twice and was not surprising, given the informality of the place. People we'd never seen before said "Goodbye" to us as they left.

Asking our petite waitress about the clientele, she said they were "fac"—university people—generally between 20 and 50 years of age.

❖ *Chez Gladines: an experience everyone should have at some time in their visits to France. If you think the French are reserved, formal, even stuffy, take a look at them here.*

Hawai
82 ave. d'Ivry, 75013 Paris (01.45.86.91.90)
Métro: Porte d'Ivry
Open daily 10:30 A.M.–3:00 P.M., 6 P.M.–11:00 P.M.

This is a book about French bistros and restaurants, places where you can enjoy French cuisine. But one night when Parisian friends offered to take us to a true remnant of colonial France, a place they describe as "la cantine de Saigon," we could not refuse.

"Little Vietnam" is what our French friends call Hawai and the area around it, and that's what it seems to be. In Hawai there's no attempt at decor: the look is basic, even brutal. Cheap paper covers formica tables, the walls are lined with ordinary-looking mirrors, a piece of hollowed-out bamboo holds spoons and chopsticks on each table. Plastic-coated menus are thrust at you briefly before being grabbed away: you're expected to make choices in seconds. Food is slapped down in front of you and, if you're lucky, you might get a thin paper napkin.

Yet Hawai is full of noisy, happy diners, French as well as Asian. Why?—it's authentic. Hawai is to Vietnamese restaurants in Paris what Katz's is to New York delis. Waiters at Hawai rush around with the signature dish, the huge white porcelain bowls of soup that must hold a gallon of the steaming broth. Our Parisian friends joked that some of the food must also have a taste of *pouce de serveur* (waiter's thumb), so slapdash is the service. The same friends come here in the morning and see people consuming bowlfuls of the nourishing stuff, a typical Vietnamese breakfast.

If you want soup, it starts at 6 euros for the one most people order, *soupe aux boulottes de boeuf.* A spring roll is 4 euros—and it is good, delicately flavored with shrimp, rice noodles, a little lettuce, and mint. There are *brochettes de crevettes* (shrimp on a skewer) for 8 euros, and a dish of *pate imperial "nem,"* or crunchy, greasy little rolls, fried with a filling of ground pork and served with *nuoc-mam,* a dipping sauce, for 6 euros. One friend ordered the *riz au porc grillé,* grilled pork ribs with rice and carrots, with a light coating of flavorful sweet-and-sour sauce.

The highlight of our meal was when the bowl of soup was served, or, one should say, slammed down unceremoniously in front of us. The *plat de résistance*, which almost everyone orders, looked like a gallon of flavorful beef broth with thin slices of beef, noodles, sliced onions, and cilantro. "Une nourriture très parfumée" (very savory food), commented our friend, finding the soup appetizing but in such an impossibly large quantity that he could only finish half of it.

❖ *Hawai: service minimal if not rudely brusque, decor nonexistent, but this feels like the real thing from the back streets of Saigon. Always full despite its shortcomings.*

Chez Louise
55 rue Barrault, 75013 Paris (01.45.80.92.44)
Métro: Corvisart
Closed weekends and in August

Near the Place d'Italie in the 13th district, Chez Louise is not a place you'd happen upon by accident, being off the beaten path and not in a tourist district. That is unfortunate, because their 10-euro menu is one of the best values we've seen.

Chez Louise has the simple bright honesty of a local restaurant. At lunch three courses are available for 10 euros, at night just two. Wines are affordable and good: a *demi* of red, white, or rosé from the South is only 5 euros.

The *mousse Saint-Jacques* was a light hors d'oeuvre, a molding of scallops and cream with *crème fraîche* and chives. *Concombres à la crème* were very fresh, like just-sliced cucumber. Accompanying them was a *baguette* that tasted as if it had come right from the oven.

We were pleased with our main dishes; an *escalope de dinde* was sautéed crisp and golden, with tagliatelli and, surprisingly, tartar sauce on the side. Topped with tomato and parsley, it was well-flavored and substantial. The *grenadier* (a delicate white-fleshed sea fish) in a subtle sauce with saffron, brought raves from the friends who'd ordered it—and were then forced to share. *Boeuf bourguignon* had been slowly simmered in its broth rich with beef and tomato flavors, and could be cut with a fork.

Desserts were admirably done: the *crème renversée aux pruneaux* in a red wine sauce had a flavor of cherries, red wine, and probably a touch of liqueur. The *charlotte aux poires* came with pear and chocolate sauce, artfully divided across the plate. Later we asked the chef how he had made this, and heard knowledgeable discourse on *crème anglaise, crème montée, gélatine, poires,* and *Poire Williams,* all of which had gone into this delicate and delicious dessert. The *tarte au chocolat* was less successful, rather too sweet, but it must have been popular, as only one portion was still available.

❖ *Chez Louise: unbeatable prices for quality food. Worth seeking out if you don't mind a walk from the métro.*

La Régalade
49 ave. Jean Moulin, 75014 Paris (01.45.45.68.58)
Metro: Alésia
Tue–Fri noon–2:00 P.M., 7:00–midnight, Sat eves only,
closed August

Way off in a remote corner of the city, near the end of the métro line going into the southern reaches of the Left Bank, there's a restaurant where it's almost impossible to get reservations. With some luck, we finally achieved a 7:00 P.M. booking. We were seated with other foreigners and found ourselves in a corner near a Texan man with the girth and dramatic presence of an Orson Welles. He was already tucking into a *pigeon rôti* and a bottle of Côte Rôtie.

La Régalade has a simple, bistro interior. It's small, with little tables clustered together. It has a homey look, with huge breads and bottles of wine clustered around a sort of pillar in the center of the room. The service was warm and friendly, the waitresses ready to translate or explain the menu.

This is one of those rare places where you have the feeling that all you have to do is sit back, fasten your seatbelt, and see what the person behind the scenes will do to amaze you.

When our gazpacho came to the table, we were presented with a large plate bearing a small, icy *sorbet de tomate* in the center. We looked at it aghast. Was this evening going to be an experience of nouvelle-cuisine-type deprivation? But no—next the waiter brought a huge terrine of green gazpacho, composed of *morue* and *cresson* (salt cod and watercress) to surround the icy sorbet and to feast on almost indefinitely. The other hors d'oeuvre was a delicately-flavored *foie gras de canard en gelée*, beautifully presented with portions of prunes and currants surrounding the foie gras for added flavor contrasts, all in a lightly flavored aspic.

One main dish, *lieu* (pollock) came in a rich sauce with *girolles* (wild mushrooms). The other was a perfectly cooked *pièce de boeuf*; this is a place that takes your order about how you want your steak cooked seriously. An unusual sauce of *anchois*, *pommes* and *girolles* (anchovies, apples, and wild mushrooms) heightened the flavor. For wine we chose the 17-euro Crest Côtes de Roussillon, a rich red from the South, which went nicely with both meals.

While tasting these rare dishes we were entertained by our neighbor. A born raconteur, he was enjoying a *hachis parmentier boudin noir* (meat loaf of blood sausage and potatoes) and said after that it was one of the best he'd ever tasted. With a little encouragement, he went on in detail about a fascinating character he'd worked with, the great Texas criminal lawyer Racehorse Haynes: "He could do anything he wanted with a jury," he said, adding a little ruefully, "The only thing he couldn't do was pass on his talent."

Then came individual puffed and golden Grand Marnier soufflés, a perfect conclusion to a memorable meal. But in the manner of the great restaurants, La Régalade hadn't quite finished with us: just before we asked for the *addition*, a small basket lined with a napkin was delivered to our table. In it, two madeleines (shell-shaped cakes). In Shakespeare's England, rosemary is for remembrance. In Proust's Paris, it's the madeleines.

❖ *La Régalade: one of the best bistros in Paris. Reserve early.*

Le Temps des Cerises
30 de la Butte aux Cailles, 75013 Paris (01.45.89.69.48)
Métro: Place d'Italie
Mon–Fri noon–3:00 P.M., 7:30 P.M.–11:00 P.M., Sat eves only
No reservations

Le Temps des Cerises is popular. Too popular. A look inside and we knew we had a problem. The place was hectic, earsplitting, and jammed; we edged our way in and were told it would be at least a half-hour wait for the three of us. French families with children were crowded at the long tables and heaping plates of *crudités*—raw vegetables, a popular starter—were being carried past.

When we finally got to a table at 10:15, Le Temps was still full of loud diners, young people speaking at the tops of their voices because it was the only possible way to be heard.

We noticed that the 12-euro menu featured *boudin* and *androuillette* (blood and chitterling sausage), but at 18 euros there were other possibilities. This menu offered good hors d'oeuvres: the *saumon* was an impressive plate, with large slices of smoked salmon, *crème fraîche*, black olives, tomatoes, sliced cucumbers, and, a surprise, little slices of fresh mango. *Tarte à l'indienne* was a cooked vegetable tart (eggplant, zucchini, onion, etc.) with a dash of curry, served with a large lettuce salad. The *féroce de morue* was a small dish of cod, with chopped parsley, black olives, basil, and *crème fraîche,* with avocado binding the mixture and a touch of hot pepper adding piquancy.

Huge plates of *filet mignon de porc* (pork filet) came with giant helpings of crisp gold French fries, the pork with an artichoke and cream sauce, cooked perfectly, moist, tender, and delicious. Little quails—*caille aux cerises*—had a flavorful sauce strongly imbued with the flavor of the black cherries which accompanied them, along with red leaf lettuce and a heaping portion of *frites*.

Desserts were brought just as we were starting to think nervously about the last métro, one of us receiving a cheese plate with not one but three cheeses: Cantal, Saint Nectaire, and Fourme d'Ambert, another getting *bavarois aux framboises* (raspberry bavarian), in a *coulis* of raspberries, and the third the coffee ice cream dessert, *liégois au café*. Hastily downing desserts (we hoped to catch that métro after all), we left after midnight.

❖ *Le Temps des Cerises: in a down-to-earth setting, food of surprising subtlety. Excellent value.*

PRIVILEGE AND PROSPERITY: THE 15TH & 16TH ARRONDISSEMENTS

Neither the working class nor the poor have any place in this perpetual garden party which goes on year in year out between the place Victor Hugo and the Seine. All the ceremonial occasions of Passy-Auteuil see the same troop of guests... they confer on the social events of the seizième arrondissement a slight air of comic opera which is not without charm.

—Léon-Paul Fargue

The 16th arrondissement is richer in fine apartments and great mansions than it is in bistros. Although it is home to some of the great and famous, a curious dullness pervades the area. You can walk for blocks without finding an inviting café or a newsstand. Wealth acts as a shield, insulating the denizens of the 16th from dirt, noise, and the unexpected, but also from the excitement and stimulus of the outside world. Cars disappear into underground lots, nannies appear at regular intervals to walk dogs and children, and a heavy Sunday silence lingers over all.

People who live in the 16th district always seem to mention it in much the same way that Harvard graduates will casually slide their schooling into a conversation. Both the 15th and 16th districts seem more spacious, more private in a sense than other districts, and both feel like a newer part of Paris. There are good bistros here, but considering the wealth of the population, fewer than one might imagine. Rents are high and young chefs struggling to develop a clientele usually can't afford them.

Writer Julien Green remembered growing up in Passy, a suburb in the 16th district just west of the Eiffel Tower.

He found the old townhouses with their gardens enchanting. But he remembered another section of Passy less favorably: "The other Passy, the prosperous Passy, I loathed even as a child. There was a kind of wealth that made me want to weep because of a certain quality of severity and arrogance in those strutting balconies, unwelcoming carriage entrances, and sumptuous porter's lodges."

Other writers made their homes in the 16th district. Molière lived in a house at what is now 62 avenue Théophile-Gaultier. One evening his guests—they might have included Racine and La Fontaine—had drunk more than they should. They decided impulsively to commit suicide en masse by throwing themselves in the Seine. Molière got them to hold off until the following day, when, as he said, their act would be seen by the public and would make more of an impression. The project was put off indefinitely.

Like the 16th, the 15th district is not an area for pleasure-seekers. There's nowhere in the area to go for fun. Quiet and bourgeois, with a few small parks (the French call them "squares"), the odd hospital and several schools, the 15th is not a quarter you're likely to frequent unless you're visiting a friend or making an effort to go to a good restaurant. It's a pleasant part of the city but not especially memorable for the visitor.

Some dining possibilities in an expensive area:

Bélisaire
2 rue Marmontel, 75015 Paris (01.48.28.62.24)
Métro: Convention
Mon–Fri noon–2:00 P.M., 8:00 P.M.–11:00 P.M., Sat dinner only, closed Sun and August

We'd already been let in on the secret about Bélisaire: it's a favorite restaurant of some top officials at the nearby Cordon Bleu, the famed cooking school. When we went there to try out this little bistro on a side street, it was not hard to understand why aficionados might want to keep it quiet.

Small—rustic—welcoming is the feeling at Bélisaire. Good smells from the kitchen waft toward you as you enter this

friendly place, and you know you've come to the right spot.

The lunch menu changes daily, and a recent one promised intriguing starters: *gratin de moules aux épinards* (mussels with spinach), *poêlon d'escargots à la crème* (sautéed snails with cream), *crème glacée de poivrons verts* (cold green pepper soup). They could be followed by *pavé de saumon poêlée aux courgettes* (salmon sautéed with zucchini), *foie de veau poêlé* (sautéed calf's liver), *bavette sauce au poivre* (steak with pepper sauce), *confit de canard* (preserved duck), and a choice of desserts.

Crème glacée de poivrons verts was a delicately-flavored, cold cream soup made from green bell peppers and potatoes, but with a refined aspect that didn't seem to owe its origins to either of these humble ingredients. *Gratin de moules,* served hot in a small cast-iron dish, was intense and satisfying, with flavors of mussels and cheese.

The *dos de saumon* on a bed of zucchini and eggplant came with an artistic dusting of pepper. An intriguing treatment of a classic: *dos de saumon* prepared with care and imagination, the first-rate salmon hot on its bed of vegetables. The *bavette sauce au poivre* for the meat-eater in the party was a flavorful steak with a good sauce, accompanied by a ramekin-shaped mound of scalloped potatoes.

Dessert was similarly above our expectations. We chose an *entremet poire-caramel,* layers of pear, *génoise,* and caramel. Accompanied by a caramelized wafer, it was an assembly of the luscious flavor of fresh pears at their peak of ripeness with fine-textured white cake and a caramel glaze.

A young and gifted chef, Matthieu Garrel, is responsible for the culinary surprises emerging from the kitchen of this small bistro. He likes to cook with seafood and is intent on pleasing his clientele, a combination that is sure to earn him a reputation.

❖ *Bélisaire: cooking in the great tradition of old France.*

Le Bistro d'Hubert
41 blvd Pasteur, 75015 Paris (01.47.34.15.50)
Métro: Pasteur
Open daily 12:30 P.M.–2:30 P.M., 7:30 P.M.–10:30 P.M., except Sat lunch

The setting chez Hubert is attractively simple, like Martha Stewart's idea of a Provençal kitchen: white tables and chairs, simple blue, yellow, and white tablecloths, and a terra cotta tile floor, the sort you see in the South. On one side, old armoires in dark wood and a white glass-fronted kitchen cupboard, displaying old porcelain canisters, jams, and *eaux de vie.* On the other side, strings of garlic, an old madeleine mold, bright red peppers, and other useful things.

The ambiance is at once relaxed and busy: the clientele are, for the most part, casually-dressed French people. This was a Saturday night, not unseasonably warm, but we saw very few coats and ties around. The young staff are kept busy running to the open kitchen where you can watch energetic young cooks at work.

A 23-euro menu weekdays at noon offers no choices; a larger menu is available weekday evenings at 28 euros. On Saturday nights only the 32-euro menu is available. One unusual feature of this bistro is that it offers both a "traditional" and a "contemporary" menu, all of the dishes described in loving detail, so you can choose from old-fashioned or modern fare.

Our friendly server brought us a pre-starter of duck pâté with slices of toasted baguette. Following was the *gâteau de crabe,* well-presented and flanked by hearts of palm and little slices of sweet red pepper, drizzled in an attractive pattern with a vinaigrette topped with chives. The *carpaccio de taurillon argentin* (thin slices of smoked beef from Argentina) was attractively presented but tasted curiously bland. A comment brought a salmon mousse layered with onion and tomato, as delicious as it looked.

Main dishes on the contemporary side of the menu were mostly fish, and were tasty and appealing: a *pavé de thon* (sautéed tuna) looked like beef filet on a bed of spinach, surrounded by an artistic sprinkle of the sweet sauce made from balsamic vinegar, with zucchini and carrots in a dish on the side. A generous portion of *morue* (salt cod) was topped with crisp fried sprouts and slivers of crisp onion, all in a delicately-flavored sauce.

The amusing wordiness on Hubert's menu extends to desserts: what would be a *fondant au chocolat* anywhere else is here a *sublime de chocolat caraïbe aux griottines à l'eau de vie, sabayon d'orange et nougatine au sésame.* A special effort is made to present food attractively; the above-mentioned dessert came shaped like a leaf, topped with a mint leaf, with three small cherries on the side, and an orange sauce. (The three cherries took up seven words in the menu: *aux griottines à l'eau de vie).* But the desserts tasted good and were an appropriate conclusion to a good meal.

❖ *Bistro d'Hubert: imaginative offerings for a largely BCBG (yuppie) crowd.*

Café Dapper
in Musée Dapper, 35 bis rue Paul Valéry, 75016 Paris
(01.45.00.31.73)
Métro: Victor Hugo
Open daily 11:00 P.M.–7:00 P.M.

The Musée Dapper is Paris's museum of African art. The museum is well worth seeing, but the café downstairs is interesting in its own right. Sleek and modern, with colors of chocolate brown and deep cream, it's so posh that the tables swing about on ball bearings.

The café offers appetizing, low-priced lunches and friendly service. A typical lunch might be salad, with small salads at 5 euros, and larger ones for 8. You can create your own salad, asking them to put on a plate ingredients that you choose from a list, creating combinations that might include items like grated carrots, tabouli, endives and Roquefort, celery with walnuts and apples, cucumbers and chives, potatoes and tuna with mayonnaise.

Food is remarkably good and very inexpensive for the area. There's a 5-euro *soupe du jour*, a quiche at the same price, and hot pasta for 8 euros. Lunch *formules* or fixed-price menus allow you a quiche-and-salad lunch for as little as 8 euros. Wine is available by the glass, and bottles are fairly priced.

❖ *Café Dapper: good food and surprisingly low prices in a sophisticated setting. Ideal for a pleasant lunch with friends.*

Le Directoire
41 rue Alain Chartier, 75015 Paris (01.40.45.08.02)
Métro: Convention
Open daily to 1 A.M.

Le Directoire is a bar-brasserie that's popular with working people in the neighborhood. It has a large terrace sheltered by a purple awning. The same flamboyant color is carried on in the wicker chairs. Inside, enlarged prints from old postcards give you an idea of what life in the neighborhood was like many years ago.

Well known for serving good *croque-monsieurs,* Le Directoire also offers reasonably-priced soup at 5 euros, quiche for 6, and a plate of *jambon du pays* or cured country ham, for 7 euros. The famous *croque-monsieurs* (hot toasted ham and cheese sandwiches) come in at 6 euros, with a *croque-madame,* which is simply a *croque-monsieur* garnished with a fried egg, at the same price.

❖ *Le Directoire: good for a drink or even a small meal.*

L'Os à Moëlle
3 rue Vasco da Gama, 75015 Paris (01.45.57.27.27)
Métro: Lourmel
Tue–Sat noon–2:00 P.M., 7:00 P.M.–11:00 P.M.,
closed August

L'Os à Moëlle attracts the inquisitive gourmet that lurks in each of us. How many times have you wanted just a taste of something special, a hint of novelty, a subtle surprise? L'Os will give you that and more, in numerous courses.

The 32-euro tasting menu changes daily and offers the diner many small dishes to try, the creations of Thierry Faucher, the gifted chef. We started with *amuse-gueules,* small cream puffs with a slight favor of cheese—light and tempting. We went on to taste a cold soup: first we were served a few melon balls with shreds of Parma ham, then the cold melon concoction was ladled in, and we savored the sweetness of summer cantaloupe at its peak, with shreds of ginger and ham to accentuate the flavors.

"Ça a été?" asked our waitress, and we responded yes, the soup had been good.

Next three succulent oysters, lightly cooked and served on the half shell with herb butter. A third course had us baffled until it appeared: *moelleux de homard à la pommes écrasées et sa crème* consisted of a light fluff of whipped potatoes in the middle of a lobster-colored cream sauce, the potatoes concealing little chunks of lobster.

The main dish was *suprême de canard poêlé au miel et épices,* a little piece of duck served hot on a sizzling platter with allspice, honey, and sauerkraut. The duck was good, although slightly underdone for our tastes. (Sharper knives would have helped us to deal with it.)

Then the cheese course: a round of white *fromage fermier* accompanied by a few leaves of lettuce. Tasty with the slightly sourdough flavor of the accompanying *pain de campagne* (country bread).

Desserts are a speciality of L'Os à Moëlle, and this is why you're asked to make your choice when you first arrive. We had ordered *quenelles au chocolat* and *baba au rhum.* The *quenelle* was a large shell-shaped serving of chocolate mousse on *crème anglaise,* with a light sifting of cocoa and a few caramelized almonds on the side. Rich and delicious. Rum babas were tiny, served with strawberries, blackberries, and a puff of whipped cream, an appealing combination.

L'Os à Moëlle presents a plain setting for serious dining. Diners there are right to be intrigued by each night's offerings, seeing what a talented chef can find in the market and translate into a memorable meal.

❖ *L'Os à Moëlle: sample the creative offerings of a dedicated chef.*

Parvis du Musée d'Art Moderne de la Ville de Paris
11 ave du President Wilson, 75016 Paris (01.53.67.40.47)
Métro: Alma Marceau
Tue–Fri 10:00 A.M.–5:30 P.M., weekends to 7:00 P.M.
No credit cards

The café of this modern art museum is a hidden treasure in the pricey 16th arrondissement. At the end of the street, at 11 avenue du Président Wilson, you find a large, imposing museum with cashiers waiting for you to pay to get in. But to eat in the café, you don't even need to enter the museum proper. Simply ask, "Le café?" and go in the direction they point.

You'll enter a café with a spacious outside terrace, sheltered by arborvitae and large tent-like parasols over elegant modern teak tables and chairs. There's a view of the river and of the Eiffel Tower.

You could just have a drink—coffee is 3 euros, a soft drink 4—but if you're there around lunchtime, you may be tempted to try the salads: large salads available for 10 euros include chef, curried chicken, and garden salad. Hot dishes including quiches are a possibility too.

Seeing young business people around us lunching on enormous salads, we decided to order one. The 10-euro chef's salad—on a base of greens were slices of ham, cheese, tomato, turkey, and a topping of a whole hard-boiled egg—was large enough to share. Very tasty. Our friend enjoyed a mixed salad of Auvergne ham and Parmesan cheese on greens. "Lovely—delicious—divine," she trilled.

In the afternoon the Café becomes a *salon de thé,* with a good selection of desserts at 6 euros; typically there are several tarts, fresh fruit salad, and various ice cream sundaes to enjoy with tea or coffee.

❖ *The Café du Musée de l'Art Moderne: well worth a stop—far preferable to the pricey establishments on the Champs-Elysées.*

Le Petit Rétro
5 rue Mesnil, 75016 Paris (01.44.05.06.05)
Métro: Victor Hugo
Mon–Fri lunch and dinner, Sat dinner only,
closed 2 weeks in August

Le Petit Retro was recommended by a friend who lives in the 16th district. "They have lovely *langoustines,*" she said. *Langoustines* (prawns) weren't on the menu when we went there, but we did enjoy Le Petit Retro's charming ambiance while we scanned the menu for possibilities.

The first thing you notice here are the tiles, stylized Art Nouveau poppies on old tiles on the walls and ceiling of the front room. Apricot petals and dark-green leaves with burgundy touches swirl with a grace and a freedom that Mucha himself might have approved, all against the background of white and yellow.

A long zinc bar is crowned with a champagne bucket bearing fresh flowers that complement the tiles, repeating the colors of yellow and white in chrysanthemums and asters. Large green plants in the corner carry on the feeling of freshness and life.

A little awed by the setting, we had a moment to contemplate the *ardoise*, where the lunch menu was chalked up, before it disappeared and we had to make choices. For lunch that day, *crème glacée de concombre* (cold cucumber soup) and *ravioli de tomate et ricotta* (tomato and ricotta-stuffed ravioli) were possible hors d'oeuvres; main dishes were *rascasse aux ravioli* (scorpion fish with ravioli) and *beignets d'agneau et pommes dauphinois* (lamb fritters and scalloped potatoes), with *clafoutis de fruits frais* (cake of fresh fruit) for dessert.

A small number of French customers were sitting near the door when we entered—elderly, well-fed denizens of the 16th district.

Intensely-flavored cold cucumber soup was a promising start: a generous serving came with color added by a garnish of cherry tomatoes and flat-leafed parsley. The other hors d'oeuvre, a pasta salad, was being consumed with relish by a young Parisienne.

A fair range of wines was offered, 4 euros or more by the glass or 14 euros by the bottle, with a few half bottles available.

The scorpion fish or *rascasse* had been cooked in olive oil and was served with a large helping of ravioli and bright touches of tomato and scallions. The piece of fish was undersized, the pasta bland. Lamb chops in puffed "beignet" coatings were more successful. They had good flavor, the crisp coating giving added interest to this dish, which was served with precisely-sliced potatoes and crisp *haricots verts*.

An unusual *clafoutis*, a cake made not with the usual cherries but with apples and bananas on a bed of *coulis de fruits rouges* (red fruit sauce) appeared for dessert. A satisfactory conclusion.

❖ *Le Petit Retro*: cuisine familiale *in a very attractive setting.*

Le Tie Break
36 rue de Danzig, 75015 Paris (01.45.31.07.99)
Métro: Convention
Mon–Fri noon–2:00 P.M., 7:30 P.M.–10:00 P.M., Sat dinner
only, closed August

"Eating here could be as cheap as eating at home," reports Katherine, who lives in the area and put us on to this budget find. An 11-euro evening menu gives you an hors d'oeuvre and *plat*, or a *plat* and dessert, and a quarter carafe of rosé or red wine, a beer or mineral water. Not only that, there's a good range of possibilities, with salads, herring, the classic *oeuf mayonnaise*, and a *terrine maison* to start.

Main dishes typically include pork with mustard sauce, steak with pepper sauce, a *brochette de boeuf*—beef on a skewer, *androuillette grillée* (grilled chitterling sausage), and the fish of the day. Desserts are the usual classics with a few surprises.

While waiting with friends, we took in the Tie Break's ambiance. The look is of provincial France, with the old-fashioned wooden bar, red-and-white checked tablecloths, and linoleum floor. A large mosaic of a soccer player gives one the idea of the proprietors' lively interest in sports.

Hors d'oeuvres were very fresh and attractively displayed on lettuce. At noon, besides the regular menu, salad lovers enjoy giant salads. For 8 euros one can choose a *salade paysanne*, with tomatoes, bacon, cheese, green beans and corn, a *salade landaise*, duck breast, gizzards, tomatoes, green beans and lettuce, or a *salade exotique*, of ham, turkey, pineapple, and Gruyère cheese.

The *cabillaud* (fresh cod) was in a good sorrel sauce with white rice and green beans. Properly cooked, it was served in a generous portion: an outstanding meal for the money. The *escalope de dinde* was also well done, a tasty turkey cutlet breaded and sautéed, in a cream sauce.

Desserts at Tie Break are excellent: particularly impressive was the *gâteau au citron et framboise*, a bavarian cream with layers of lemon and raspberry on a cake base, served in a bright *coulis de framboise*, or raspberry sauce. Not the sort of thing one expects to find in a budget restaurant. The *mousse au chocolat* was just as we like it, intense flavors of bittersweet chocolate in a creamy-textured mousse.

❖ *Le Tie Break: outstanding value at minimal prices. Art lovers who come here will want to see La Ruche, a place that once sheltered some of the greatest artists of the twentieth century, only a block away.*

Le Totem
Musée de l'Homme, 17 Place du Trocadéro, 75016 Paris
(01.47.27.28.29)
Métro: Trocadéro
Open daily noon–midnight

You can unpack your Jean-Paul Gaultiers and your Issey Miyakes's—here's a place where you can wear them and feel right at home. Le Totem, the restaurant on the ground floor of the Musée de l'Homme, attracts a large number of young, tanned, and sophisticated Parisians. It's a dramatic room, and carefully set spotlights provide the illusion of being on stage. Everyone should feel comfortable, however: Totem is a friendly place with a buzz of happy sounds.

For an incomparable view of the Eiffel Tower and the city behind it, you need only to order coffee for 3 euros or some other drink on the terrace at Le Totem. If you're just a little hungry, still on the café–*salon de thé* side, they offer antipasto, *salade niçoise*, or a cheese plate for from 7 to 12 euros. You sip your drink on a breezy terrace overlooking the Place de Trocadéro.

The Eiffel Tower is an artist's version of a triangle, lit up against the blue fading into purple of the night sky.

Intermittent sparks of flash bulb lights around are its glowworms, our age's homage to Monsieur Eiffel. You think of all the people you wish were there with you to take in so incomparable a view.

Incomparable, that is, except to the Parisians, several of whom sit with their backs to the Tower.

Behind us is the Musée de l'Homme, with the serene strong lines of its Art Moderne origins. As the sky darkens and takes on shades of coral, the tower lights up. It's the quintessential symbol of Paris.

❖ *Le Totem: a view you should not miss. At dusk watch the twinkle of lights coming on all over the city.*

Le Troquet
21 rue François Bonvin, 75015 Paris (01.45.66.89.00)
Métro: Cambronne
Tue–Sat noon–2:00 P.M., 7:30 P.M.–11:00 P.M.

At Le Troquet the chef, Christian Etchebest, is a hefty young fellow who looks as if he'd be more at ease behind the wheel of a semi than dabbling in the culinary arts. But Etchebest, who worked with Christian Constant at Le Crillon, creates a refined and innovative cuisine that has people coming from all over to this little bistro on a side street in the 15th district.

A long, rectangular room with tables around the edges filled with BCBGs (yuppies) in animated conversation, Le Troquet has high ceilings and Lalique-style light fixtures, no two alike, suspended from the ceiling.

One day the fixed-price menu choices were *gaspacho façon Troquet, marbré de sardines avec péquillas* (gaspacho with slivers of sardine and peppers) followed by *morue façon Bascayenne* (salt cod Basque-style), *caille façon crapaudine* (breaded and grilled quail), and cheese or dessert. Lunch is 22 euros for three courses, 24 for four, and dinner for 30.

Starters were excellent: lightly spiced gazpacho with tiny diced vegetables, colorful and crunchy textures, the flavor of tomato enhanced with a little balsamic vinegar. The *marbre de sardines* was marinated sardines cleverly presented as a *roulade*, rolled with sweet red bell peppers and tiny diced vegetables, all bound by thinly sliced zucchini. Beside the sardine-and-vegetable roulade was a garnish of lightly sautéed greens.

Morue façon Bascayenne was cod served on a purée of tomatoes, rich and concentrated; the *caille façon crapaudine* was crisp portions of quail on a sauce of a pleasing intensity with touches of sweetness, complex and scrumptious, with potatoes, peas, and carrots served in a separate ramekin.

Service at Le Troquet is friendly without being intrusive, the "Ça a été?" (How was it?) being asked after, not during, the meal.

Desserts looked like something from *Gourmet Magazine*: a *compôte de rhubarbe* was stewed rhubarb with citrus undertones, topped by a *quenelle* of strawberry sorbet and encircled by a rhubarb-flavored syrup. The whole was a more delicious rhubarb dessert than one could ever have imagined. The other dessert was a large almond-flavored macaroon filled with vanilla cream—surely some real vanilla beans featured in its creation—served on crunchy, lightly grilled apricots. A delightful ending to a memorable meal.

Chatting with the chef afterwards, we brought up the subject of bistros, and he was generous enough to recommend some of the very stars of this collection, other chefs trained by Christian Constant at Le Crillon. Constant and others like him have inspired a generation of young chefs who have revolutionized the bistro scene in Paris.

❖ *Le Troquet: one of the outstanding new bistros of Paris. Exceptional cuisine at reasonable prices.*

ESCAPE FROM CONVENTION: THE 17TH & 18TH ARRONDISSEMENTS

Night is coming on, the night of the boulevards, with the sky as red as hell-fire and from Clichy to Barbès a fretwork of open tombs. The soft Paris night, like a ladder of toothless gums and the ghouls grinning behind the rungs.... It's in the night that Sacré-Coeur stands out in all its stinking loveliness. Then it is that the heavy whiteness of her skin and her humid stone breath clamps down on the blood like a valve.

—Henry Miller

ook up toward Sacré Coeur, rising like a white exclamation point into the northern sky, and you're looking at Montmartre. Unlike its sister districts, Montmartre is an area apart, a hill where narrow streets circle around, dilapidated buildings remain standing, where the poverty that has clung to the hill would inspire an Aristide Bruant to celebrate the unfortunate, the little, forgotten people of Montmartre in his songs. Here in the stillness of the side streets you can imagine that on some parts of the hill there are still clusters of windmills turning in the wind of early dawn, instead of the two which survive to our day.

Rue Lepic runs around the slope, with the more famous windmill, the Moulin de la Galette, at number 77. This former cabaret, immortalized by the Impressionists, can best be glimpsed from rue Tholozé. Just south of the other remaining mill, Moulin Radet on the rue Lepic, is the Place Emile-Goudreau. At number 13 of this Place was the Bateau Lavoir, which once sheltered Picasso, Max Jacob, Juan Gris, Georges Braque, Guillaume Apollinaire, and others. Here in 1906

Picasso started his own revolution by creating the first Cubist work, *Les Demoiselles d'Avignon.*

Montmartre has remained a village unto itself, somehow resisting being drawn into the city. There's a vast tolerance here, tolerance even for the Place du Tertre, where the clichés in oil and acrylic are sold, and the price of a cup of coffee equals that on the rue St. Honoré or the Café de la Paix.

Outside of the turbulent Place du Tertre, Montmartre keeps its own special and distinctive character. Go farther away from the Place and you will see what we mean. The sense of being in a town rather than a capital city is palpable around the Lapin Agile, that picturesque old cottage, where you can imagine young Picasso paying his way with a Harlequin painting to gain entrance to the singing and revelry within.

> *The Place des Abbesses with its Métro station, the théâtre de l'Atelier, which looked like a toy or a stage set, and its bistros and small shops, seemed to the inspector far more the genuine working-class Montmartre than the Place du Tertre, which had become a tourist trap...*

—Georges Simenon, *Maigret & the Saturday Caller*

If you admire Art Nouveau, the best approach to Montmartre is by métro to Abbesses. You emerge into daylight at one of the best preserved of Hector Guimard's remaining métro entrances. In the same square you can study an Art Nouveau church, St. Jean-L'Evangéliste.

On the lower slopes of Montmartre, the little bistros and restaurants retain the ambiance of local hangouts possibly not unlike those in your own neighborhood; the proprietor greets you with a warmth that does not seem feigned, and you find yourself in a milieu that you would enjoy going back to.

What is there to see at the top? Sacré-Coeur, of course; the Place du Tertre that gives the visitor struggling through the loud and frenzied crowds a good opportunity to discover how masochistic he or she can be; the Lapin Agile; possibly the Musée de Montmartre; a few artists' addresses; and, other than that, the whole city of Paris, spread out before you in all of its splendor when you stand near Sacré Coeur looking down the hill.

> *Around ten thirty a drumroll announced the floorshow. The lights went out, the projectors focused on the dance show, which was then invaded with a triumphant yell by the cancan dancers in a flourish of flying skirt....*

—Georges Simenon, *Les Anneaux de Bicêtre*

Below on the boulevard de Clichy is the Moulin Rouge. "The last word in sin and iniquity," decided William Faulkner in a letter written in 1925, explaining, "It is a music hall, a vaudeville, where ladies come out clothed principally in lip stick." The Moulin Rouge is no longer the last word in anything, but its eye-catching façade with lights and posters of the latest attraction liven an extent of the boulevard Clichy that is dedicated mostly to drab sex shops and bars.

In the 1920s, some residents of the 18th district were famous men in the making who all seemed to know each other. Toulouse Lautrec and Aristide Bruant were friends. Salvador Dali lived at 7 rue Becquerel with Gala, the wife of the surrealist poet Paul Eluard. When Dali first came to Paris in 1927, he met Pablo Picasso and Joan Miró. Dali was also friends with the Spanish filmmaker Luis Buñuel.

A cousin to the 18th district is the 17th, on the western side of Montmartre. Part of the 17th has something of the same character as the 18th: part of it is more chic, with neighborhoods good enough for anyone and better than most of us are used to, near the Arc de Triomphe. We have seen elegant apartments in the 17th with high ceilings, parquet floors, and the elaborate carved wood panels that the French call *boiserie*. But for us the 17th is associated with our memories of the modest *quartier populaire*, with street markets and a large immigrant population selling and haggling over the merchandise, near the Place de Clichy and La Fourche.

A professor who still lives near the Place de Clichy used to joke about the increasingly colorful character of her area. "Il y a des travesties qui sortent la nuit," she remarked. "On peut les voir vers minuit" (Transvestites go out at night—you can see them around midnight). She kept a large black dog of indeterminate origin which she referred to as her "grosse bête"—large beast. He was, we suspect, kept more for reasons of style than to ward off transvestites or anyone else. His black coat stood out in the small apartment which she had painted white even to the floorboards.

With the village air of the narrow side streets and the well known, over-publicized nightclubs of "Gay Paree," the 17th and 18th districts are a study in contrast. They also appear to be places where working artists could continue to exist. If the nightlife, so well documented in the paintings of Toulouse-Lautrec and the Impressionists, still continues to thrive, might not the creativity be still alive in countless little ateliers?

When most people think of Montmartre their images are of mysterious windmills and can-can dancers in nightclubs, bad painters and areas of kitsch crammed together in the Place du Tertre. They might remember Sacré Coeur, the smelly tourist buses clustered near the Moulin Rouge, and maybe even Picasso and Utrillo. But there's another Montmartre, a part of Paris that's residential, middle class, very respectable, and surprisingly quiet. It's a place where people don't drive like madmen and the painter is probably someone who comes by to touch up the doors and windows.

If you're looking for the "real" Montmartre, try these bistros:

L'Eté en Pente Douce
23 rue Muller, 75018 Paris (01.42.64.02.67)
Métro: Anvers
Open daily noon–midnight

If you've ever trudged through the more tiresome parts of tourist Montmartre, pushing your way through crowds and stepping briskly past the art shills who insist on painting your portrait, L'Eté en Pente Douce will be a breath of fresh air. Not all the way up to the top, it's halfway up on the lesser known eastern slope of the hill, There's an excellent view— a park across the street and the lower town down the flight of stairs. (If you don't want to attempt those stairs yourself, try the gentler slope of rue Feutrier).

On the day we went there with a friend, we found a charming café in green and white with a glassed-in terrace and small green tables and chairs, the sort you see in parks, within and without. Little mosaic tiles cover part of the walls with a design of cherries, flanked by impressive borders of retro green. Above is a remarkable ceiling, with extraordinary vintage tiles.

A nice surprise was the prices: the *plat du jour*, a substantial *pintade* (guinea hen) with sautéed potatoes and a little green salad, was only 8 euros. Otherwise there was a vegetarian quiche at 7 euros, *saumon fumé* (smoked salmon), and *filet mignon* (a pork filet) for from 9 to 12 euros.

Servings were large: a quarter of *pintade* was accompanied by an abundance of potatoes and a salad involving greens, carrots, celery, and beets. "Very French and very delicious," announced our friend. The house-made bread, a *pain de seigle*, was dark and substantial. At L'Eté en Pente Douce they bake their bread in the old-fashioned baker's oven, still there from the days in the nineteenth century when this was a bakery.

The service is competent and friendly, and the waiter anticipated our needs. After we'd sat talking over coffee for a long time, he came by with a carafe of chilled water that was just what we wanted.

❖ *L'Eté en Pente Douce: a warm welcome and good* cuisine familiale *halfway up the hill to Sacré Coeur, in a lovely part of old Montmartre not often seen by tourists.*

L'Etrier Bistro
154 rue Lamarck, 75018 Paris (01.42.29.14.01)
Métro: Guy Moquet
Tue–Sat noon–2:00 P.M., 7:30 P.M.–10:30 P.M.,
closed August

This is a quiet, classy little bistro, with whitewashed walls, white floor tiles, and framed botanical prints of fruit above the bar area. Dark green paper tablemats over white linen and green trellis-patterned Giën china are a good contrast with all of that white. Huge windows, too large for traditional café curtains, are covered by an expanse of light, gauzy fabric, swept up here and there by ties of raffia. A nice touch is the small bunch of flowers at each table.

This little restaurant offers a refined and inventive cuisine. The lunch menu is one of the better bargains we've found. Three set lunch *formules* or menus are possible, at 13 and 19 euros. At night there's a 28-euro *prix fixe* menu.

The *escabèche de thon* hors d'oeuvre was unbelievably good for a tuna salad, made as it was with fresh tuna combined with dried tomatoes, onions, and served on little toast rounds with salad greens; one serving of this would be enough for two diners. A *polenta d'aubergine et courgette* was a light, warm, and tasty appetizer, the vegetables layered in polenta and served with crisp greens.

The *parmentier de haddock* was like a *brandade,* the fish combined with mashed potatoes and with diced parsley and chives contributing color and flavor. This in a rich and delicious *beurre blanc* sauce. The roast chicken was well flavored and accompanied by small roast potatoes.

Desserts were good too: a *fondant d'amandes et citron,* an almond-studded cake, was pleasantly light and served with *crème anglaise.* A *tarte aux abricots* had an intense fruit flavor, not marred by excessive sugar, and was complemented by the custard sauce.

❖ *L'Etrier Bistrot: unexpectedly good cuisine in the 18th arrondissement.*

Iroko Bar
7 rue Boursault, 75017 Paris (01.45.22.35.25)
Métro: Rome
Mon–Sat noon–2:00 A.M.

Fed up with the usual café or bistro? Then head north, to métro stop Rome, just west of the Place Clichy to experience something very different.

The first thing you see upon entering the Iroko is just another bar with highly colored walls. But the second room is special: an authentic wagon or train car from the Orient Express of 1925, with polished mahogany woodwork and a feeling of the gilded age. Have you ever read Agatha Christie's *Murder on the Orient Express* or seen the movie? That's what we're talking about. It's not the Jazz Age that's evoked in this old train car, but the richness of the early twentieth century, Edwardian elegance in warm woods, heavy brass luggage racks, curving ceiling, and charming alcoves. Adding to the feeling of time warp, of being in a phantom train speeding toward Constantinople, are the real train sounds coming in from the outside: the Iroko is just beside and above some real railway tracks, and we hear trains en route from Gare St. Lazare to Normandy.

The menu is fairly simple: hors d'oeuvres run from 7 to 8 euros and are generally salads or melon with Parma ham. *Plats,* mostly between 11 and 17 euros, include *émincé de poulet caramelisé* (chicken in a caramelized sauce), *saumon et poireaux* (salmon and leeks), *foie de veau poêlé* (sautéed calf's liver), and *tartare de boeuf* (raw ground round steak). Desserts at 6 euros are conventional: fruit salad, *crème brûlée,* and *moelleux au chocolat,* the last the partially-cooked cake.

But you can have an Orient Express experience for the price of a drink, or, if you're a little hungry, for trying one of the reasonably-priced omelets. We sampled the *émincé de poulet caramelisé,* chicken in a dark, rather sweet sauce, reminding us of various sweet-and-sour Asian sauces. Served with a round of basmati rice and small wedges of tomato, it was exceptional for bar food. A half bottle of rosé, the Côtes de Provence at 8 euros went well with the chicken. Other wines available included a Bordeaux and a Cheverny for 14 euros each by the bottle, or 4 euros by the glass.

❖ *The Iroko Bar: if you're a railway buff, a fan of mysteries, or just like historic places, this little bar-restaurant is for you.*

Aux Négociants
27 rue Lambert, 75018 Paris (01.46.06.15.11)
Métro: Lamarck-Caulaincourt
Mon–Fri lunch, Wed–Fri dinner, closed weekends, August

If you think that this *bistro à vins* looks vaguely familiar, it very well could be. It's long been a favorite of Paris-based photographers and journalists, and the walls are covered with extraordinary photographs taken here, some of them by well-known people. This is Montmartre, but it's the more authentic and less touristy part behind the hill; you can be sure that there will never be tourist buses parked nearby. Almost everyone who comes in is a regular and the clientele look interesting even for Paris. A film director might reject some of them as being too exaggerated in appearance.

Who are they? Workers from the area, intellectuals, and wine-lovers, but no tourists when we've been there: a pity, since Aux Négociants deserves a wider public. Some of the people who wander in look very intriguing—a lanky brunette in black posed against the bar and a white-haired, mustachioed gent near us chatted with the proprietor about a certain vineyard. There were cluckings of tongue and shakings of head over the news that it had recently been sold—"Vendu—il fait la retraite" (Sold—he retired).

Evidently they don't feel they can rely on a newcomer to produce the same quality product.

Aux Négociants is one of the city's best wine bars. Proprietor Jean Navier knows his wines, as you gather from spending some time here.

A few *plats* are available for people requiring more sustenance than the grape. On a recent visit, we chose *saumon aux courgettes*, a light and pleasing combination, with salmon making up the center and grated zucchini the outside of a terrine that included homemade mayonnaise; the dish was perfect on a warm day, and just right with the hearty *pain de campagne*, supplied in generous quantities. Accompanying it was a salad of lettuce and tomato with a light vinaigrette.

Plats are generous: a large quarter of chicken came with yellow beans and an enormous amount of flavorful rice. The emphasis at Aux Négociants is less on presentation than on flavor, and a very discriminating crowd leaves well pleased with what they get.

For years this has been a two person operation, with Monsieur serving at the bar and waiting on tables, and Madame cooking in the kitchen. But this time we glimpsed a young *cuisinier*—it's just as well that the burden of cooking doesn't fall on just one person.

The wine list emphasizes wines of the Loire, with prices running from 3 to 5 euros a glass. Most are available only by the glass or the bottle, and some good choices are available on takeaway.

The dessert of the day, *tarte maison aux abricots*, was, at 6 euros a portion, very popular with the regulars. One near us asked Navier what was in it. He shook his head and responded with typical, poker-faced humor: "Tu veux l'essayer? Risqué. Impossible à décrire" (You want to try it? You're taking a risk. Impossible to describe).

Risky or not, the man's pretty companion ordered one and consumed it with gusto.

❖ *Aux Négociants: honest food at good prices in authentic bistro surroundings. Worth the short walk from the métro.*

Le Nord-Sud
Place Jules-Joffrin, 79 rue du Mont Cenis, 75018 Paris
(01.46.06.02.87)
Métro: Jules-Joffrin
Open daily noon-1:00 A.M.

A vivacious young woman who works at the world-famous Cordon Bleu cooking school in the 15th district mentioned this brasserie near her home in the 18th. "It's very typical," she said. "The cuisine is O.K., but the desserts are nothing special. Everybody gets the *steak-frites*."

We were impressed to find the Nord-Sud open in August and packed with happy diners. There are staid-looking older French people from the neighborhood, the odd tourist, young mothers with children or dogs—sometimes coping with both at the same time.

This is no designer bistro; the look here is flashy, with brass and plastic imitating burled walnut. Incongruous paper tablecloths in pale pink clash with about everything in sight. Mirrors, lights, loud music, old photos in gaudy frames—the Nord-Sud has it all. A brasserie is usually a happy place, and the Nord-Sud, with its loud music and flashy interior, is no exception.

Outside there's quiet Square Jules-Joffrin, with the real life of the 18th arrondissement passing by. There's a good view of the church Notre Dame de Clignancourt, and of the Mairie (town hall) of the 18th. A concierge sits reading on a park bench. Buses 80 and 85 go by, and a newstand on the corner attracts the locals.

Next to us, a lovely young leather-jacketed Parisienne attacked her *steak-frites*, evidently the house specialty. Lunch specials also offered *grandes moules farcies* for 7 euros, melon and country ham for 9, and mixed salad for 8. Substantial dishes, the *plats*, were from 11 to 19 euros, and included *poissons panés à l'aioli* (breaded fish with garlic mayonnaise), *lapin et tagliatelle* (rabbit and pasta), and *entrecôte au poivre, pommes frites* (pepper steak and French fries).

Six *moules farcies*, delectable in a garlic butter sauce sprinkled with parsley, were served along with slices of the good baguette. A *rumsteak*, in a delicious caper sauce, was served with a delicious helping of hot, crisp *frites* and green beans.

While we were finishing lunch, the elegant young woman opposite paid for hers. She left her *addition* on the table: only 8 euros for a plate of steak and French fries, with a little lettuce on the side. Amazing! At this point we noticed that the really good buys at Nord-Sud are featured under "Buffet Chaud" on the back of the menu.

❖ *Le Nord-Sud: outstanding value in a neighborhood hangout.*

Le Petit Caboulet
6 Place Jacques-Froment, 75018 Paris (01.46.27.19.00)
Métro: Guy-Môquet
Mon–Sat 11:30 A.M.–2:00 A.M., closed 1 week in August

The first thing that catches your eye at Le Petit Caboulet, this otherwise traditional-looking bistro in the 18th, are the flashy, vintage advertising signs all over. Signs like "Dunlop—Pour Aller Vite," "Byrrh: l'apéritif" and the cobalt-blue and white, "Chocolat Menier."

The 10-euro lunch *formule* was very appetizing: an attractive salad of *crudités*, with bits of red and green bell pepper, accompanied by beet and avocado on a base of green and purplish lettuce. This was followed by *cabillaud* (cod). The fish came with pasta in a light butter sauce, garnished with red bell peppers and chives. Delicious!

The house red, or *pot lyonnais*, was modestly priced if rather rough. Better-known varieties are available on the extensive wine list.

If the wine or dinner fixed-price menu doesn't appeal to you, try ordering a *plat* with a better-known wine. There are several tables outside, and "On peut manger dehors?" (Can we eat outside?) is a question one hears repeated often.

❖ *Le Petit Caboulet: good value in an attractive bistro.*

Au Relais
48 rue Lamarck, 75018 (01.46.06.68.32)
Métro: Lamarck-Caulaincourt
Tue–Sat lunch and dinner, closed 2 weeks in August

When most people think of Montmartre, their images are of mysterious windmills, can-can dancers, and nightclubs like the Moulin Rouge. But there's another Montmartre—very middle class, respectable, and surprisingly quiet.

There are some small bistros here, where people expect good food and not necessarily a culinary vision. One of their favorites is Au Relais, a family-run bistro. The friendly owner and chef Edouard Martinez is ably assisted by his wife, Marie-Jeanne, who waits on the tables.

Upon entering, you have a choice between the somewhat staid but attractive nonsmoking section in the back, and the more typically bistro section in the front. The look at the back is sleek and glossy with mirrors, Provençal-inspired tablecloths, romantic-looking framed prints, small black-and-white photos. It looks like an old bistro that was redone in Deco style.

To start, the gazpacho was a large bowl of the intense flavors of the South: tomato, garlic, green pepper, cucumber, and olive oil in a pleasing combination. The other starter of *chèvre chaud* was also generous: three rounds of chèvre, the warm and pungent goat cheese on dark toast surrounded by greens with an olive oil vinaigrette. Our *plats* were an excellent value—the *bavette* a huge steak sautéed with shallots, the duck many slices of *magret*, or duck breast, both richly flavored and accompanied by a quantity of crisp fried potatoes.

Wines available include Spanish reds from Valencia, the house specialty, at 13 and 18 euros a bottle. There's a good selection of the wines of Bordeaux, with some wines available in smaller quantities and at very reasonable prices by the carafe.

Desserts are a specialty here: Au Relais offers a better-than-average dessert list. We saw two typically svelte Parisiennes digging avidly into large plates of dessert, one *profiteroles*, the other a sundae garnished with lashings of dark chocolate.

A clientele from the hill frequents Au Relais. Residents of the quarter that come in regularly include individuals from show business, as well as literary and professional people.

❖ *Au Relais: a charming neighborhood bistro with good, sustaining food.*

Brasserie Wepler
14 Place de Clichy, 75018 Paris (01.45.22.53.24)
Métro: Place de Clichy
Open daily noon–1:00 A.M.

These are not the days of Henry Miller, an old habitué, and one cannot imagine him in the splendid marble and glass interior of Le Wepler in our time, studying the 23-euro menu. (On the other hand, one can picture him cadging a drink on the plainer brasserie side, where hors d'oeuvres are about 6 euros and main dishes double that amount.)

Inside are warm colors of soft persimmon, a minimum of formica imitating burled walnut, waiters hurrying to and fro in their classical black and white. It's an elegant interior, with large globe-shaped lights in brass fixtures. On the terrace, a number of high-pressured businessmen enjoy an animated lunch. A burly but pleasant headwaiter ushers us to a good table near the window.

A light lunch, the *midi-express* at 16 euros, offers an entrée and main dish or main dish and dessert. This is a seafood brasserie, but classics include sauerkraut. There is an elegance

in the heavy white linen on the tables, the café curtains an intriguing shade of ochre, the plates advertising Wepler–Paris–Montmartre.

Service is efficient and professional: the young men in their penguin attire correct but not particularly friendly. The food makes up for any deficiencies. It starts with a *salade de pêcheur*, an imposing plate with mussels, shrimp, black and green olives, tomatoes, and frisée lettuce artistically arranged and crowned with parsley-sprinkled lemon. In the salad there's a generous quantity of seafood with good-tasting vinaigrette liberally laced with lemon.

The *plat* is a large portion of hot *julienne* (sea burbot) with fresh pasta on the characteristic Wepler plate. Garnished with tomato and parsley and accompanied by sauce Béarnaise, it is satisfying, warming, and delicious. A couple near us are served a large, impressive platter of *langoustines*, beautifully presented on ice with lemons and dark bread. "C'est formidable," murmurs one of them.

So if you find yourself in the shabby, rather sordid surroundings in the area of the Moulin Rouge, walk or take a bus a little farther north to the Place de Clichy and the Wepler.

❖ *Brasserie Wepler: sustaining brasserie fare in an elegant setting.*

OUT OF THE LOOP:
THE 19TH & 20TH
ARRONDISSEMENTS

From the top of our hill in Ménilmontant we could look down on the heart of Paris, as if we had seats in the highest balcony of a theater.... This distant world seemed to us... like the private paradise of the bourgeoisie, the rich, the aristocrats and all their grand doings. It was the Paris of History. We others were actually like the peasants of the capital, humble and self-effacing, and as if held apart, kept in our places on the fringe.

—Maurice Chevalier, *My Paris*

The 19th and 20th arrondissements are an outer ring of districts, made up largely of Belleville, Charonne, and Ménilmontant. These villages became part of Paris only in 1860, when people dispossessed by Haussmann's new boulevards crowded into the outer suburbs. Much was lost in the transition. There had been cabarets and *guinguettes*, cafés with music and dancing, and people in the neighborhoods tended to know one another. Now the area took on some aspects of a slum, infested with thugs who called themselves "apaches." In recent years the districts have been a place for modern architects and their experiments.

Maurice Chevalier and Edith Piaf both came from the outlying town of Ménilmontant. Chevalier remembered that his mother, the family's sole support, had to work hard as a seamstress, sewing all day and sometimes through much of the night. This gave young Maurice freedom to explore the area, to get to know the local merchants who would sometimes give him a treat, a croissant or even a slice of horsemeat sausage, when he went out to buy the family's food.

He remembered the area with affection. It was not central Paris, it was not at all glamorous, but the town hall looked imposing and the church beautiful in the eyes of a child. Sundays were special occasions when his mother would take her sons to a café near Place Gambetta, and all would share French fries and a small beer. Afterward on the walk back, they would find something to admire about the Père Lachaise Cemetery, which they passed on their way.

Still, Chevalier admitted that life in this district was far from easy:

> In these rough, crowded, vital districts, peopled by hard-working and hard-living Parisians of every degree of human decency, I came to learn, just like a boxer, how to dodge, to guess, and to avoid as many knockouts as possible.... from my surroundings in Paris when I was a little street kid, I formed a very good idea of everything I came to know later as a performing artist and even more as a citizen.

When he was relating his reminiscences about a childhood in the early part of the twentieth century, Chevalier could see that his district was already changing and becoming unrecognizable. He was doubtful about what was happening to the streets he knew so well, noting, "A new architecture has moved in and... it begins to reject any memories of the past."

> Whenever you leave Paris for a few months, you invariably find on your return that it has been brutally improved here and there, with the modernizing of some old façade or with an entire edifice replaced by a huge hole, indicating one more skyscraper to come or an altitudinous new apartment house of the type the French call "de grand standing," meaning luxury flats.

—Janet Flanner *Paris Journal*

Whether you like the changes here or not depends on your attitude toward modern architecture or possibly your capacity for accepting change. The 19th arrondissement has been a fertile ground for enthusiasts of modern design. Here the Cité des Sciences et de L'Industrie was created. The most eye-catching feature of this whole complex designed by the architect Adrien Fainsilber is the Géode, an enormous shiny ball, its triangular steel plates acting as mirrors which cast strange reflections of the area about it.

The Parc de la Villette was once one of the city's main stockyards. Now it has Explora, an extraordinary science museum, with interactive exhibits on astronomical and ecological themes, talking robots, a planetarium, and more. The area outside is dominated by large structures designed by Swiss architect Bernard Tschumi. Some of them are called "follies." These structures start with red three-story cubes of ten meters square and emanate out from that. It takes more of a stretch of the imagination to see the follies at the Parc as part of our conventional picture of Paris. The paved expanse with red follies, bridges, and slides has become a gigantic playground for children, who love the color and the novel experience of unlimited room to run about under the watchful eyes of their parents.

If your interest in science or modern design draws you to this part of Paris, a place to stop for refreshments could be:

Le Café de la Musique
Place de la Fontaine aux Lions, 213 ave. Jean-Jaurès, 75019
Paris (01.48.03.15.91)
Métro: Porte de Pantin
Open daily 8:00 A.M.–2:00 A.M.

If you like modern design, and still haven't recovered from the razing of the first Café Costes near the Pompidou Museum, you might want to visit the Café de la Musique. This highly-styled café from the Costes brothers is another one of their experiments in world-class sophisticated design.

At Le Café de la Musique colors are muted: inside are pale wood tables and a matching floor. You're seated in a large elegant room done in cool colors—grayish-green velvet chairs, greenish glass, a skylight over the modern bar. Cool, too, is the behavior of the waiters. But if you're a true devotee of the Modern, you won't let that affect you. Outside, the old gray cobblestone terrace supports countless rows of chrome and wicker chairs around circular steel tables under white umbrellas. One looks out, alas, over one of the bleakest and loneliest vistas in Paris, an exercise in the intentional abrasiveness of modern architecture, but because of the attractions of La Villette, thousands of people come here.

In the Café, hors d'oeuvres, including salads, start at 7 euros and up. *Plats*, which include ground round steak, tuna and salmon, are between 14 and 19 euros. Drinks also start high, at 5 euros. In theory coffee is only 3 euros, but our requesting "un peu de lait" (a little milk) with it doubled the price—something that has not happened elsewhere.

When we visited the café it was almost deserted, with just a trio of elegant designer types, in jacket and tie and bluejeans, sipping beer a short distance away. Outside some of the local people were there with their small children, a situation made more understandable after we'd walked around La Villette and discovered the slides and playgrounds that appeal to the very young.

❖ *Le Café de la Musique: sleek, modern, and over-priced.*

Le Petit Belleville
12 rue des Envierges, 75020 Paris (01.44.62.92.66)
Métro: Jourdain
Mon–Fri lunch, Tue–Sat dinner

Entering the Petit Belleville is like taking a trip back in time. Accompanied by two French architects, we found ourselves discovering a *café-chantant* from the past. Le Petit Belleville is not much to look at: you see a long, narrow room lined with tables pushed back against the walls—the reason for their placement becomes apparent later. Dark cream walls are covered with momentos of "greats" from the area: well-worn record jackets from old Edith Piaf and Maurice Chevalier albums, framed black-and-white photos of the same. It's a modest little hangout which on weekends is transformed into a joyous old-time *café-chantant*, where working-class men and women celebrate the end of the work week, singing old songs to the loud strains of accordion and a lead singer.

The food at Le Petit Belleville is on the average-to-good bistro level. A decent meal can be made from an 11 to 13-euro *plat*, preceded, if you wish, by a *salade parisienne*, with

ham, or perhaps a *salade auvergnate*, from 6 to 8 euros.

The friendly proprietor, who enjoys practicing his English, came by to answer questions about the menu and to welcome us to his bistro. When we'd approached the Belleville at 7:45 P.M., he was kind enough to suggest that we come back later, as the music doesn't get started until after 9:00 o'clock on Friday and Saturday nights.

And what a show there was! Dressed in a costume of quirky individuality, the accordionist—a perky blonde— filled the bistro with her voice and music. First she made sure everyone could join in, handing out photocopied sheets of words. Most were for songs from long ago, ballads with catchy tunes and bawdy lyrics that the strait-laced -looking locals bellowed with gusto.

A few people got up and danced: most stayed where they were, singing and laughing and finishing their meals, ordering dessert or another bottle of wine. Loud, raucous music and laughter filled the air; conversation became impossible, and we concentrated on trying to sing with the accordionist and guess at the naughty nuances in the songs.

❖ *Le Petit Belleville: a look at old times in Maurice Chevalier and Edith Piaf's Paris. Family-style cuisine and great fun.*

Lou Pascalou
14 rue des Panoyaux, 75020 Paris (01.46.36.78.10)
Métro: Ménilmontant or Père Lachaise
Open daily 9:30 A.M.–2:00 A.M.

Lou Pascalou is a bar off Ménilmontant. It's also a joyous romp into the past.

To get here you'll have to walk down boulevard Ménilmontant, a lively and untidy street lined with all sorts of ethnic restaurants. Ordinary people live out here. Dogs bark. Children cry. Old ladies lug their packages out of the Arab grocery across the street. There is a life and a vitality here, even late at night, that you can't find in the more exclusive parts of Paris.

On the way we pass old, dilapidated apartments with no balconies, just a rail in front of the window, and others which lack even that. Just as the search seems fruitless, we spot rue des Panoyaux, and a little way along see how this small street, with an exaggerated curve and V-shaped Place, becomes a haven, with lively-looking restaurants and bars.

Lou Pascalou is one of the best. The inside of the large old café has been painted in the deeply warm colors suggestive of the late nineteenth century, the red earth tones of terra cotta, faded browns of the South, the richness of old varnish. Along one wall is a long rounded bench with dark wooden slats, reminiscent of seats in the old métro. A strangely curved wooden bar balances the othe side of the room, and a pressed tin ceiling remains from another era. Strange spidery metal chandeliers cast a golden glow through the large windows.

Drinks here are fairly priced: wines 3 to 4 euros a glass, with Sauvignon and Côtes du Rhône at the low end, Médoc at the top. Even in the evenings coffee is only 2 euros, with soft drinks a little more. An impressive list of beers is available, as well as the usual daunting French apéritifs like pastis, Ricard, Pernod, Suze, etc. If you need more sustenance, simple café food is available day and night: sandwiches at 3 euros include *jambon* (ham), Gruyère, Camembert, and *saucisson* (dry salami). The 5-euro salads are niçoise and chicken.

The regular clientele are young professionals of the artistic variety, including actors and people working in television and the film industry. People go to Lou to relax; we heard a lot of laughter around us on the welcoming terrace. So if you're in the 10th to pay your respects to Oscar Wilde, Colette, Jim Morrison, or just to scope out the neighborhood, Lou Pascalou is a nice stop.

❖ *Lou Pascalou: well worth a trip to the 20th.*

Le Rendez-Vous des Quais
10 quai de Seine, 75019 Paris (01.40.37.02.81)
Métro: Jaurès
Open daily noon–midnight

In the dark and grubby northeast reaches of the city, one little expects to come upon something like the Rendez-Vous des Quais. Despite its location in a high-tech MK2 cinema complex, the Rendez-Vous has a romantic terrace where you sit on the planks of what looks like a ship's deck, looking out at the water of the canal. Overhead an ironwork canopy suggests a railway station in the country. A cordoned-off perimeter with heavy rope brings to mind the sea as well as lines at movie theaters.

There was a queue when we arrived to find the café full at 10:30 P.M. on a Sunday night. For the Rendez-Vous des Quais is a café, with better-than-average café food available most of the day and into the night. Some people just stop by for a drink, a glass of wine, perhaps, at 3 euros, or a *demi*, a carafe at 9 euros.

Our salade du Rendez-Vous des Quais was enormous, a real value at 10 euros, rare roast beef topping slices of white bread, and that on a large green salad with grated carrots, tomatoes and hard-boiled eggs. The *entrecôte Béarnaise et frites* was a large, thin, very flavorful steak, with an ample portion of crisp fries and a small pot of Béarnaise sauce.

The look was quietly romantic, with bushes and little trees around the perimeter, lights, reflections from the water, and young couples soulfully gazing at one another—when they weren't discussing the symbolism in the latest film. Service was very friendly, and our requests for salt, pepper, and more Béarnaise sauce was promptly fulfilled.

Note: The Rendez-Vous des Quais is appealing during the daytime, when you don't have to deal with the sinister-at-night aspects of nearby métro station Stalingrad, and, to a lesser extent, Jaurès. It's lovely in the afternoons. On a return visit we took a Parisian friend there for coffee and she was charmed: "It doesn't look like Paris!" With the tranquility and the view of the water, this could be a café in a provincial town.

❖ *Le Rendez-Vous des Quais: good value in a surprisingly attractive setting. An "in" place for the upscale locals. At night, proceed with caution.*

Le Saint-Amour
2 ave. Gambetta, 75020 Paris (01.47.97.20.15)
Métro: Père Lachaise
Open daily to 10:30 P.M.

We first heard about the Saint-Amour years ago in the course of researching a book about Paris cafés. This bistro was warmly recommended by an intellectual Parisian with a profound knowledge of the city. It seemed an unlikely choice. Nothing about the exterior of Le Saint-Amour is appealing, and the interior is even worse, recalling one of the more garish New Jersey diners, or possibly the studied kitsch of a restaurant scene in a gangster movie.

But low prices combined with the quality of first-rate produce from the Auvergne gives this brasserie serious appeal. Budget-minded travellers will go for the three-course express menu priced at 9 and 12 euros, and served until 9:00 P.M.

The 12-euro menu offers hors d'oeuvres and *plats*, typically a choice of a specialty of Auvergne. Dessert in the set menu offers bistro classics like *mousse au chocolat* and *crème caramel* as well as *tarte aux pommes maison* (homemade apple pie). With the three courses this menu offers a quarter bottle of rosé, Pays du Var, red wine from Castalou, or mineral water. Jean-Louis Rouchet, the proprietor, has a particular interest in wines of the Southwest, and offers a carefully chosen variety.

Since the hour was late, we took just a *salade Auvergnate* and an *assiette de charcuterie*. The salad was large and very good, a platter heaped with *jambon du pays* (cured country ham), Cantal cheese, walnuts, hard-boiled egg, and boiled new potatoes on a bed of greens. The *assiette de charcuterie* (plate of cured meats) was fresh and tasty with ample quantities of pâté, *saucisson* (dry salami), thin slices of the excellent country ham from Auvergne, and pickles. Both choices gave us a taste of excellent produce from Auvergne, and an exceptional value.

The *tarte bourdaloue* was a fine example of Auvergnate pastry. The young waitress described it as a "tarte aux poires légèrement chauffée, servie avec chocolat." It involved layers of thinly-sliced pears with almonds on pastry, served warm with a dark chocolate sauce, rich without excessive sweetness. A satisfying dessert.

❖ *Le Saint-Amour: good simple food in an unlikely-looking setting.*

MAIGRET'S BISTROS

Paris reveals itself to Maigret. It shows itself in bistros and brasseries, by chance encounters and strange coincidences. This was the discovery of Georges Simenon's brillant Chief Inspector. For Maigret, the background checks and surveillance that are standard procedure often start in bistros. There was nothing self-indulgent about Maigret's frequenting of them, although the amount of alcohol that he put away would have provoked a *crise de foie* in a lesser man, and in his later years became a cause for alarm in his good friend Dr. Pardon.

The secrets of Paris were more accessible from the bar of a bistro. From his first case onward, certain police procedures came more easily to Maigret in the relaxed ambiance of a local hangout. And the description of the café or bistro he patronizes during a case can lend a fine exactness to the locale. We picture the Marais and the Place des Vosges, delineated for us by the mention of three familiar drinking-places in *L'Amie de Madame Maigret*: "In a square that everybody knew, there are the three cafés, one on the corner of the rue des Francs-Bourgeois, the Grand Turenne opposite, and, about 30 meters away, the Tabac des Vosges."

No longer called the Tabac des Vosges, the bistro on the corner could still be called Maigret's because of its close identification with the Chief Inspector of Simenon's stories. Now known as Ma Bourgogne, this warm and venerable watering place with the dark, massive beams overhead dominates a corner of the Place des Vosges, a square currently even more fashionable than in Maigret's day. Wealthy and privileged people can be victims of crime, just

like anybody else, and his work would take him into districts like this, where someone might, perhaps, exact payments for concealing damaging information, or try to hasten the demise of a wealthy relative.

In certain of Maigret's adventures, the great detective gives such attention to the *cuisinier's* and sommelier's arts that one wonders how he could keep a clear head for solving the crimes. England's Sherlock Holmes was lean and spare, leading a Spartan regime, paying little attention to what or when or if he ate—most of Mrs. Hudson's scones were consumed by Watson. Holmes's French counterpart recognizes the importance of the table in the life of any civilized man. And Sherlock had no wife, no kindly Madame Maigret to welcome him with a bistro-type dish simmered all morning, its aroma wafting down the stairs to welcome him when—and if—he would come home to lunch.

The Maigrets' tastes on the occasions when they dine at home together run to the *cuisine grand-mère* that makes up the classic bistro food. In *Maigret and the Loner*, Maigret goes home for lunch to find that his wife had made *coq au vin*, one of his favorite dishes. In another story, a day off on a weekend is made special by the food: Madame Maigret has prepared a beef stew. It is simmering in the blue-tiled kitchen, making their apartment fragrant with the scent of herbs. Old-fashioned dishes are perceived as best, and for a dinner with their friends the Pardons, Madame Maigret made an excellent *boeuf bourguignon* which became the center of conversation.

> *Maigret had been only a detective when he had made a sally that was often repeated to newcomers to the Quai des Orfèvres. Told to watch a banker... he had said to his chief: "To understand how his mind works I must breakfast with financiers."*

—Georges Simenon, *Maigret Has Doubts*

Trying to understand the thinking of all types of suspects and victims, whether financiers, racketeers, petty criminals, or call girls, the whole gamut of society that becomes mixed up in murder, Maigret's investigations familiarize him with all of Paris and he patronizes bars and bistros throughout the city. His local near work is the Brasserie Dauphine in the Place of the same name. He sends down to the Brasserie for beer and sandwiches when he's conducting the marathon questioning of a suspect which often leads to a confession and terminates his work on a case.

When he has more time, he can savor the simple cuisine there: he remembers that the brasserie has distinctive odors and in *Maigret and the Headless Corpse,* identifies the dominant ones as the smell of Pernod around the bar and coq-au-vin simmering in the kitchen. On another day he perceives a scent of wines from the Loire Valley, and an aroma of herbs, particularly tarragon and chives.

A case on the rue St. Dominique in the 7th arrondiss-ement brings Maigret closer to the seat of power; with Janvier, he picks a restaurant on the rue de Bourgogne, patronized by officials from nearby ministries. Here they start a meal with asparagus and proceed to ray in brown butter. Near the Parc Monceau in the 17th district he remembers walking with Madame Maigret not long after their marriage, looking at the elegant houses overlooking the park. The young Maigrets imagined the privileged way of life that went on behind those façades.

Other stories take Maigret to the seamier parts of Paris, in particular the 18th district. In *Maigret Has Scruples,* he notices a pimp waiting in the detention center and thinks that he "had Place Pigalle written all over him." He remembers working on the boulevard de la Chapelle, where, beneath the elevated métro, night after night there were "familiar shadows." Maigret thought he knew what the women were doing, waiting around there, but that it was much more difficult to work out what reasons such men could have for hanging about doing nothing, men of all races and ages, who came out in the evenings when it was dark and cold.

Closer to home Maigret frequents a bistro on the Place de la République, near the family apartment on boulevard Richard-Lenoir in the 11th district. In *Maigret's Little Joke,* he decides to spend his vacation quietly in Paris while spreading the word that he and Madame are enjoying the beaches at Les Sables d'Orlonne. He starts to follow a murder case, reading the morning papers on a relatively deserted café terrace on the Place.

In the course of the Maigrets' Paris vacation, they make their way to Montmartre and stop for a drink at the Place du Tertre. There they notice three cafés dominating the square.

Maigret notices that the square had changed since he was young, that it still seemed amusing, like a fairground, but more vulgar than ever.

Starting with his first case, Maigret acquired the habit of dropping into a bistro wherever his work might take him. Often his purpose was to gather information. In *Maigret's First Case*, young Maigret is trying to observe the activity in a building where he thinks a murder has been committed. He spends hours trapped in a bistro called the Vieux Calvados, feeling that he has become the victim of a generous—or sadistic—proprietor who keeps pouring him glasses of Calvados, the Norman liqueur of almost lethal potency. He is tormented by doubts, asking himself if it is worthwhile "to hang around all day in a bistro, in order to watch a house where nothing happened?" Maigret could not foresee that some day, although chief of the special squad with police officers under his command, he would continue to do lookouts himself, following a suspect through the streets and waiting in small bistros for hours on end.

> *Having crossed Place de la Bastille, he was passing a little bistro on his way down Boulevard Henri IV.... As he went past... Maigret's nostrils were assailed by a gust of fragrance which was forever to remain with him as the very quintessence of Paris at daybreak: the fragrance of frothy coffee and hot croissants, spiced with a bit of rum.*

—Georges Simenon, *Maigret and the Spinster*

Caught up in an investigation, Maigret considers ordering sandwiches from the Brasserie Dauphine, but decides instead to try the Henri IV, a little bar opposite the statue, where he orders a ham sandwich and is recognized by the waiter. Later on the same day he makes do with a sandwich and beer at La Coupole, a famous brasserie on the boulevard du Montparnasse, while he ponders the case.

In the evening, a little self-conscious now at being accompanied by Spencer, an American criminologist who has come to Paris to study his methods, Maigret finally stops to eat in a bistro near the Porte d'Orléans, with a zinc counter, a few marble-topped tables, and sawdust on the floor. The proprietor, a pleasant man with a blotchy complexion, comes and shakes hands with Maigret. His wife Mélanie produces a substantial meal, starting with *cèpes à la bourdelaise,* the mushrooms fresh from the country, and proceeding to *coq au vin.* With it, the proprietor suggests, "Your usual Beaujolais, Superintendent?" and Maigret accepts.

The young American questions Maigret to learn his views on the psychology of murderers, and is surprised by his thinking on the question. Maigret asks whether he is talking about murderers before or after they've committed the crime, because before they're not yet guilty, and they might live 40 or 50 years of their lives behaving just like everyone else:

> "What makes you think, Monsieur Spencer, that just killing one of his own kind should change a man's character from one minute to the next?"

> "So what it comes down to," said the American, "is that a murderer is a man like any other."

After they've found the murder victim's cache of thousand-franc notes and Maigret is fairly sure of who the murderer is, he receives a lesson in the differences between himself and the congenial American. Maigret suggests that they drop into a nearby bistro for a glass of something while they're waiting for their streetcar:

> "I'll have a Calvados. What about you?"

> "Would they have such a thing as a glass of milk, I wonder?"

> Maybe that explained how a man of thirty-five had managed to retain a complexion as rosy as the muzzle of a young calf.

Sometimes a bistro or brasserie is crucial to the plot of a Maigret story. La Coupole, on the boulevard du Montparnasse, is almost a character itself in *Maigret's War of Nerves.* The story begins with a prisoner escaping from the maximum security section of the Santé prison. The escape is secretly engineered by Maigret, who has been convinced for some time that the wrong man was condemned to die for murdering a wealthy American woman. A day before his execution, Joseph Heurtin finds his cell door open and the guard nowhere near. A note had appeared in his food two days before, suggesting that escape would be possible at 2:00 A.M., when a rope ladder and a disguise would be at hand.

Maigret's unconventional approach to trying to solve the crime is put to the test when an article appears in *Le Sifflet*, one of the evening newspapers, exposing his carefully planned scheme and stating that it was the police officials themselves, along with the judicial authorities, who presided over this "pseudo-escape."

Who could have leaked the information? Maigret finds that the editors at *Sifflet* had received a letter written on stationery from one of the cafés. He narrows the source down to the Coupole.

To solve this case, Maigret has to spend time at the Coupole. He is intrigued by the brasserie, so different from the small bistros he usually frequents. His observations give us an excellent description of many Parisian brasseries today:

> The place was writhing with humanity.... Four waiters were all shouting at once, accompanied by the clatter of plates and tinkling of glasses. Snatches of different languages broke out on all sides. Yet somehow the whole scene—customers, barmen, waiters, the room itself—gave the impression of a homogeneous whole.

A wealthy and socially prominent American couple, Mr. and Mrs. Kirby, enter. The arrival of these people in their luxurious sports car with their other signs of conspicuous wealth makes Maigret think of the escapee Heurtin, that pathetic figure, the strange-looking young man who was somewhere in the city with just over twenty francs in his pocket.

Further work on the case leads Maigret again to the Coupole, to the Pelican, a small bar on the rue des Ecoles, to other bistros on the boulevard du Montparnasse, and, finally, to the house where the murder had been committed and where the real murderer gives himself away.

Some of Maigret's time in bistros, when he isn't actually questioning a barman or a proprietor about a suspect, a victim, or possible witness, is spent getting a "feel" for the place. In *Maigret's Memoirs*, the great detective relates his ideas on the subject: "You have to know. To know the milieu in which a crime has been committed, to know the way of life, the habits, morals, reactions of people involved in it, whether victims, criminals, or merely witnesses. To enter into their world without surprise, easily, and to speak its language naturally."

This is why Maigret feels that the police are not wasting their time when they spend years pacing sidewalks. Theirs is the serving of an apprenticeship, different from other apprenticeships because it goes on for a lifetime, as the variety of settings in Paris is almost infinite.

Maigret's patronage of bistros allows us insights into the man himself: he can manage to keep going on beer and sandwiches—how many beers and sandwiches has he had sent up from the Brasserie Dauphine during the course of an interrogation, for example?—but he prefers home cooking. Used to the *cuisine familiale* at home in the apartment on boulevard Richard Lenoir, he is able to appreciate good food when he finds it.

The pleasure of the ordinary bistro, its sights, sounds, and smells, are celebrated in *Maigret Bides his Time*. Inside Chez l'Auvergnat, an old-fashioned bistro with a zinc counter and a jovial, mustachioed owner, Maigret notices sausages, chitterlings, and gourd-shaped cheeses. Hams with grayish rinds hang from the ceiling, and there are enormous flat loaves of bread from the Massif Central. Cooking is done by the owner's wife. The lunch menu changes daily, chalked on a slate blackboard. This day Maigret samples *rillettes du Morvan, filet de veau, fromage,* and *tarte tatin*, served by the owners who are clearly proud to entertain such a famous customer.

Maigret's bistros still exist in Paris. Some of them are easy to find: obvious, well-known, named in the books. Others need a little searching out, but are worth the effort for Simenon enthusiasts and on their own merits:

Le Bar du Caveau
17 Place Dauphine, 75001 Paris (01.43.54.45.95)
Métro: Cité
Mon–Sat 8:30 A.M.–6:30 P.M. May–Sept; Mon–Fri.
Oct–April

Situated in the Place Dauphine behind the Palais de Justice, this is almost certainly the original of the Brasserie Dauphine patronized so often by Maigret. Here are old stone walls, venerable beams, an old oak bar, brass-edged marble café tables, and charm. The clientele are mostly French: two men standing and talking at the bar looked to be almost caricatures of middle-aged French government officials. High above them was a shelf with numerous carefully arranged bottles, conveying the fact that this is a wine bar with serious wines. They are available by the glass, the *demi,* and the full bottle.

Small basic lunches are served at low prices. For only 7 euros, you can get tabouli, salad, and *crème caramel. Tartines* (open-faced sandwiches) on *pain poilâne* are from 3 to 4 euros, and *oeufs brouillés* (scrambled eggs) with grilled *pain poilâne* and salad, 6 to 7 euros, depending on whether you want ham with them. Wine by the glass ranges from 3 to 4 euros, and beers from 3 euros and up.

While eating we had a chance to appreciate the quiet refinement of this little bistro tucked away into one of the most coveted parts of the great city. An oil painting, large enough to be a mural, conveys some of the feeling of what life by the Seine must have been like years ago. Old wooden boxes contain glossy magazines about food, wine, and the good life in general; the daily newspapers hang near the door. The dour barman did not affect anyone's pleasure at being in this idyllic retreat.

❖ *La Bar du Caveau: an idyllic spot on the Ile de la Cité, the most historic part of Paris.*

Ma Bourgogne
19 Place des Vosges, 75004 Paris (01.42.78.44.64)
Métro: Bastille
Open daily 8:00 A.M.–1:30 A.M.

The original name was the Tabac de la Place des Vosges. Warm and welcoming interior. Prices reflect the important location, but a drink at the bar is still a bargain. Avoid peak times, when it's next to impossible to get near the bar. A coffee and croissant on the *terrasse* is a nice beginning to a day in Paris. This bistro, formerly a *tabac*, is specifically identified in *L'Amie de Madame Maigret.*

La Coupole
108 blvd du Montparnasse, 75014 Paris (01.43.20.14.20)
Métro: Vavin
Open daily to 2:00 A.M.

Dining at La Coupole is, for better or worse, one of the quintessential experiences of being in Paris. It's an institution, a legend, an artistic memory, an historic monument, and it's a restaurant where everybody goes. It has a New York-midtown Manhattan sort of flavor. It's festive, it's fun, it's bright, it's glossy and glittery. It's also noisy, swarming with Parisians and tourists alike, and it virtually shouts, "I'm important and famous!" Everybody has been here, and it's no use listing their names.

La Coupole is not a bistro, but a brasserie important enough to come up in several mysteries. Also La Coupole has been an historic writers' and artists' gathering-place from its beginnings in 1927. It quickly became a favorite of the American expatriates. The main floor was a brasserie and thirty-some artists, Léger included, contributed their skills to the decoration of the huge room. Since 1988 it has belonged to the Groupe Flo.

La Coupole is a vast room, generally believed to be the largest restaurant in all of France, with high ceilings, elegant lighting, and a remarkable floor in Deco-patterned tile. The

interior is broken up by pillars and banquettes. There are suspended lights with Deco lines, Deco curves in the molding around the ceiling, and a ceiling the color of a pale *café-crème*.

The food is sometimes described as *cuisine industrielle*, but in our experience, the Groupe Flo food, while never very creative, can be surprisingly good. Going there on a Saturday night with friends, there was little option for us but the 32-euro menu, which included three courses and wine or mineral water. Starters were *foie gras*, oysters, or *carpaccio de tomates*. In our party of six, somebody ordered each of the possibilities, and they were all good: the *foie gras de canard* delicious with accompanying cubes of aspic, the *carpaccio de tomates* a dish in which the tomatoes were covered with a round of *fromage blanc*, and the whole surrounded with a circle of green pesto sauce and topped with chives.

For *plats*, the well-flavored salmon on a bed of cooked red and green peppers was served hot in an ironware dish with little boiled potatoes. *Canard confit* (literally "preserved duck") was duck which had been cooked a long time and tasted delicious, the meat falling off the bone. The rumsteak was tasty in a rich brown sauce with mushrooms and a purée of potatoes.

Desserts included a spectacular *soupe aux fraises*, a bowl of strawberries sliced in half, in a strawberry purée, topped with a scoop of strawberry ice cream garnished with mint.

All of us were satisfied. Flo cuisine pleases most people: it provides consistency and a certain level of competency. It's an institution. You've been dining at a legend, and it's not bad. It's glitzy, glossy, and fun.

❖ *La Coupole: You'll eat better elsewhere—if you pay the price—but you'll remember La Coupole.*

La Patache
60 rue de Lancry, 75010 Paris (01.42.08.14.35)
Métro: Jacques Bonsergent
Open daily 6:00 P.M. –2:00 A.M.
No credit cards

Almost certainly the "dingy-looking bar" described in *Maigret and the Headless Corpse.* "The ceiling was low and blackened with smoke, and the walls were grimy. Indeed, the whole place was murky, except for faint patches of sunlight here and there."

This bar is an old photographic postcard brought to life. It has a reputation for boisterous patrons, mediocre folk music, and, some might add, nineteenth-century sanitary conditions. One of a kind. Worth seeking out if you want to see what an ordinary nineteenth-century Paris café looked like.

Au Pied de Fouet
45 rue Babylone, 75007 Paris (01.47.05.12.27)
Métro: Sèvres-Babylone
Mon–Fri noon–2:30 P.M., 7:00 P.M.–9:30 P.M.,
closed August

A different location, but similar in spirit to the little restaurant on the rue de Miromesnil described in *Maigret Hesitates* as a relic of former days. The menu was chalked up on a slate, and "Each of the regulars had his napkin in a pigeonhole and frowned when someone took his seat."

Le Royal Turenne
24 rue de Turenne, 75004 Paris (01.42.72.04.53)
Métro: Chemin Vert
Open daily 7:30 A.M.–midnight

This is the café mentioned in *L'Amie de Madame Maigret* as "Le Grand Turenne." The Royal Turenne gives you a superb people-watching vantage point, something Maigret would need. During the few minutes we were there, slender young Parisiennes moved past like silent deer, a bald gentleman wearing a business suit and carrying *Le Monde* rounded the corner on rollerblades and then whirled down the street.

Here are the venerable brass-edged café tables, the old bar and exposed stone, and a good view of the bright façade of L'Escurial across the way. In fact, under the blue-and-white striped parasols of Le Royal Turenne, you have a choice spot for reconnoitering the whole neighborhood.

Here you can stop for a 2-euro espresso or try a *croque monsieur* for 5 euros. Times have changed, and now you can even get Coca-Cola and hot dogs. But Maigret was not a person to be disturbed by change; he had travelled, he'd been to New York and enjoyed the pubs of London, so a few American innovations would not be likely to upset him. Still, his favorite *consommation* at Le Royal Turenne would most likely be a beer, at 5 euros or possibly a glass of wine, at 3 euros.

If it's around lunchtime, this simple café has a *plat* du jour which could be an economical meal with a carafe d'eau (ordinary water) and perhaps a small coffee to finish. One day recently the special was *poulet rôti*, with fries and green beans, for 9 euros.

❖ *Le Royal Turenne: a classic café for observing street life in the Marais.*

Le Sélect
99 blvd du Montparnasse, 75006 Paris (01.42.22.65.27)
Métro: Vavin
Open daily 7:00 A.M.–3:00 A.M.

One of the most historic of the literary cafés, this name comes up several times in the Maigret mysteries, notably in *Maigret Mystified* when Nine, the murder victim's mistress, waits in vain for him to keep a rendezvous with her there, not knowing that the wealthy man who's supported her is dead. Typically, Maigret is more sympathetic with her than with the victim's other associates and even lends her money for a taxi. Le Sélect is described elsewhere on pages 78–80.

Taverne Henri IV
13 Place du Pont-Neuf, 75001 Paris (01.43.54.27.90)
Métro: Pont-Neuf
Mon–Fri noon–3:00 P.M., 6:30 P.M.–8:30 P.M.,
closed August

A famous winebar on the Ile de la Cité with a notoriously grumpy proprietor. Noted for the variety of its wines and for the good sandwiches on pain poilâne. Worth a visit. Here Maigret goes for a ham sandwich during a rainy day in *Maigret and the Spinster*. It was a day when he felt the need to get out of his office and the usual sandwiches ordered up from the Brasserie Dauphine just wouldn't do.

ROMANTIC BISTROS

"Oh! To wander Paris! Such a lovely, delectable experience!"

—Balzac, *La Physiologie du Mariage*

It should always be seen, the first time, with the eyes of childhood or of love.

—M.F.K. Fisher, *The Gastronomical Me*

It must be something about the light in Paris: something rather unusual, a softness, an ethereal, diffused quality, a glow that illuminates faces and flowers and creates a mood. Alone among cities, Paris is still associated with romance, love for the young and the not-so-young, where the beauty all around hints at romantic possibilities.

Magic exists here, and not only in the great places of recognized importance, the palaces and mansions and exclusive haunts of the privileged. It can be elusive, but is to be found as surely in the perfume from a shower-sprinkled flower, a view of the Seine from one of its bridges on a cloudy day, the sinuous curvings of a métro entrance or a wrought-iron balcony, an expanse of chaotic grass with violets competing with the orderly rows of trees in a park.

Under the spell of Paris things said and felt take on a greater significance. Life is charged with a particular energy, an intensity not to be found in any other place. Stay in Paris for a week, and, while time races relentlessly on, as it does everywhere, you are left with the sense that you've lived and felt much more than the experience of a few days.

Paris is a special place for lovers, too, who flock everywhere in this great city. They meander hand-in-hand along the narrow streets, they embrace beside the Seine, they exchange long, soulful glances across rooms and at train stations. (Increasingly, too, when apart they shout sweet nothings at each other over cell phones.)

But there remains something reassuringly old-fashioned about romance. The most modern Parisian bride is choosing to be wed in a Victorian froth of white lace and silk; she has no doubt been courted across the tables of traditional family bistros, familiar haunts that lure one with their promise of cozy intimacy.

Picasso celebrated love in many of his paintings. An American reporter found that he had something eloquent to say about it too. Janet Flanner, Paris correspondent for the *New Yorker* magazine, remembered that she used to see Picasso during her first years in the city. He too was an habitué of the bistros: "After 1945 he began coming to the Café de Flore at night. He always sat at the second table in front of the main door, with Spanish friends. I would sit where, without seeming to, I could view his remarkably mobile face with its amazingly watchful eyes."

In the mid-1950s Flanner happened to be in Cannes. She met the artist son of an old friend and learned that Picasso had given the young man a gift, a sketch of his infant son. He had promised to sign and dedicate it if the father stopped by. They went to the great artist's villa, and Flanner, not wanting to intrude, stayed behind in the car. Summoned twice to come in, she told of walking into the art-crowded salon and being recognized by Picasso:

> ... with a loud cry of astonishment, [he] shouted: 'You! Why didn't you ever speak to me in the old days at the Flore? For years we saw each other and never spoke, until now. Are you just the same as you were? You look it! By now he had his arms around me and was thumping me enthusiastically on the shoulders. "You look fine, not a day older," and I said "Nor do you," and he said, "That's true; that's the way you and I are. We don't get older, we just get riper.... Tell me, do you still love the human race, especially your best friends? Do you still love love?" "I do," I said, astonished at the turn the monologue was taking. "And so do I!" he shouted,

laughing. "Oh, we're great ones for that, you and I. Isn't love the greatest refreshment in life?" And he embraced me with his strong arms, in farewell.

Flanner and Picasso are gone now, but like them, you can still find the romantic Paris that remains to be enjoyed.

Start with morning coffee with croissants in an historic café—we might pick the unspoiled Sélect; walk on the historic Ile Saint-Louis or the Ile de la Cité, indulge in a ride around Paris at off-peak hours, not with tourists in a group but with Parisians on a regular bus route that's special—we like the 29, which sweeps past the Café de la Paix and the old Opéra, and the 96, with its views of Notre Dame, the Marais, and the Place Saint-Sulpice. En route, spot the small streets and little galleries which you wish to return to and explore on foot together; share a boat trip on the Seine; pick up a snack from a vender or at a boulangerie, and take it to enjoy in a green place, perhaps the Jardin du Luxembourg; indulge in hot chocolate or tea and a pastry in the afternoon in the gilded luxury of a good *salon de thé*; explore the stalls of the *bouquinistes* along the Seine, and find a postcard or print of old Paris that's good

enough to be a special keepsake; finally, walk near the river when the lights begin to glow all over the city at twilight.

"A walk through the Paris streets was always like the unrolling of a vast tapestry from which countless stored fragrances were shaken out," wrote Edith Wharton. You will sense the romance in these narrow streets with the cobblestones underfoot and the sky above, the fanciful Old-World façades of countless little shops shining, a painter's palette of deep and luscious tones—cobalt blue, hunter green, umber, burnt sienna. And there are endless surprises along the way: a massive brass door knocker in the shape of a lion, an unexpected niche in an old wall with an unlooked-for saint or Virgin and Child, a morning splash of color in a market vender's stall, the oranges, reds, and yellows of artfully piled fruit in a marvel of balance and symmetry, a glimpse of a courtyard with trees and flowers, an old-fashioned bistro with its original zinc bar and an affable proprietor.

When you leave the modern noise and nervous intensity of the tourist world and turn into the Place Dauphine, you'll hear birds singing and leaves rustling. It's an exquisite place, almost unnaturally quiet and unhurried, a part of Paris most visitors never enter. Though a few feet away you glimpse tourists searching for Notre Dame and the Conciergerie, here it's like finding yourself in an especially quiet provincial town on a lazy Sunday afternoon.

There are several restaurants on the Place: our favorite is

not a restaurant but a wine bar, the **Bar du Caveau,** at 17 Place Dauphine. Inside is a room of real charm, where you sit on a classic bentwood chair at a marble-topped, brass-rimmed café table. You brush against ancient stone walls and notice on one side a Romantic-influenced oil painting of early Paris by the Seine. It's a special place for drinks and low-priced lunches in an enchanting corner of the city. (Further details in "Maigret's Bistros," page 226).

If you were going by the **Bistro du Peintre,** not far from the Bastille at 116 avenue Ledru-Rollin, 75011 Paris, you'd almost certainly say to your partner, "Remember where we are—we've got to come back here sometime." This bistro recalls the Paris of romantic legend, the Belle Epoque with Toulouse-Lautrec and Sarah Bernhardt. Large swirling Art Nouveau-shaped windows cover the front and massive oak cabinets carved into quasi-organic floral forms are punctuated by highly polished brass. It's a charming place with cuisine that is honest, basic, and good. *Pichets* of the house wine are more than adequate. *Plats* around 11 euros might include simple bistro fare like *brandade de haddock* or a *pot au feu* (stew). In the afternoon you can enjoy this setting for the price of a cup of coffee or a glass of wine. It's open every day until 2:00 A.M. except for Sunday, when it closes at 8:00 in the evening.

Do you want to take someone special to a romantic garden, once the private retreat of a Rothschild? The special

someone could be you yourself, when you need to get away from people and traffic and noise. Perhaps you could use an hour with a special person amongst green spaces and flowers. Then try the **Café du Centre** in the Museum of Photography at 11 rue Berryer, 75008 Paris (01.42.56.22.48). It's open daily from noon to 6:00 P.M.

The food here may be café-style but the surroundings most definitely are not, for this magnificent mansion is the former home of Solomon Rothschild. This great house and beautiful garden, almost front on the rue du faubourg St. Honoré, the most elegant street in Paris and home to Hermès, Gucci, and the British Embassy.

The Café du Centre has a minimalist modern interior, with an extraordinary metal bar that's like abstract sculpture. But for us the treasure in this place is its garden. You can enter the garden area from the street behind, and when you do, you'll discover a lovely and almost rural spot right in the center of Paris. The Café du Centre offers sustaining lunches and a view of hedges and flowers at prices that don't reflect the expensive 8th arrondissement, or the exclusive location: salads are 8–9 euros, an omelet 8, and pasta a little more.

Possibly you just want a drink as a pick-me-up. In the afternoons the Café is a *salon de thé,* with coffee and a large pot of tea for around 3 euros. There's a separate list of numerous teas, including Earl Grey and lapsang souchong, so if you're English—or simply love the brew—you can indulge yourself here.

Wines are available by the glass from 3 euros, with a *demi* carafe, large enough to share, for 9 euros.

While you sip whatever restorative you've selected, you sit under big white umbrellas on tangerine or pale lemon sorbet-colored chairs designed by Philippe Starck. It's a great place for a lazy afternoon and you don't have to know a Rothschild—all you need is 3 euros for a cup of good coffee. If you call ahead and reserve, you can also have the chef's special of the day.

Sometimes romance has little to do with appearances. Consider the **Café les Deux Moulins**, open daily at 15 rue Lepic, 75018 Paris (01.42.54.90.50), Métro: Abbesses. The

look of this café is shiny, glitzy, and cheap—no aspiring young actresses or lanky long-haired models lurk about here. But this was the locale for the movie *Amélie*, in French *Le Fabuleux Destin d'Amélie Poulain*. It's the story of a French girl who works in a drab little café and spends her spare time trying to do good things for people. On the way she falls in love with a rather ordinary boy. The Deux Moulins was probably chosen for shooting the film because it's larger than average, with doors on both sides that let in abundant light.

The Café les Deux Moulins is in a part of Montmartre where tourists seldom go, a rather crowded and intense working-class area without much of the usual Parisian charm. But young, impressionable tourists now flock there from all over, to photograph each other in the café where Audrey Tautou, the star, worked as a waitress in the film. (Sometimes they even leave graffiti in the washroom—little notes for "Amélie" telling how she has touched and inspired them.) While many of the tourists are Japanese schoolgirls, some are also Europeans and Americans.

The Café les Deux Moulins is memorable, with a circular lowered part of the ceiling glowing with an almost luminescent canary yellow, set off by the upper ceiling in blue.

A dramatic neon tube zigzags above the bar. Tables are unabashed formica. The real barmaid is an unsmiling blonde of a certain age, tending bar with a lean French waiter. No one courts the late afternoon crowd with Amélie-style charm, but the Deux Moulins still gets more than its share of customers. If you have wine or a beer at an inside table it's about 3 euros; a coffee in the same place would be 2. Fair prices for a neighborhood hangout that made it into the big time.

It may be that the most romantic spot in Paris to sit and sip coffee is by the outdoor café, **Café Les Gaufres** (75006 Paris, 01.43.26.13.65, RER Luxembourg, open daily until sunset), at the northern end of the Luxembourg Gardens. The nineteenth-century-style metal and glass building looks

like nothing more than a large gazebo, with olive chairs and tables spreading out around it. In the summer, you'll sit somewhere outdoors at a table under a tall tree, watching the dusky light filter down through layers of translucent green foliage. On even the warmest summer days the breezes feel cooler here.

Our server was clad in the garb of the classic French waiter, even down to the corkscrew emerging from his pocket. He might have been an old actor hired for the role. The 2-euro coffee is drinkable if not special, and if you wish to spend more than your day's allowance, they can bring you champagne.

In an unlikely location just off a busy boulevard, there's a place of unusual charm. **Le Clown Bar** (see pages 153–154) is a tiny *bistro à vins* between the République and the Bastille. Here you can raise a glass of simple country wine, taste a snack, or enjoy a full meal right next door to the Cirque d'Hiver (Winter Circus), where Hemingway would sometimes practice boxing with his friends. We like to think that afterwards his bruised fists might have cradled a drink at the Clown Bar, although it's not exactly his sort of place. Too much charm.

The walls in the two small rooms are covered with spectacular old tiles from 1919, many of them depicting clowns in assorted comic poses. They remind one of pictures in old children's books, especially those illustrated by Kate Greenaway. Original vintage posters of clowns and other circus memorabilia complete the picture. At night during warm weather, the doors open and a young crowd spills over onto the sidewalk, but inside the low lighting and lovely setting suggest romance.

L'Etrier Bistro (see pages 197–198), is an almost ideal neighborhood bistro in the less-visited part of Montmartre. It's small, bright, and intimate, a light and airy place, offering delicious cuisine.—the owner once worked at the Élysee Palace. Developed from what was once a storefront and with only ten small tables, L'Etrier is cleverly decorated with white walls, white floor tiles, and fine lace curtains tied back with raffia. Flowers adorn each table and classical music plays softly in the background.

One of Paris's prettiest little bistros is tucked away in a lovely residential area near the Ecole Militaire, not far from the Eiffel Tower. The **Fontaine de Mars** at 129 rue St. Dominique, 75005 Paris (01.47.05.46.44) was named for the old fountain beside the outdoor terrace. On warm summer days most visitors choose tables there, but the room inside has its own special charm and a radiance born of many years of service. Highly polished nineteenth-century oak cabinets, antique brass, and simple plaid curtains suggest an old-fashioned local bistro. It's a quiet and civilized setting suitable for romantic conversations. Patrons tend to be well-tailored and soft-spoken. An especially likeable little bistro, open daily from noon to 3:00 P.M. and 7:30 P.M. to 11 P.M.

Le Julien, or **Restaurant Julien**, is a glorious Art Nouveau brasserie in a grubby district. Go anyway for its fabulous interior and a feeling of Parisian life in the early 1900s. More details on page 132.

Very few tourists come to the 10th arrondissement where no fancy boutiques or impressive monuments exist to draw their attention. All the more reason, then, to choose for your rendezvous a quiet little bistro with pleasing touches, **Le Parmentier** (see pages 135–136). A few tables are more widely spaced than usual in a room that reminds us of a restaurant in a small provincial town. Relatively inexpensive, especially at lunch, Le Parmentier offers sophisticated cuisine—if you can detach your attention from your significant other long enough to taste the food!

Paul, at 35 rue Tronchet, 75008 Paris (01.40.17.99.54), is open Monday to Saturday from 7:30 A.M. to 8:00 P.M. At first, this seems a most unlikely choice. What you see when you pass Paul is a bustling bakery, with people lined up at peak times to sample the sandwiches and pastries. But go in sometime, fight your way past the line, and try the upstairs dining room.

Here you find yourself in a charming dark-paneled room with a high ceiling and large windows framed by red and gold curtains. Outside the department store, or *grand magasin,* Au Printemps, is partially obscured by trees. Against the dark paneling, framed photos attest to a quieter time when the streets weren't dominated by traffic.

Paul is a good choice for young people without much money, for a couple enjoying a second honeymoon, or for anyone who wants quality food at low prices. Here you can have a meal for little more than the cost of dessert somewhere else. It is full of knowledgeable Parisians who have found a cozy and comfortable place for lunch, away from the crowds on the boulevard. The friendly staff are dressed in bakers' white, their heads crowned by small toques.

A lunch one day included pasta, dessert pastry and wine for 11 euros, but you could do just as well ordering à la carte. Soups are 4 and 6 euros, tartines or open-faced sandwiches 7. A *tartine jurassienne* included bacon and delicious cheeses melted on top; a *tourte landaise* for 6 euros was puff pastry with tomato sauce, peppers, ham, and cream. A *tourte trois fromages* included blue cheese from Bresse, Swiss, and *fromage blanc*, like a light cottage cheese. The *assiette de charcuterie* at the same price included several types of ham and a side salad.

And the bread! Despite our best resolutions, we had to ask for the bread basket to be refilled. No one, not even the slender Parisiennes seated on our right, could ignore the bread. Paul also provides a generous crock of salted butter. Another elegant outpost of Paul is on the rue de Buci in the 6th district (see page 75).

Le Temps des Cerises is the perfect small Parisian bistro, a little gem hidden away in the touristy Marais. Its popularity with the locals makes Le Temps too chaotic to be romantic at lunch, when people from the quarter flock there to wolf down the daily specials in the warm ambiance enhanced by the friendliness of the proprietors. But Le Temps is perfect for a mid-afternoon pick-me-up, or for a drink and a snack to sustain you in your meanderings through the picturesque 4th arrondissement. Described in more detail on pages 43–45.

A hundred and some years ago, Montmartre was a small village just north of Paris, known for its bawdy entertainment and artistic freedom. Today the town looks much the same, but it has been completely infested by foreign tour groups. The center of this frenzied activity is the Place de Tertre, a small-town square now completely jammed with restaurant tables, itinerant artists, and bewildered foreigners milling about, trying to make sense of it all.

Le Vieux Chalet (4 rue Norvins, 75018 Paris, 01.46.06.21.44, métro Auvers) is everyone's idea of a typical French restaurant—and there it survives, in the most unlikely location of all among the sidewalk artists and souvenir stands. From the métro station Auvers, take the funicular up to Sacré Coeur, then go left onto Place du Tertre and rue Norvins. Waves of people surge past, but in the old chalet, with its dark beams, whitewashed walls, and warm red-and-white checkered tablecloths, you feel secure. Safe from the crush of tourists outside, you could be in a country inn. The menu is simple, with predictable starters like pâté, sardines, minestrone, *pamplemousse* (grapefruit), and *salade de tomates* (tomato salad). There are the reliable classics to continue: *steak de boeuf grillé* (grilled steak), *côte de porc* (pork chop), and *poulet rôti* (roast chicken).

And the surprise was not the menu but the prices—even on a Saturday night, the 15-euro menu was in force.

A tureen of steaming minestrone was presented with a large, flowered soup plate; a small plate with sardines was garnished with tomatoes and lemons, and included a basket of sliced baguette. Both were satisfying beginnings, followed by a quarter chicken hot and crisp, with sautéed potatoes. The steak, with similar accompaniments, was also large, with a good smoky flavor of the grill. Desserts are simple, the 15-euro menu permitting a cheese or dessert finish. We decided on dessert, a choice of fruit or ice cream.

Service is friendly and attentive; the manager-owner speaks fluent English, and enjoys chatting about the Vieux Chalet. "It's over a hundred years old," he told us. So this restaurant was here in this village when Utrillo painted his views of the streets and when Picasso went by on his way to the Lapin Agile.

The wine list is surprising. There are some perfectly decent wines for from 9 to 12 euros, and a few very unexpected bottles—a Lafite Rothschild, a Cos d' Estournel, all from good years. When we asked about this, the manager mentioned that he had bought up several private wine cellars.

A final word:

As you go through our pages about Paris bistros, you'll realize that a separate chapter about romantic restaurants wasn't really necessary: there are so many of them, thanks to the genius of the French for creating places where one is made to feel special. So whether you like the old stones and weathered beams of historic drinking-places, prefer quiet garden retreats that seem to have been created especially for you, or love the flamboyant decor of a great brasserie for celebrating in a setting that's festive, you can find just what you've been looking for in Paris.

BIBLIOGRAPHY

Angelou, Maya. *Singin' and Swingin' and Gettin' Merry Like Christmas*. New York: Bantam Books, 1989.

Beauvoir, Simone de. *The Prime of Life*. Cleveland and New York: World Publishing Company, 1962.

—. *After the War: Force of Circumstance, I 1944-1952*. Trans. Richard Howard. New York: Paragon House, 1992.

Baldwin, James. "Equal in Paris." in *The Price of the Ticket: Collected Nonfiction, 1948-1985*. New York: St. Martin's Press, 1985.

Boyle, Kay, and Robert McAlmon. *Being Geniuses Together, 1920-1930*. San Francisco: North Point Press, 1984.

Campbell, Barbara-Ann. *Paris: A Guide to Recent Architecture*. London: Ellipsis London Ltd., 1997.

Charters, Jimmie. *This Must Be The Place: Memoirs of Montparnasse*. As told to Morrill Cody. New York, London: Collier Books, 1989.

Chevalier, Maurice. *My Paris*. Photographs by Robert Doisneau. New York: Macmillan Co., 1972.

Courtine, Robert J. *Madame Maigret's Recipes*. Trans. Mary Manheim. New York: Harcourt, Brace Jovanovich, 1975.

Ducongé, Ada Smith, and James Haskins. *Bricktop*. New York: Atheneum, 1983.

Fabre, Michel. *From Harlem to Paris: Black American Writers in France, 1840-1980*. Urbana: Univ of Illinois, 1991.

Flanner, Janet. *Darlinghissima: Letters to a Friend*. New York: Random House, 1985.

—. *Paris Journal, 1965-1971*. New York: Viking, 1972.

—. *Paris Was Yesterday 1925-1939*. New York: Viking, 1972.

Green, Julien. *Paris*. Trans. J.A. Underwood. New York: Marion Boyers, 1991.

Haine, W. Scott. *The World of the Paris Café: Sociability among the French Working Class, 1789-1914*. Baltimore and London: Johns Hopkins UP, 1996.

Hansen, Arlen J. *Expatriate Paris*. New York: Arcade Publishing, 1990.

Himes, Chester. *The Quality of Hurt*. New York: Thunder's Mouth Press, 1971.

—. *My Life of Absurdity.* New York: Thunder's Mouth Press, 1976.

Hughes, Langston. *The Big Sea.* New York: Thunder's Mouth Press, 1940.

Littlewood, Ian. *Paris: A Literary Companion.* New York: Harper and Row, 1988.

Marshall, Paule. "Chez Tournon: A Homage," in *The New York Times* Oct. 18, 1992.

Miller, Henry. *Letters to Anaïs Nin.* New York: G. P. Putnam's, 1965.

Morton, Brian N. *Americans in Paris.* Ann Arbor: The Olivia and Hill Press, 1984.

Russell, John. *Paris.* New York: Harry Abrams, 1983.

Schlosser, Eric. *Fast Food Nation.* New York: Houghton Mifflin, 2001.

Shirer, William L. *Twentieth-Century Journey: A Memoir of a Life and The Times, 1904-1930.* New York: Simon and Shuster, 1976.

Simenon, Georges. *Maigret and the Black Sheep.* Trans. Helen Thomson. New York and London: Harcourt Brace Jovanovich, 1976.

—. *Maigret and the Headless Corpse.* New York: Hamish Hamilton, 1955.

—. *Maigret and the Spinster.* New York: Harcourt Brace Jovanovich, 1977.

—. *Maigret's First Case*, in *Maigret Cinq.* Trans. Richard Brain. New York: Harcourt Brace Jovanovich, 1977.

—. *Maigret Hesitates.* New York: Harcourt Brace Jovanovich, 1970.

—. *Maigret's Little Joke*, in *Maigret Cinq.* Trans. Richard Brain. New York: Harcourt Brace Jovanovich, 1965.

—. *Maigret's Memoirs.* Trans. Jean Stewart. New York: Harcourt Brace Jovanovich, 1985.

—. *Maigret Mystified.* Trans. Jean Stewart. Middlesex, England: Penguin, 1964.

—. *Maigret's War of Nerves.* Trans Geoffrey Sainsbury. New York: Harcourt Brace Jovanovich, 1940.

Stein, Gertrude. *Paris France.* New York: Liveright, 1970. First published in 1940.

Stovall, Tyler. "Harlem-sur-Seine: Building an African Diasporic Community in Paris." *Stanford Electronic Humanities Review* 1997. vol. 5.2 (1997).

Wright, Richard. "There's Always Another Café." *Kiosk*, vol. 10, 1953.

GLOSSARY

Useful terms: the following does not pretend to be an exhaustive list of the foods you'll find in bistros, simply a few basics that will help to get you started comprehending French cuisine.

l'addition: the bill
agneau: lamb
ail: garlic
aloyau: beef loin grilled on a skewer
amande: almond
amuse-gueule: cocktail snack
anchois: anchovy
ancienne, à l': in white sauce
andalouse, à l': with garnish of calmar (a small squid), tomatoes, peppers, and eggplant
andouille: cooked tripe sausage
andouillette: similar to above
aneth: dill
asperge: asparagus
assiette: plate
avocat: avocado

baba: rum-soaked sponge cake
bar: sea bass
barbue: brill, flat sea fish
basquaise, à la: with tomatoes, peppers, garlic, and cured ham
basilic: basil
batavia: type of lettuce
bavarois: Bavarian cream dessert
bavette: beef flank steak
Béarnaise: Hollandaise sauce with tarragon, spices, and shallots
Belle Hélène: pear with ice cream, topped with chocolate sauce
beignet: doughnut or fritter

beurre : butter

beurre blanc: sauce flavored with white wine, shallots, vinegar, and fish stock

bien cuit: well done

bière: beer

bifteck: beef steak

bisque: thick soup

boeuf: beef

boeuf bourguignon: beef stew

boudin: blood sausage

bouillabaisse: Mediterranean fish soup of various fishes, tomatoes, garlic, etc.

brouillé (oeuf): scrambled eggs

cabillaud: fresh cod

caille: quail

Calvados: apple brandy

canard: duck

carafe: decanter, pitcher

carafe d'eau: tap water

carotte: carrot (*rapée*: grated)

carpaccio: appetizer of slices of raw cured beef

carte: menu

cassis: black currant

cassoulet: white bean stew with duck, lamb, or sausage

cèpe: type of wild mushroom

chantilly: whipped cream

charcuterie: cured meats

Charlotte: creamy fruit dessert made with gelatin

chèvre: goat (*fromage de chèvre:* goat milk cheese)

choux-fleur: cauliflower

choux: cabbage

coeur: heart

contre-filet: upper filet of sirloin steak

coq: rooster

cornichon: pickle

côte: rib of beef or pork

courgette: zucchini

crème brûlée: custard dessert with caramelized topping

crème caramel: caramel custard dessert

cresson: watercress

crevette: prawn or shrimp

croque-madame: open-faced toasted ham-and-cheese sandwich topped with fried egg

croque-monsieur: toasted ham-and-cheese sandwich

cru: raw, uncooked

crudité(s): raw vegetables

daube: meat stewed in red wine, onions, and herbs

daurade, dorade: sea bream, a white, delicate fish

de campagne: country-style

dinde, dindon: turkey

eau: water

échalotte: shallot

émincé: thinly sliced

entrecôte: beef ribsteak

entrée: hors d'oeuvre, starter

épinard: spinach

erable: maple

escargot: snail

espadon: swordfish

estragon: tarragon

faisan: pheasant

farine: flour

faux-filet: sirloin steak

fermier: farm; free-range

feuilleté: puff pastry

figue: fig

fines herbes: mix of herbs including chives, parsley, tarragon, and chervil

flan: tart made with eggs and milk, sweet or savory

foie: liver

foie gras: fattened goose or duck liver

frais: fresh, chilled

fraise: strawberry

framboise: raspberry

frit(e): fried

frites: fried potatoes, French fries, chips

fromage: cheese

fumé: smoked

galette: pancake

garni: garnished, usually with vegetables

gaspacho: cold soup usually made with tomato, cucumber, onions, and sweet pepper

gâteau: cake

gaufre: waffle

génoise: sponge cake

gésier: gizzard

gibier: wild game

gigot: lamb

girolle: apricot-colored wild mushroom

glace: ice cream

gratin dauphinois: scalloped potatoes, sliced, with cream cheese

grenouille: frog

griotte: sour cherry

grondin: gurnard, a marine fish used in bouillabaisse

groseille: currant

haché: chopped, minced

hareng: herring

haricot: bean; *haricots verts:* green beans

huile: oil

île flottante: dessert of caramel-coated egg whites in custard

jambon: ham

joue: cheek

jus: juice; *au jus*: in its cooking liquid

kasher: Kosher

lait: milk
langoustine: large prawn
langue: tongue
lapin: rabbit
lard: bacon
laurier: bay leaf
légume: vegetable
lotte de mer: monkfish
lieu: pollock
loup: European bass

macédoine: mixture of diced vegetables or fruit
mâche: lamb's lettuce
madeleine: small cake baked in shell-shaped mold
madère: Madeira
magret (de canard): duck breast
maître d'hôtel: head waiter; *sauce maître d'hôtel*: butter and
    lemon sauce
mangue: mango
maquereau: mackerel fish
marc: brandy
marchand de vin: sauce with red wine and shallots
marron: chestnut
médaillon: small round slice
menthe: mint
menu: a set-price menu, as opposed to the *carte*
mer, fruit de: seafood
meunière: sautéed with lemon juice and parsley
miel: honey
millefeuille: puff pastry; a Napoleon filled with custard
moëlle: bone marrow
Mont Blanc: chestnut cream dessert
morille: morel mushroom
morue: salted cod

noix: walnut, nut
norvégienne, omelette: baked Alaska
nouilles: noodles

oeuf: egg
onglet de boeuf: similar to flank steak
osso buco: veal shin braised in white wine with tomatoes, garlic,
    and onions

pamplemousse: grapefruit
paincomplet: whole-wheat bread
pan bagnat: round flat sandwich with
    tuna, anchovies, and olives
Parmentier: potato-based dish
Pastis: anise-flavored, before-dinner drink
pâte: pastry
pâté: seasoned, cooked meat
pâtisserie: pastry
pavé: thick slice
pêche: peach
pichet: pitcher or jug for wine
pintade: guinea fowl
pistou: Provençal sauce of basil, garlic,
    and olive oil; also a rich bean soup
plat: main course, dish
poire: pear
pois: peas
poisson: fish
poivre: pepper
poivron: bell pepper
pomme: apple
pomme de terre: potato
porc: pork
poulet: chicken
praline: caramelized sugar with almonds
pression: draft beer
prix: price
prix fixe: fixed-price menu

quart: quarter
quatre-quarts: pound cake
quenelle: dumpling
queue: tail
quiche: tart with eggs

raifort: horseradish
radis: radish
raie: ray fish
raisin: grape
râpé: grated
rascasse: scorpion fish, used in bouillabaisse

rillettes: meat, often pork
ris: sweetbreads
riz: rice
rognons: kidneys
rognon blanc: testicles
rosbif: roast beef
rôti: roast
rouget: red mullet
rumsteak: rumpsteak

sabayon: frothy sauce of white wine, egg, and sugar
sablé: sweet biscuit or shortbread
safran: saffron
salade: lettuce
salé(e): salted
Salers: highly regarded beef from Auvergne, also cheese
sang: blood
saucisse: sausage
saucisson: dried salami-type sausage
saumon: salmon
sauvage: wild
sec, sèche: dry
seigle: rye

tartare, steak: raw ground beef
tartine: open-faced sandwich
terrine: dish used for prepared meat, seafood, vegetables, etc.
thon: tuna
truffe: truffle
truite: trout

vacherin: meringue cake with ice cream and whipped cream
viennoiserie: pastries
vin: wine
vinaigre: vinegar

xères: sherry

yaourt: yogurt

zeste: outer peel of citrus fruit, zest

INDEX

Allard vii
Altitude 95
    in Eiffel Tower 101–102
Angelou, Maya 89
Ardoise, L' 2–3
Arletty 125
Astier 142–143
Atelier Renault, L' 103
Auberge de Jarente 25–26
Avant-Goût, L' 167–168

Babylone, Au 104–105
Baker, Josephine
    adopted by French 87
    early success of 87, 99
    final comeback 88
Baldwin, James
    and Les Deux Magots 83
    and Café de Flore 91
    and Brasserie Lipp 91
    imprisonment 84–85
Balzar, Le 57–59
Baracane-Bistro de L'Oulette 27
Bar du Caveau, Le 226
Bar des Théâtres 100
Bascou, Au 24–25
Bâteau Lavoir, Le 191
Beauvoir, Simone de 55–56
Bélisaire 178–180
Biche au Bois, La 144–145
Bistro, definition viii-ix
    etiquette in xii
    new bistro x–xi
    see individual names
Bistro d'Hubert 180–181
Bistro de la Gare 59
Bistro d'Opio, Le 60

Bistro de Paris 105–106
Bistro du Peintre 237
Bofinger 27–29
Bons Crus, Aux 4
Bontemps, Arna 87
Bookinistes, Les 60–61
Boubal, Paul 56
Bouillon Racine 61–62
Bourgogne, Ma 217, 227
Bourgogne, Restaurant de
    126–127
Brasserie, definition ix–x
Brasserie de L'Ile St. Louis 29–30
Brasserie Lipp 63–65, 91
Brasserie Wepler 205–206
"Bricktop," Ada Smith du Conge
    86
Buisson Ardent, Le 65–67

Café du Centre 238
Café Charbon
    description 148–150
    started renewal of 11th 142
Café Dapper 182
Café des Délices, Le 67–68
Café Denon, in Louvre 12
Café les Deux Moulins 239
Café Flo in Au Printemps store
    127–128
Café de Flore 56, 72–73, 91
Café les Gaufres 240–241
Café du Marché 108–109
Café Mollien (Louvre) 12
Café de la Musique 209
Café du Musée Jacquemart-
    Andrée 106–108
Café de la Musique, Le 209–210

Café Noir 5–6
Café de la Paix 125
Café Viaduc, Le 161
Callaghan, Morley 166
Cartes Postales, Les 6–7
Camelot, Au 145–146
Camille 31
Chardenoux 150–152
Charpentiers, Aux 68
  celebrities at 69
Charters, Jimmie 52–54, 164
Chartier 61, 122–123
Cheminée, La 147
Chevalier, Maurice
  dreams of becoming acrobat
    140
  memories of 20th 207–208
  visits Cirque d'Hiver 140
Clos des Gourmets, Le 110
Closerie des Lilas, La 55, 69–70
Clown Bar, Le 153–154, 241
Conran, Terence xi
Coupole, La 221–222, 227–228
Cullen, Countee 81, 86

Dame Jeanne 154–155
Dauphin, Le 8–9
Denise, Chez 17–19
Directoire, Le 182–183
Dôme, Le 54, 165

Ellington, Duke 89
Encrier, L' 155–156
Endroit, L' 32
Epi Dupin, L' 70–71
Eté en Pente Douce, L' 195–197
Etrier Bistrot, L' 197–198, 241

Faulkner, William 193
Fitzgerald, F. Scott
  apt. rue Tilsitt 97
  description of Right Bank 1
  meets Hemingway 55

Flanner, Janet
  about Josephine Baker 88
  comments on Ritz 1
  encounter w. Picasso 234
  sees Paris changing 208
Florès 111
Folies Bergère 123
Fontaine Gourmande, La 34
Fontaine de Mars, La 112–113,
    242
Fous d'en Face, Les 35
Fresque, La 9–10
Freud 166

Green, Julien 20, 177–178
Gladines, Chez 168–170
Grille, La 128–130
Grizzli, Le 36–37

Hangar, Le 37–38
Hawai 171–172
Haynes 91–93
Hédiard 100
Hermès 100
Hemingway, Ernest
  commenting on cafés 53
  Closerie des Lilas 54–55
  reactions to Lipp 63
  sitting at Dome Café 165
  The Sun Also Rises 53
Himes, Chester
  arrival in Paris 82
  frequents Le Tournon 82
  writes at Le Sélect 95
Hughes, Langston
  arrives in Paris 85
  difficulty finding work 85
  memories of Montmartre 86
Hugo, Victor
  at home Place des Vosges 22
  saved by café owner 141

Iroko Bar 198–199

Jacques Melac (bistro à vins) 157
Joyce, James 54
  at Fouquet's 98
Julien, Restaurant 131–133, 242

Lescure 10–11
Lina's Sandwiches, Marais 38–39
Lou Pascalou 212–213
Louise, Chez 172–173
Louis Philippe, Le 39–40

McAlmon, Robert 53–54
McKay, Claude
  appreciates cafés 86–87
Maigret, Jules
  bistros essential to 216
  and La Coupole 221–222
  familiarity w. Paris 218
  frequents Dauphine 218
  and the Henri IV 220
  identifies with suspects 216
  and Royal Turenne 230–231
Marais, description 20–23
Marcel, Chez 73–74
Marine, La 134
Martin, Florence 54
Michel, Chez 130–131
Miller, Henry 55, 191
  life in 9th district 122
Molière 178
Montmartre 191–195
Monttessuy, Le 115–116
Morgan, Ted, formerly Sanche
  de Gramont 141

Négociants, Aux 199–200
Nord-Sud, Le 202–203

Orwell, George work at Lotti xi
Os à Moêlle, L' 183–184

Parmentier, Le 135–136
Parvis du Musée 184–185
Pascalou, Lou 212–213
Patache, La 229
Paul (bakery and salon de thé)
  75, 243–244
Paul, Chez (bistro) 152
Petit Belleville, Le 210–211
Petit Caboulet, Le 203–204
Petite Chaise, La 116–117
Petit Keller, Le 158
Petit Retro, Le 185–186
Petit St.-Benoît, Le 76–77
Pharamond 12–14
Pied de Fouet, Au 113–114
Philosophes, Les 41–42
Picasso 194, 234
Proust, Marcel
  at Ritz 1
  meets Joyce 98
Polidor 94–95
Prune, Chez 136

Reconfort, Le 42–43
Régalade, La 173–175
Relais, Au 204–205
Reminet, Le 77–78
Rendez-Vous des Belges, Au 137
Rendez-Vous des Quais, Le
  213–214
Royal Turenne, Le 230–231
Rubis, Le 14–15
Russell, John 65
  comment on boulevards 124

Saint-Amour, Le 214–215
Sainte Marthe, Le 137–138
Sartre, Jean-Paul 55–57, 72–73
Savy, Chez 118
Sélect, Le 78–80, 95, 232
Square, Le 119–120
Square Trousseau, Le 160

Tambour, Le 15–16
Tartine, La 45–46
Taverne Henri IV, Le 232
Temps des Cerises, Le, 4th arr.
    43–45, 244
13th arr. (Butte aux Cailles)
    175–176
Tie Break, Le 187–188
Tir-Bouchon, Le 16–17
Totem, Le 188–189
Tour de Montlhéry, A la, (Chez
    Denise) 17–19
Tournon, Le 82, 95–96
Troquet, Le 189–190
Trumilou 47–48

Valet de Carreau, Le 48–49
Vieux Chalet, Le 245
Villaret, Le 162–163
Vins des Pyrenées, Les 49–51

wine, ordering xv–xvi
Wright, Richard
    argument at Deux Magots
        83–84
    choosing a café 90
    patronage of Tournon 96
    visits Polidor 94–95

Zola, Emile
    description in *Nana* 123